Meeting Faith

W. W. Norton & Company • New York • London

Meeting Faith

THE FOREST

JOURNALS

OF A BLACK

BUDDHIST NUN

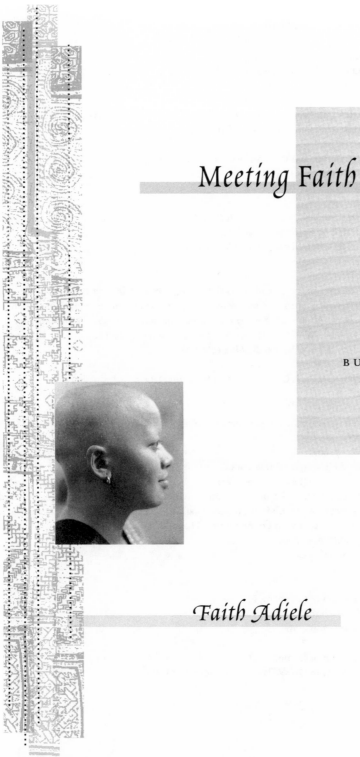

Faith Adiele

Since this page cannot legibly accommodate all the copyright notices, page
289 constitutes an extension of the copyright page.

For information about permission to reproduce selections from this book,
write to Permissions, W. W. Norton & Company, Inc., 500 Fifth Avenue,
New York, NY 10110

Manufacturing by The Maple-Vail Book Manufacturing Group
Book design by Barbara M. Bachman,
based on an original concept by Shari DeGraw
Production manager: Anna Oler

Some of the material in this book has appeared, in different form, in the
following publications: *Creative Nonfiction; Fourth Genre: Explorations in Nonfiction; Iowa Alumni Magazine; Life Notes: Personal Writings by Contemporary
Black Women* (W. W. Norton, 1993); *Ploughshares; Transition: An International
Journal;* and *Tricycle: The Buddhist Review.*

Library of Congress Cataloging-in-Publication Data

Adiele, Faith.
    Meeting faith : the forest journals of a black buddhist nun / Faith Adiele.—1st
ed.
            p. cm.
Includes bibliographical references.
    ISBN 0-393-05784-4 (hardcover)
    1.Adiele, Faith. 2. Spiritual biography—United States. 3. Buddhist nuns—United
States—Biography. 4. Buddhist nuns—Thailand—Religious life. 5. Monasticism and
religious orders for women, Buddhist—Thailand. I. Title.
    BQ940.D34 A3 2004
    294.3'91'092—dc22

                                                                    2003024575

W. W. Norton & Company, Inc.
500 Fifth Avenue, New York, N.Y. 10110
www.wwnorton.com

W. W. Norton & Company Ltd.
Castle House, 75/76 Wells Street, London W1T 3QT

1 2 3 4 5 6 7 8 9 0

for Annie Phillips Slabach

&

Adanna Grace Adiele

&

Holly Joanne Hanson Adiele
the three who taught me faith

Contents

Acknowledgments

THE FIRST STEPS down any long path require faith. When embarking upon my ordination journey, I was asked to take refuge in the Three Gems of Buddhism. I took additional solace in three wise teachers—Ajarn Boon, Maechi Roongdüan, and later on, Patricia A. Foster. In life, I have always taken refuge in my mother, she who gave me my name and the guts to use it.

I cannot thank Patricia Bell-Scott enough for insisting that I drag my journals out of a drawer. Not only were she and Marcia Ann Gillespie the first to read these scribblings, they were also the first to suggest my story might be of interest.

I am deeply indebted to Jen Hofer, who volunteered to wade through a virtual stranger's journals and then solved my structural woes with characteristic brilliance; Samantha Chang, who generously read several early drafts; Shari DeGraw, who spent her own time designing the perfect layout; and Courtenay Bouvier, who quite wisely saw that we needed to meet each other.

Further along the way, I was lucky enough to encounter three more incomparable gems: my agent Lynn C. Franklin, my editor Jill Bialosky, and my chair Dave Bartholomae. In addition to them, I have been blessed by such cheerleaders as Stuart Dybek, Molly O'Neill, Sapphire, Coco Fusco, Dee Morris, Christi Merrill, Leslie Roberts, and Toi Derricotte. And where would I be on the path without great friends like Michael Melcher, Z. Z. Packer, Nasir Naqvi, Unoma Azuah, Ronald Palmer, Summi Kaipa, Susan Freireich, Carrie Messenger, Laura Serna, Lisa Olivarez Slabach, Lisa Zeidenberg, Bennett Singer, Julia Sullivan, Marah Gubar, and Kieran Setiya?

Many thanks to Marcia Lippman for allowing me to pair my words with her gorgeous portraits of Thai Buddhas, and to old pals Eric Azumi, Jim Flint, and Scott Sester for the generous use of their photographs.

I am additionally grateful for funding and support from the Yaddo Corporation, the Virginia Center for the Creative Arts, the Willard R. Espy Foundation, the Sacatar Foundation in Brazil, and the Millennium Award from *Creative Nonfiction*.

Meeting Faith

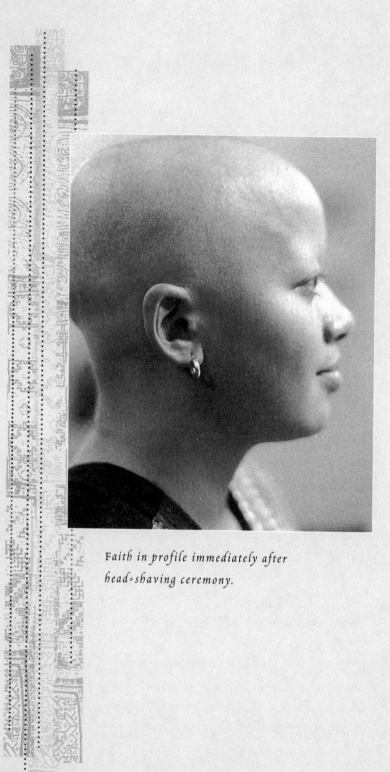

Faith in profile immediately after
head-shaving ceremony.

Stripping: A Preface

DESPITE THE NAME FAITH, I'm an unlikely candidate for spiritual aspirations. Strangers are surprised to learn that I spent a Lenten season as a Buddhist nun in the Thai forest. Their eyes widen, taking in all of me, as mine drop, seeking the floor lights marking the exit. I dread the questions, but even more I dread my stock answers, chanted like an unholy mantra. Yup, I'm not Asian. Nope, I'm not some New Ager on a holy trek to the food co-op. Nah, I don't particularly believe in religion. I don't even believe in camping. To complicate matters further—their eyes narrow, homing in on me—I am black. Physically soft. Pierced! And what they may not know—addicted to African dance grooves, snacks involving processed flour *and* sugar, good jewelry, and bad television.

Friends, too, are surprised to learn the details. It's no secret Faith lacks discipline. She can't even make it to the gym—forget about enlightenment! Anyone who knows me knows that I couldn't have risen at three-thirty each morning and spent nineteen hours a day in meditative practice. Aren't I the one always saying that seven-thirty comes but once: dinnertime? I certainly didn't go from sitting fifteen minutes in meditation to seventy-two hours at a stretch. *How many hours?* Nope, not Faith! The only thing to suggest that otherworldliness might be possible is a quaint refusal to smash bugs and an inability to keep shoes on my ringed, painted feet. But that's not enough, is it?

Understandably, friends and strangers ask questions, the answers they expect embedded in the queries themselves: *Wasn't it hot? Weren't you lonely? Weren't you scared?* The answers are all invariably yes. Yes to hot, lonely, scared. Yes also to missing physical intimacy and movies and Pop-Tarts. And yes to my fear of everything the phrase "tropical forest" conjures—giant spiders and hissing cobras and forest fires and prehistoric monitor lizards. Yes to my fear of everything Buddhist asceticism suggests—a single meal a day, sleeping on wooden floors, meditating on decomposing corpses. Yes, yes, yes, there were times I shuddered and sobbed in a Southeast Asian night so dark I couldn't tell if my eyes were open or shut. Times I detested the Buddha and Asia and so-called personal growth. Times when nothing was more terrifying than the prospect of sitting with the contents of my own mind for nineteen hours a day. But (and here's the part friends can recognize in the stranger that used to be Faith) I was even more afraid of failure. And why not? It seems downright un-American to fail. Furthermore, failure nearly killed me once.

ༀ

THERE WERE TWO REASONS I found myself in the Thai forest, stripped of my curls and eyebrows and sporting strange undergarments. The first was, surprisingly, comfort. I'd been to northern Thailand before—my junior year of high school—and the experience had satisfied my lifelong quest for fairness. For me at that time, Thailand was a place that worked in a way that America, for all its immigrant narratives about hard work paying off, did not. It was a place where merit was truly rewarded.

At age fifteen, my obsession with getting the hell out of small-town America was finally within reach: I had made it into the final round of applicants for the Rotary Club International Exchange Program. After I plowed through a barrage of questions about global affairs and cultural sensitivity, my answers honed sharp with teenage determination, the selection committee invited my mother into the Holiday Inn conference room. Together we did a tag-team perform-ance about my upbringing: how she supplemented my public school education with home schooling from her old college history and an-thropology and religion textbooks; how I'd petitioned the school board to be allowed to study both Spanish and French; how we dressed in makeshift rebozos and saris and dashikis for our monthly United Nations Day dinners and tried recipes for crêpes and piroshki and kimchee from the Time-Life international cookbook series at the library; how neither of us expected me to be homesick. We dissem-bled a bit when it came to my picky palate; after all, we both knew that when push came to shove, I'd eat blood soup and fermented fish paste and roasted beetles. Dammit, I'd been raised to travel!

The Rotarians shot approving glances around the table, and I could tell I had the scholarship. I was about to become a junior ambassador ("Rotar-ree, Rotar-rah, my knapsack on my back!" to lift from the official Rotarian songbook) and spend a whole year out-side my hometown, the Land That Time Forgot. A whole year in the world! I quivered with delight.

A pleasant-faced, well-groomed man raised his hand. "I have one last question." I fastened bright, attentive eyes on him.

"Do you anticipate any problems stemming from Faith's race? Most of the world assumes that Americans are white." He smiled. "We of course know that's not the case, but how will you handle those expectations, Faith?"

My eyes sought out my white mother, who blinked her icy Scandinavian blues. Had she forgotten I was black, or was she get-ting ready to take him out, despite his reasonable phrasing?

"That's an interesting question," she said. "Faith's blackness never even occurred to me until I was waiting there in the hall and noticed that every other applicant was white."

I held my breath, willing this to be the one battle she walked away from. We had a chance. She was apple-cheeked and blue-eyed and cowlicked, a farmer's daughter like their own mothers, and looked genuinely rueful about her discovery. As I prayed feverishly, she let out a slow chuckle. The Rotarians followed suit. Then it was my turn.

I was ready. This was the question I had been answering all my life. Who better to represent America than I? Who was more American than the offspring of two New World poles—a mother descended from Scandinavian immigrants and a student father from newly independent Africa? Who more up to the task of proving herself? To the task of translation? I could do it in my sleep. Every day I was an exchange student in my own country.

And you, I surely intimated to the table of white men and women, imagine how progressive *you* will look!

Afterwards, on the phone, our local Rotary Club president was ecstatic. Here we came, a tiny rural club from eastern Washington State with the only black candidate, and swept the entire Northwest Inland Region, Canada included! "No one has ever scored so high on adaptability," he raved to my mother. "She'll be able to take her pick of countries. Anywhere she wants!"

That night we sipped the closest thing to champagne our town offered. As long as I could remember, my mother and I had dreamed of international travel, her dream blurring into mine, my opportunities hers. We decided that I should spend the school year in Europe, developing my French, while she saved money to join me in the summer. We would visit Finland, my grandmother's homeland, and Sweden, my grandfather's, during the midnight sun. Or I should spend the school year in Latin America, perfecting my Spanish, and we would meet in Mexico at the Ballet Folklórico. All that hard work had paid off; it was simply up to me to pick!

A second call came as I sat at the kitchen table poring over Time-Life's *World's Great Religions*. The Rotary adviser assigned to me sounded tentative and apologetic. "There's been, uh, a change in plans," he reported. "You're being sent to a small town in northern Thailand." He said it twice, pronouncing it once *Tai-land* and once *Thigh-land*.

In the silence of my caught breath, he pressed on. "This town, Chiangrai, has been having problems. None of the American exchange students can adapt. They can't eat the food, learn the language, stand the heat. They cause their host families trouble. Rotary Thailand is considering canceling the entire exchange program."

"But what about getting to choose?" I demanded, finally able to speak, more concerned with equity than with the possibility of being sent to a place I knew nothing about (other than the fact I was fairly certain it did not abound with thighs). "I was told that I ranked high enough—"

"You did," my adviser confirmed. He sounded like a very nice guy who wished he were anywhere but on the phone with a teary teenager. "And I'm terribly sorry. But you're their last hope. If you can't adapt, they'll give up on the Thailand program."

And so it began. Already I suffered from migraines and chronic after-dinner burps ("Nerves," the doctor had said with a shrug). Now I'd been enlisted to save Thailand.

Eventually a more rational thought presented itself: "Hey," I blurted, "where's Thailand?"

It was 1979, pre–adventure travel, pre–mountain treks, pre–Pan Asian cuisine. Way before embroidered Burmese backpacks and Indonesian rayon sarongs and Pad Thai takeout. Years in advance of the Travel Channel and Hmong refugees and canned coconut milk. Where the hell was Thailand?

I could almost hear the man wince, a crack like static. "I think it's near Vietnam." He paused. Crack. "And Cambodia."

Scenes of fire flared in my mind. Self-immolating monks aflame in busy Vietnamese streets. The Napalm Girl running down the road, flesh sizzling. American GIs burning green villages. We were just four years out of Vietnam, the homeless vets collecting behind Seattle's Greyhound terminal, flasks in paper bags tucked beneath the stumps of arms. Vietnam had invaded Cambodia, ending four years of Khmer Rouge rule. The stories were just trickling out. One-fifth of the country's population dead of forced labor, starvation, murder. Children sent to war. Heaps of skulls along the border.

I gripped the table. I was going to die. I had scored the highest in the entire Northwest Inland Region and my reward was being sent to war.

"Please," the man pleaded, "I'm sure Thailand's interesting. I'm sorry to say that I don't know much about it, but . . ." He petered off.

My mother appeared in the doorway, chestnut hair askew, eyes magnified behind thick glasses. "What? What?" she mouthed.

In the midst of the war reel running in my head, a second, pettier thought emerged. The other exchange students didn't have to be the best, and yet in the end they were packing their bags for France and England and Costa Rica, while I, who earned my number one ranking, was off to the Hanoi Hilton.

When an hour later my mother rushed in, red-cheeked and breathless from her speed-walk downtown, toting a stack of library books about Thailand, I was still moaning about my intention to leave the United States and move to a country where merit damn well got rewarded. For a week I sulked, refusing to let her tell me anything about my new home.

Eventually, of course, curiosity got the better of me. I watched her devour the library books and send away for travel brochures. I overheard her crow, "Never been a colony!" on the phone. I saw my grandfather drop off his World War II photographs of the Philippines. Finally I ventured into her room, a veritable camp headquarters with maps and reconnaissance photos of Southeast Asia.

"Do you want to hear about Thailand?" she asked, eyes lighting up.

I nodded, unable to fight the blood I had inherited, feeling it warm to the pulse of adventure.

"Great!" She grabbed her notes and hopped onto her bed, patting the spread next to her. "It's truly fascinating!"

And once I opened myself to the idea of some unknown country near Vietnam and Cambodia not yet on tourist maps, I too began to see the possibilities. This was virgin territory, literally uncolonized, unconquered, unexplored. The best Rotary had to offer had tried and failed. Now I, at fifteen the first black ambassador, was being sent in to do the job. I had been raised to love the quest. *Tell me I can't, and I must* was practically our family motto. I had no intention of failing.

And so it was that I found myself a few months later, at age sixteen, standing in the Chiangrai post office, my school uniform wilting in the humidity. Chiangrai, the tiny capital of Thailand's northernmost province, is one point marking an infamous geometry—the Golden Triangle of opium poppies blooming between Thailand, Burma, and Laos. Except for a white Peace Corps volunteer who taught English at the local high school (the ubiquitous tall, pale, pointy-nosed man), no one in Chiangrai had ever seen a foreigner. Certainly not a black female one in the standard Thai schoolgirl uniform of white blouse, navy pleated skirt, and black Mary Janes.

The postal officials were no exception.

"How do you find Thailand?" A clerk with a lean, youthful face posed the question in English. He flashed a mouthful of brilliant teeth, obviously speaking for the huddle of workers behind him. They strained forward in their khaki uniforms, arms intertwined, men with men, women with women.

"*Suay maak,*" I replied. *Very beautiful.* I'd been in the country less than a month, but I knew the proper answer. And truly, the Golden Triangle with its temples of saffron-clad monks, its blood-red poppies on carpets of green, even Chiangrai town itself with its pastel stucco houses beneath bowers dripping with hibiscus and Raspberry Ice bougainvillea, was breathtaking.

The cluster of delicate-boned men and women giggled appreciatively, gentle as a flock of laughing thrushes.

I flitted the telegram I'd been trying to send all day. Chiangrai's telegraph had been down since morning. Every hour, my school counselor, Ajarn Supatra, got permission to take me out of the girls' school where I was an exchange student for the year and escorted me to the dim wood-and-cement post office to beg them to try my telegram just one more time.

The smiling clerk disregarded the fluttering telegram, asking instead, "What do you think of Thai people?"

I stifled a sigh. This was Question Two of the Trinity of Visitor Inquiry. First were questions assessing Thailand's merits as a country, the correct answer being *Very beautiful*. Then came those regarding the merits of its citizens (as tourism increased, a variation crept in querying the beauty of its women); the correct answer here was *Very friendly* (or later on, *Very beautiful*). Last would be solicitous concern about the visitor's ability to eat spicy Thai food, the correct answers being, "I love it!" or "Boy, it sure is hot!"

"Wonderful people," I assured my audience, trying not to cry. "Very friendly."

The khakied crowd nodded in unison, though one astute soul noted, "She seems distressed. What does the telegram say?"

The clerk lifted the page from my hand and studied it. *"Dear Mom,"* he read, his hollow cheeks rounding out to pronounce the unfamiliar English *o*, *"please forgive—"*

"No, please," I begged, holding up my hand and then folding it away to stop myself from snatching the telegram. "If you could just send it . . . ?"

Ajarn Supatra intervened, the picture of Thai femininity and charm with her soft voice and matching flowered blouse and skirt. "Americans are very private," she explained, spreading her pearly nails across the bow at her throat. "Apparently this message is very urgent, though she won't say what it is."

She laughed, a sound like one of Chiangrai's hidden mountain waterfalls flowing over smooth stone, and I couldn't tell if she was mocking me or appeasing them. The Thai, it seems, are always laughing—at fatness, sadness, life. I wondered if she was speaking English so that I would learn something about Thai society, or out of respect for me, so that I would know how she was presenting me.

She rooted around in an embroidered clutch and laid some coins on the counter, an assortment of bronze and silver disks with profiles of the king. I hadn't yet received my allowance from the local Rotary Club, which meant I couldn't afford to send my own telegram—or bribe the clerk for the retries.

It was embarrassing, for someone like me, to rely on strangers, as was the truth that there was no emergency, really (at least, I suspected, not one that would qualify as such to a laughing Thai). Thailand's most commonly used phrase is *Mai pen rai,* which translates loosely as, *It doesn't matter, No problem, Never mind, Don't worry.* So how could I have explained that my childhood friend Cheryl (and not my mother) received my first letter home, and my mother, furious, hurt, had decided to lash out? Every few days her letters arrived, smoldering blue airgrams that traveled halfway around the world to declare her rage and humiliation. They were my only mail (being the Anointed One not having inspired the appropriate responses from Cheryl).

Each day I waited, half dreading, half hoping, for hot words from home in a tiny upcountry town where I was the first black person anyone had ever seen, where seventy percent of the language was rendered in tones I couldn't yet hear, where laughing crowds formed every time I ventured into the streets. I was used to being different, but nothing had prepared me for that.

In a culture that possesses a sparse psychological vocabulary at best, how could I have explained that I was an only child with a single parent who shoved angry notes under my bedroom door enumerating my childhood transgressions? That I was the grandchild of an immigrant Swede who disowned his only daughter for becoming pregnant by a black man. That if I didn't fix the situation, spending a stranger's money to send a series of apologetic telegrams, my mother would leave, just as my father had. At sixteen, I was as foolishly terrified as a child.

Ajarn Supatra draped a soft arm over my shoulders. We were nearly the same height. *"Mai pen rai,"* she said, as if she could sniff the complex cycle of worries seeping out of my pores. *Everything will be fine.*

There was an outburst of sharp whispers and hisses, then a hush as the postmaster himself threw open his office door and stood in the doorway beneath the portrait of the king. Chin aloft, he surveyed the knot of workers, who quickly disentangled themselves and scurried in all directions. The women closest to the door placed their palms together and bent forward, the Thai gesture of respect. The postmaster's uniform gleamed with gold braid; his belly bulged impressively over his belt.

My clerk snapped up off the counter, his boyish demeanor disappearing along with the wide expanse of teeth. He held the telegram inches away from his nose, feigning study.

The postmaster spotted us at the counter and narrowed his eyes. *"Farang!"* he hissed, as do all Thais upon spotting someone different. Shouting the word "foreigner" at the subject itself appears to be a biological imperative, almost a communal form of Tourette's.

He extended an imperious finger in our direction and wriggled it at me.

I caught my breath.

"Ask the *farang* if she likes spicy dishes!" he shouted. "Can she eat Thai food?"

§§

THE SECOND REASON I found myself ordained in the Thai forest, stripped of contact with friends and family and having taken a vow of silence, was failure. In the five years between my high school exchange and my sophomore year of college, the expectations of Holiday Inn Rotarians melted into benign nostalgia. Thailand had taught me my role as the Adaptable Foreigner, and richly rewarded my efforts. Not-yet-discovered Southeast Asia was a great place to be free, or rather to be so alone, so *farang,* that little was required of one. The entire society, beginning with Buddhism itself, was based on earning and rewarding merit. Glowing with confidence after my year, I'd fastened my sights on home, on the last great bastion of American meritocracy—a university education. And it was there, at Harvard, the ultimate American institution to which I had won a scholarship, that I would learn failure—and nearly die in the process.

Though the events driving my second trip to Thailand are more recent than the first, they're harder to remember. I recall a few hazy images: I'm twenty-one, creeping through the courtyard of my dorm with a raincoat over my head. Two friends flank me, guiding my steps and holding the coat in place. It's dark beneath the coat and quiet, my friends' voices muffled and singsong. The plan is to get into Harvard Square and avoid being spotted by a professor who wants to help me pass his class.

The class, a special seminar on international human rights, is the exact course I imagined when I imagined college as my salvation from rural life. The focus is Southeast Asian refugees; the classroom is in my own dormitory; the professor is willing to let me write about my high school exchange experience in Thailand and my current volunteer work with Cambodian and Laotian refugees. All I need to do is go explain my chronic absences and incomplete work. Each week after class he stands in the courtyard outside the classroom, waiting.

Beneath my raincoat, I stagger and sweat. If I could explain, don't you think I would? My two friends giggle and steer, amazed at the lengths to which I will go to fail.

All that spring, I cried. Even when raging at my boyfriend for imagined transgressions, or teaching English to refugees who woke each morning to find their memories as barren as the bombed territory they'd fled, or ladling soup to the homeless outside Harvard's wrought-iron gates, or staring numbly at my worried mother during the rare vacation when I could afford to go home, I was really crying.

Besides nearly killing me, college taught me several things. Namely, that external identity mattered. Being black mattered. It determined where to get off the Boston subway without receiving a baseball bat to the head. Being the biracial child of a single, white mother determined which whites would beg me, breezily, to integrate certain spaces and which blacks would turn their backs, stage-whispering about "messed-up Oreos." Being female determined the number of times I would cross my professors' minds, and the number of men who would grope me, curious for integration of a sort. Being from the rural Northwest encouraged peers to smile at my accent and unfamiliarity with the *New York Times*. Being on financial aid meant I spent my vacations huddled in dormitory rooms with the heat turned off, my afternoons serving Faculty Club highballs to pinstripe-suited recruiters who placed their tips wearily in my hand with a whispered confession: "You're probably better off where you are." Yes, the outside mattered, and it all mattered more than what I believed did.

The spring of my sophomore year, the spring before I headed to Thailand for the second time, I was already sick from the long Boston winter—skin pale, legs bowed like a sailor's. In a desperate bid to save myself, I orchestrated a foolproof exit. My plan, if I could call it that, was brilliant in its simplicity. I committed myself to an exhausting mesh of responsibilities—classes, independent study projects, volunteer extracurriculars, work-study jobs. My net was taut, intricate. Then, once everybody expected great things of me, I jumped ship. The splash could be heard all the way to Washington, where my mother was trying to teach gang kids to read, all the way over to Nigeria, where my father was arrested in the coup that ended democracy for the next sixteen years.

I can scarcely remember the details. All that remains is the after-pain, a faint throb whenever I try to force myself to remember, a silent slide show: There I am, "floating," i.e., rudderless, unattached to any rooming group, my roommates having dumped me at the last minute. There I am, my family's up-by-your-bootstraps hopes dashed. There I am, at three in the afternoon—still in bed, the covers pulled over my head.

It began during Harvard's notorious reading period. While other students scrambled to master an entire semester's worth of information in two weeks, aided by yachtloads of pharmaceuticals, I sat in my room with the phone blaring off the hook, too depressed to finish my term papers or take my exams, and too scared to get a dial tone and ask for help.

By the time exam period washed in, I'd given up any pretense of treading water. Slowly I began to sink. It would be years before I realized what actually happened, before I recognized the signs— waking up already weak from tears, days spent in bed, avoiding friends—of my breakdown. The self hadn't sunk. It, along with an entire raft of values, had hit bottom and shattered. Bits lay scattered among the wreckage, too small to recognize. Divers returned from the murky depths, shaking their heads. I surfaced occasionally, at night or beneath a coat.

Once it was too late to salvage my college career, I plugged the phone back in and waited, shivering like a wet dog, for Harvard to respond to its wasted investment in my potential. A lifelong perfectionist, I took a certain dull pride in my commitment to complete failure. An official directive arrived expressing sympathy for my father's imprisonment and disapproval over my behavior. I was told to leave campus for a year.

During short bursts of sugar highs, I packed my bags, thinking it wasn't enough to leave campus. The site of failure was so much wider. And so, mismatched socks trailing out of my grandfather's army duffel, I chose true exile. I would leave Cambridge, New England, the United States, North America, the entire Western Hemisphere!

When I fled my country, I didn't take a map. I wasn't looking for anything. I sensed, without yet being able to articulate it, that Harvard represented the very essence of the West that didn't work for me. All I knew for sure was that I was drowning, a constant pressure on my chest to choose between things I could not choose between—black or white America, material or spiritual gain, gender or racial allegiance, beauty or safety, myself or others—choose, choose! With each dichotomy I sputtered, taking on water. For the first time in my life, I was lost. Even if I could swim, where was the shore?

So why the Thai forest? In my haze, I remembered Thailand. I remembered that Eastern culture opposed oppositionals, that ambiguity flowered like orchids. If I wanted golden temples and green mountains in the morning, followed by massage parlors and opium dens at night, where was the conflict? If I wanted to squat at the clash of cultures, in the crazy gray zone, who would tell me no? There I could be brown—not interwoven shreds of black or white flesh only resembling it from a distance. There perhaps I could catch my breath as I prepared to do battle for my place in America.

And why a Buddhist nun? This I don't know. I'm as surprised as anyone. When I returned to Thailand, I dedicated myself to a Grand Fieldwork Project, believing that I would therein avenge my academic failure and redeem my intellect. And I did just that (yes, happily, I am no dolt). But I had no such plan to redeem myself. If I had planned to start again, it certainly wouldn't have been in a world where the independent self did not exist. How could one plop oneself down amidst mendicants seeking to renounce their egos and find one's own? How could stripping possibly save anyone's life?

If I'd been thinking, I wouldn't have chosen to erase all physical identifiers and swaddle my body in sexless layers of white cloth. (Despite sharing the American girl's love-hate relationship with her body, I balk at punishing it; feeding weakness is more my style!) It wouldn't have occurred to me to try to reconstruct an identity free of this troubling, marked body. Nonetheless, the surprising decision to ordain and what I learned during my short, short tenure as a nun revised the very premises of my life. I'd been raised to believe in myself, in intellect, in the Western tenets of self and science, and I'd taught myself not to fail. Soon everything I knew and counted on would be stripped away. As it turned out, failure was the first step toward real life.

ৡৢ

FOR YEARS I DIDN'T talk about being a Buddhist nun. The reasons varied. For one, the subject presented two Great American Conversational No-nos: Religion and Race. I'd been taught that religion was a private, touchy subject. My parents split over their differences, and our town condemned my family's liberal spiritual beliefs. Added to that, I'd been raised Unitarian, a vague, good-natured philosophy that required little of adherents save rejection of a Trinity—the very thing Buddhism espoused. In truth, Buddhism seemed fertile with shame. It wasn't a black religion, after all. God knew my connection to black America was tenuous enough, given my mixed, African parentage, Scandinavian immigrant upbringing, and privileged college life. Spending a year developing an interior life seemed like a luxury reserved for students with trust funds and time to burn. How would indulgent endeavors uplift the race? There was also the shame of having fled America. It confirmed that, like the Tragic Mulatta of literature, I was (alas! hand to cheek) weak, tainted. Frankly, I didn't need the strange looks and demands to account for myself.

Even today, with Eastern philosophies in the mainstream, ordination is an unlikely, discomfiting topic. Now the problem, in this age of Extreme Sports, Adventure Travel, and Radical Makeovers, is that I haven't changed in the way that people expect. Where I should be *über*-nun, I'm not even what is perceived as a practicing Buddhist. I don't meditate regularly; I nurse anger; I despise tofu. Dammit, I don't appear to have *learned* anything! So how can anyone learn from me?

How do I begin to explain that, though I lived the role more seriously than anything in my life, being a Buddhist nun actually had little to do with being a Buddhist or with being a nun? It was about hacking a difficult path through the jungle, clawing my way from one paradigm to another. The change was the journey itself, and anyone can get there, down any trail. This is specifically the story of a silent girl who threw off an overcoat and stripped away everything underneath. A new kind of traveler—the Hungry American—who set out in search of faith without a map. The Sarcastic American who used a journal to write her way through the trees to a new self. It has taken me all this time—more than a decade—to understand the strange decision made one afternoon in the dreaming shade of a Thai temple, as pale butterflies knocked against my warming flesh. Despite arising from failure, my decision was an act of resistance, of downright defiance. I chose life. And in telling the tale, I choose it still.

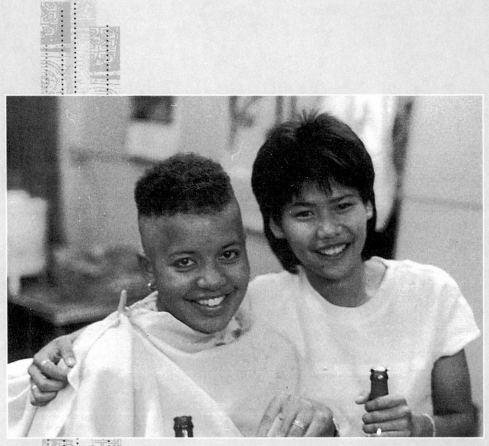

With Chong, best Thai friend, at head-shaving
ceremony, the night before the ordination.

CHAPTER ONE

❦ Killing Faith

ORDINATION SIGNIFIES DEATH AND REBIRTH FOR THE CANDIDATE.
HE GIVES UP FAMILY AND FRIENDS, ALL FORMER ASSOCIATIONS,
LEAVES OFF HIS OLD CLOTHES, IS SHAVED AND RITUALLY BATHED,
AND FINALLY RECEIVES A NEW NAME.

—*Robert C. Lester,*
THERAVADA BUDDHISM IN SOUTHEAST ASIA

JANUARY 26. I arrive at Wat Phra Singh, the Royal Temple of Northern Thailand, slightly hungover, fighting a losing battle with my clothes. I am draped in yards of heavy white cotton, which indicate little intention of adapting to Western body movement. The fitted jacket whispers angrily when I bend my arms. The stiff new sarong slyly unwraps itself when I'm not looking. The wisp of gauzy shawl slung shoulder-to-shoulder alternates between twisting tight to strangle me, incensed, and sliding off, indifferent. Worst of all, my breasts are flattened to my chest by an undergarment I am convinced traces its origin to the medieval hair shirt. Only the plastic flip-flops behave. It seems a bad omen that my attire so clearly hates me.

My Thai host mother maneuvers the new Nissan pickup into the temple courtyard and jams the gears into park with a vigor that feels like hostility. It's just the two of us; my host father will follow later with the kids. I peer out the window, terrified to leave the cab of the truck. I suspect my angry clothing has little investment in helping me carry off this deceit. How do I stand? Where do I put my

Mae—N 1. com. mother
Chii—N ascetic (of either sex)
Maechi or *maeji*—N nun

—MARY R. HAAS,
Thai-English Student's Dictionary

Thai Theravada Buddhist nuns are women who live an ascetic lifestyle by shaving their heads, wearing white robes, and following certain precepts. Most of the nuns have taken eight precepts, but some have taken ten. Thai nuns are generally known as "mae chi."

The ritual ordination of mae chi requires a woman to receive the precepts from a monk or a senior mae chi. This is usually done after they have shaved their head and donned a white robe. Mae chi may stay at home, in a temple, or a nunnery. When a mae chi wants to leave the religious life, she may do so by returning to the preceptor and again wearing lay clothes.

—NARUMON (POOK)
HINSHIRANAN,
"The Case of Buddhist
Nuns in Thailand"

It was only later that the Order lost its primitive character and became a refuge for the poor, the unsuccessful, the unmarried and the widowed, the entrants being looked upon as unfortunates who had found life too difficult.

—I. B. HORNER,
*Women under Primitive
Buddhism*

hands? What if the entire outfit falls to the ground, leaving me naked before the crowd?

I glance at Khun Mae, my tiny, bespectacled host mother, who finally cuts the engine. Though she hasn't said anything since two nights ago when she ordered me into the truck and drove in grim silence, lips pursed as they are now, to the house of Ajarn Boon, my fieldwork supervisor and ordination sponsor, I know that she still must doubt my ability, question my resolve.

"She doesn't know what she's doing," she railed that night to Ajarn Boon. "If she breaks the precepts, our family's *kamma* [karma] will be jeopardized for having helped her." She was a born-again Buddhist, zealous in her hunger to make up for lost time.

And despite my anger that after all the months we've spent visiting temples and discussing Buddhism, she waited until two days before my ordination to voice her reservations, I had to agree. It's true. I have no idea what being *maechi,* a Buddhist nun, entails. I just know I must do it. I've known since the first moment I saw Wat Thamtong, a few weeks ago. Ajarn Boon and I had stumbled out of the mountain pass and into the narrow grounds with their rushing streams and ivory butterflies. As I stood panting, I knew that this was where I would live. Everything else has been incidental.

Now, at eight o'clock on the morning of my ordination, as on the night my host mother carted me to Ajarn Boon's like a bad rebirth just waiting to happen, I say nothing. Terrified as I am, I am still more afraid to admit defeat.

❧

ONE MORNING, months before I even considered ordaining, while I was still preparing my research project on *maechi,* I accompanied my host mother to a *wat* (temple or monastery grounds). At the front entrance we passed two *maechi* dressed in white, their heads and eyebrows shaved. They stood outside the door to the sanctum, clutching meager posies in the folds of their robes, faces shining as brightly as their polished heads. I lingered to smile at them while my host mother watched, a strange expression twisting her face.

Once we passed out of earshot, she leaned close. "See how they sell flowers to support themselves?" she whispered. "They can't even take the vow not to touch money!"

She explained that though circumstances force *maechi* to support themselves, using money relegates them to a lower spiritual plane. While Thailand's much revered monks receive food, clothing, and shelter from the church and devout laypeople, *maechi* are no one's concern. They're generally considered misfortunate, forgotten women. "Broken heart, broken home," Thais quip when the subject arises, implying that women ordain due to domestic problems, failed love affairs, poor health, or the loneliness accompanying old age.

Are these supposed to be "illegitimate" reasons for seeking spiritual solace? I wondered if she was telling me this to dissuade me from "wasting" my time studying female mendicants, or out of feminist outrage.

Inside, we prostrated ourselves before the altar three times and lit three sticks of incense. Like Christianity, Thai Buddhism is based on a Trinity: the Buddha (the Enlightened One), the Dhamma (His teachings and doctrine), and the *Sangha* (the ordained community). The importance of the number three runs strong throughout Thai society, even secular life. Everything must be constructed, articulated, allocated in threes, my host mother often explained.

When we left the *wat* compound, the *maechi* glanced up to say good-bye. Again I loitered, staring at them and their flowers, trying to imagine what made these hungry women smile so. Reluctantly I followed my host mother to the parking lot.

At the truck I turned to find one of the *maechi* hurrying after us. She was holding out her hand, and I patted my pockets, wondering what I'd dropped. As she neared, I saw one of her flowers pinched between her thumb and index finger. Reaching me, she tucked the golden blossom into my palm in a single smooth movement.

[*Maeji*] standards of education are very low: only forty percent have completed the required seven years of primary school and only seven percent have completed ten years. Eighty percent of them come from farming backgrounds, and the majority become *maejis* to escape worldly problems. . . . [E]lderly ones often find it necessary to beg for their sustenance, which further degrades the status of *maejis*.

—DR. CHATSUMARN KABILSINGH, "Nuns of Thailand"

The living conditions of mae chi are relatively poor. If they live in a temple, they are often automatically subordinate to monks. Most mae chi live in the poorer quarters of the temple. Their daily activities include cooking, cleaning, washing, and maintaining the temple grounds. James Hughes observes that: "In

Thailand nuns cook for themselves and for the monks, as well as performing other labour which would be forbidden if they were fully ordained. They frequently have merely replaced motherly responsibilities with those of celibate housewives, though with even more exaggerated subservience than laywomen."

—NARUMON (POOK) HINSHIRANAN, "The Case of Buddhist Nuns in Thailand"

Up until the moment of ordination, one can, of course, have no idea what being a nun entails. . . . Naturally, one will have expectations, hopes and views. One could compare it to getting married.

—AYYA KHEMA, "The Significance of Ordination as a Buddhist Nun"

"*Hai khun,*" she said, her face aglow. *For you.* And then she was gone, her bare feet crunching over the sharp gravel of the parking lot.

My host mother blinked behind her Coke-bottle glasses, speechless for once. I stared at the gift in my hand. The flower was so delicate, its veined, buttery-colored petals so thin, that it seemed to be made of paper. I turned it over and over to convince myself it was real.

Inside the car, I put the flower on the dashboard and immediately a full, heady perfume plumed the sunny car. For an instant it was summer back home on the farm and I was easing my way through a cloud of bees to reach the trumpets on the honeysuckle vine. I broke off an orange blossom and sucked the honeyed nectar from the neck.

When I felt the familiar lurch of the truck pulling off the main road and bouncing into the family compound, I opened my eyes. The flower was gone. Its papery petals had burned up in the sun, leaving nothing but a scattering of sweet, pale ashes across the dashboard like the residue of incense.

☙

AS I GAZE OUT the truck window, I imagine a cluster of *maechi* all holding fragrant, golden bouquets; instead I see a dozen laypeople inside the temple grounds. They mill about the white stone fence and stiffly manicured bushes, stirring up the packed dirt of the courtyard. As soon as we depart, the saffron-clad monks will sweep the grounds, as they do every day, twice a day.

The crowd is a mixture of Thais and Westerners: my five fellow students in the University of Wisconsin's new College Year in Thailand program—tall, studious Jim from Colorado; Angel, the raised-in-Bangkok daughter of career diplomats; tiny, laid-back Eric from Amherst; Francis, a fortyish nonstudent from Canada; and my buddy Scott from the Twin Cities, loose-limbed and wicked. Faculty and staff from Chiang Mai University. Students and travelers we have befriended. Thai host families.

The white January sun gleams cool in the morning sky. Though most of the Thais are wearing sweaters, several of the Westerners drag handkerchiefs across their brows, already overheating.

As I step out of the truck, the knot of people rushes forward. "Your hair!" comes the cry from those who missed the head-shaving ceremony last night. "Look at your robes!" They surround me, pelting eager questions.

I smile, feeling too goofy to merit all the attention. This is just a research strategy, after all. For months I've read the sparse literature available about *maechi,* planning the Groundbreaking Fieldwork Project on the identities and self-images of Thai *maechi.* I've withstood the barrage of prejudice against the wisdom of female ordination. I've visited famous *wat* and interviewed residents. I got so caught up in this double redemption, this plan to recover both my intellectual credibility and the status of Thai *maechi,* that when Ajarn Boon suggested true anthropological study required undercover work, I leapt. Asking myself, *Why not?* I willingly chose this white, unfriendly disguise.

Grateful that today is a day for ceremony, for strict attention to the intricacies of Thai ritual, I place my palms together in a steeple and bring them to my face while bowing. The gesture, known as *wai,* indicates both greetings and thanks. As the head is sacred and the feet profane, the higher up the hands touch the face, the greater the respect shown. Fingertips touching the bridge of my nose, I thank each elder for coming.

I find Jim's parents, who coincidentally arrived in Chiang Mai City two days ago as if representing America itself, among the growing number of guests. Over the summer they took pains to visit Jim separately at the apartment we shared in Madison, but now here they are—together halfway around the world at the Buddhist ordination of the girl who used to be their son's roommate.

January 18
8 Days Before Ordination
..

Preparing for ordination is much like planning a wedding. For weeks I've been studying my vows, going to the dressmaker for fittings, and dangling a list of supplies I need for entering the monastery in front of invited guests.

..

Ajarn Boon is going to be my official sponsor. He drew up a list of twenty items, things like new bath sandals, a straw sleeping mat, a flashlight, a water bucket for showers and laundry, toilet paper, and honey for the afternoons.

..

I added things that wouldn't occur to him, like antimalarial pills and tampons.

The guests write their names next to the item they plan to buy, just like in a bridal registry. The difference is that they're making merit, adding to their good karma, by aiding my spiritual journey. Maybe it's not so different after all.

..

The items should be new so I can donate them to the *wat* when I leave, and it all needs to be ready and accounted for in a week, the night before the ceremony.

..

Somehow my ordination has become *the* event of the season. Everyone, no matter how Westernized or modern or temple-shy, wants to be invited, from resident expats to tourists we meet at the Night Market. Everyone wants to provide something.

Jim's mother, an effusive, beautifully groomed matron, gasps upon seeing me. "Faith dear!" she cries, throwing her arms around my shoulders. "You look absolutely lovely without your hair!" She bends to kiss my cheek. "Or eyebrows!"

There is something reassuring about her ingenuous charm, as if looking good were the point.

Jim's father looks like an ad for American Dad. He pumps my hand a second and then returns to fiddling with the impressive array of buttons on his sleek camera. The thing looks sophisticated enough to launch missiles. I note his obvious discomfort and wonder which unsettles him most: my baldness, the Buddhist ceremony, or being in Thailand in the first place.

At the end of the line stands a professor notorious for his disapproval of Westerners. I stop short for a heartbeat and let my hands drop. I remember that we issued an open invitation to the entire social sciences faculty, our host department. Finally I manage to stagger forward.

Glaring, he thrusts out a fist as if to ward me off.

I falter, feeling my sarong slip. Why has he come? Is he the proverbial jilted lover here to stop the wedding? (Will he leap up at some point and declare that he "must speak now . . . !"?)

It takes another heartbeat to see the bag dangling from his extended fist, three more to realize that he is offering a gift. The sarong unfurls a bit more. At the back of my mind I recall something in one of my Buddhist texts exhorting postulants not to be concerned with matters of food and shelter, but rather to accept such offerings with the equanimity of one who could just as easily go without. I manage to *wai* and touch the bag, indicating my acceptance while fighting the urge to look inside. I'm not supposed to be toting around merchandise.

Moving as deftly as a Thai, Jim glides up behind me and slides the gift out of the professor's grasp. Acting on my behalf, he offers the bag around. The other guests peek inside, ooh and aah their approval.

I look up to see Ajarn Boon standing near the *wat* stairs with the abbot. He gives a quiet nod.

ତ୍ତ

ALL DECEMBER, the month prior to my ordination, Ajarn Boon took me to as many different ceremonies and *wat* as possible so that I could decide whether I wanted to ordain. As soon as I stepped into his office for our scheduled fieldwork hours, he would leap up and sweep his arm like a general preparing for battle. "To the car!"

He hurried through the open-air hallways, and I scurried behind, tracking his polyester safari suit past crowds of watchful Thai students to the battered gray Peugeot parked out back.

Sometimes we drove miles out of town, stopping to give rides to monks at the side of the road. Though I scrambled into the back, taking great care not to come in contact with them or their robes, always they hesitated.

Ajarn Boon would laugh, his trademark shock of gray hair flapping over his high forehead, slitted eyes crinkling even more with humor. *"Mai pen rai,"* he assured the monks with an airy wave. *Don't worry!*

Ajarn Boon's position in the hierarchy that governs every aspect of Thai society was unimpeachable. His identity as male, elder, a professor, and a former monk—an abbot, no less—shimmered with status. The students in the halls whispered that he used to govern his own monastery but gave it all up to marry late in life and father a child. It was considered a great honor to study with him. Despite this, he treated everyone with the same gentle amusement.

"She's an excellent student," he cajoled the monks paralyzed at the side of the road. "She knows all about the precepts."

Eventually convinced that I wouldn't violate the prohibition regarding monk-female contact and cause them to undergo lengthy purification rituals, the monks would creep into the Peugeot and relax enough to enjoy the novelty of the situation: a ride through

..

The actual event will consist of three parts: the head-shaving ceremony and blowout the night before (my bachelorette party), the big ordination ceremony in white robes at the temple (the wedding), and finally the smaller send-off, where only a dozen or so people accompany me down to the residence *wat* (the impoverished reception).

..

I'm not sure who all is coming to the latter, but it will surely include Scott and Chong, my best Thai pal, Khun Mae (my host mother), and Ajarn Boon, who's organizing the whole thing.

Ajarn Boon has done something amazing. Using his status as a former abbot (and my ambiguous status as an outsider), he's arranged for a full, formal ceremony to be conducted by the abbot of Wat Phra Singh, the Royal Temple of Northern Thailand!

..

Wat Phra Singh is the premier temple of the north and governs all the other *wat* in the region. Ajarn Boon wants to use this as an opportunity to raise the visibility of women in the Buddhist church. No ritual for a woman has ever been held at the royal temple.

..

Suddenly I'm a vehicle for advancing social concern. Of course, I hoped that my body of work would serve this purpose, but I hadn't expected that my actual physical body would.

the countryside from a Buddhist scholar (who drove like there was indeed an afterlife), with a black *farang* poking up from the backseat.

It was obvious how much Ajarn Boon enjoyed these trips, how much he missed his former monastic life. During an afternoon spent at a *wat*, I would return from assessing *maechi* quarters or helping out in the school to find him wandering the library, blinking over his glasses at thick volumes of scripture. Or sitting in the garden, his gaze somewhere in the distance. Other times, normally a man of few words, he forgot himself in lively discussions with abbots and *maechi*.

We ate silent lunches he purchased at roadside noodle stands and invariably returned late to campus. As he entered his waiting classroom, I saw the students watching me, their resentment a faint shadow behind the glossy sheen of Thai politeness.

One particular day in December we stayed in town. One of the larger temples was hosting a major ceremony for *Wan Phra* (holy day), and Ajarn Boon hoped that some interesting *maechi* would appear. And so it was that I found myself kneeling at the back of a crowded *wat* staring through clouds of incense at an albino Thai girl who was staring at a Hmong couple, who were in turn staring at me. It felt like Sweeps Night for Misfits.

All around us ordinary Thais pressed their palms together, struggling to keep their attention on the monks chanting at the front of the smoky *wat*, trying not to watch us watching each other.

The albino girl's skin was creamy as fresh cow's milk. Her hair, which fell in a sleek, straight pageboy, just like every Asian schoolgirl's, was a brilliant yellow-white. She seemed to be completely unaware of my open gaze, staring instead at the Hmong couple through narrow, pink-tinged eyes.

Like most hill tribes, the man and woman were petite and light-skinned, with pale brown hair and pinched features. Rows and rows of silver coins and red cross-stitching bedecked their black cotton clothing. Each sported a black toque with red pompoms at the corners. Silver bangles encircled the woman's arms and legs.

I wondered what led the Hmong, who are neither Buddhist nor Thai-speaking, to venture onto the flatlands and into a *wat*. I'd recently heard that Hmong women who birth twins are considered cursed and driven from the village with their families. Were they such exiles?

The couple showed little interest in the albino girl, staring instead openmouthed at me. Like most Westerners, I was larger than the average Thai and infinitely less graceful. My curly hair and bright skin turned brown by the Thai sun additionally distinguished me. Although tourism was just beginning to creep north to Chiang Mai Province, the majority of tourists were still white, male, and firmly located in the air-conditioned coffee shops, discos, brothels, fancy temples, and opium dens designed for them. I was most certainly the first black, female, Thai-speaking, sarong-wearing, *wat*-going *farang*.

After the ceremony, I found Ajarn Boon near the entrance, where he introduced me to a pale, moon-faced *maechi* who looked to be in her late twenties. Dressed in the standard white sarong and tunic blouse of *maechi,* she wore a third garment, a thick white over-robe resembling the saffron one of monks.

"This is Maechi Roongdüan," he announced, and I understood his excitement. A graduate of Chiang Mai University, our university, she was a bit of a local celebrity.

I grinned. In all my preparatory research, I had yet to meet a college-educated *maechi,* much less one so young.

Sitting so erect she seemed to be floating above the bench, she replied with a wide, twinkling smile.

"*Maechi,*" I asked in English, as Ajarn Boon had spoken, "may I ask why you decided to ordain?"

She responded immediately. "Ordained life allows me to test the truth of Buddhist concepts for myself."

Taken aback by her frankness and impeccable English, I blinked. I'd never heard any Thai—the long-haired student radicals returned

..

My decision to ordain has taken on a momentum of its own, which is both satisfying and terrifying. Satisfying, because after studying and attending so many lavish monks' ordinations at famous *wat,* with their yards of saffron cloth, loads of jasmine blossoms, joyful processionals of attending monks, and feasts, I've been a little resentful on behalf of *maechi.* Their ordination is just a quiet ritual at the residence *wat.*

..

A small boy becomes a novice, and the entire village rejoices. Women, on the other hand, are supposedly weak, worldly creatures, unfit for spiritual endeavor, their ordination a condemnation of the family system. No party for us.

..

And terrifying because, imagine, I'm to be the first woman to become ordained at Wat Phra Singh!

from forest exile, the jean-clad disco crowd, even Buddhist scholars—question a single aspect of Buddhism. Admitting a need to "test" Buddhism in this ninety-seven percent Buddhist country was tantamount to criticizing the royal family or refusing to stand at attention during the daily broadcast of the national anthem—acts to land one in prison.

Maechi Roongdüan pointed to an empty space on the bench next to her, and I accepted her invitation to sit. "Try the precept on eating," she suggested, placing a firm finger on my wrist for emphasis. "Eat a single daily meal purely for sustenance and note the difference in suffering. You are saved from having to think about whether or not you are hungry yet, what and how much you're going to eat, whether it is the most delicious food that will make you the happiest. Saved from preparing, serving, and spending the time eating; saved from washing up afterwards—all three times a day!"

I nodded. "Interesting, but if one loves to eat, where is the suffering?"

She laughed, noting that perhaps we had different definitions of suffering. We debated some more. If I could manage it, I told myself, this would be the quintessential woman in my study to contradict the "broken heart, broken home" stereotype. Unlike other cloistered women I'd interviewed, she had a strength that seemed both worldly and spiritual.

At Ajarn Boon's offer of a ride, she stood up and made a little snaking movement with her left arm; suddenly her left hand appeared from the folds of her odd robe. "We walk," she replied, interlacing the fingers of both hands and placing them against her stomach. Her body looked to be at complete rest.

"Come visit my temple sometime," she offered. "You know Wat Thamtong?"

Again I grinned. Wat Thamtong was rumored to be one of the most welcoming residences for women. Of course she lived there!

This precept [of not eating after noon] helps ordained ones to become aware of hunger and thirst, and to distinguish between bodily needs and greed, greed being basically an exaggerated notion that happiness comes from outside objects. Here the awareness evoked helps us become the lord of our body and mind rather than remaining their slave.

—SYLVIA WETZEL,
"The Function and Meaning of Vows"

Ajarn Boon nodded. "I'll bring her next week," he promised. "I've been wanting to see that place myself."

ᛒᛒ

LIKE ALL THAI BUDDHIST TEMPLES, Wat Thamtong faced east. Unlike other *wat*, however, whose survival depended on proximity to the community they served, it was virtually impossible to find. A week after Maechi Roongdüan's invitation, Ajarn Boon and I spent the better part of a day trying to reach her.

Determined to travel as she had, we took a bus eighty kilometers south to Hod Township. The bus, hot and airless, was packed with the usual commuters—market women hefting large baskets of noisy livestock, flirtatious soldiers with machine guns slung casually over their shoulders, uniformed students with prickly heat powder ringing their downy necks—all wide-eyed and chatty, excited to encounter a *farang* so far south of Chiang Mai City.

Ah, maechi, they sighed upon discovering my mission. *Broken heart, broken home!*

When the sun was orange and high in the sky, the driver set us down on a lonely stretch of dusty road and pointed to a footpath cutting through the underbrush. For another four kilometers we hiked past greening rice paddies in the blistering midday heat.

As I staggered along, eyes on the lookout for snakes, I couldn't imagine where out here a temple would be or why Maechi Roongdüan had declined Ajarn Boon's offer of a ride the week before. Ahead of us, children slipped off the backs of water buffalo and scurried down the path to announce the arrival of a man in safari grays trailed by a black *farang*. As we passed, one by one, the villagers squatting in the paddies stood up, unwrapped the scarves covering their noses and mouths, and stared.

"*Sawasdee, sawasdee khrap*," Ajarn Boon called, waving. *Hello, hello*. "Is the new *wat* this way?" And guided by their openmouthed nods, we moved deeper into the countryside.

January 23
3 Days Before Ordination
..

This is the third day I've made it on a single meal. Ordination rules stipulate that meals can only be eaten "before the sun reaches its zenith." Most *wat* interpret this to allow monks and *maechi* to eat twice a day before noon—breakfast and lunch—and to drink fortifying liquids (such as coffee with cream or tea with honey) after noon.

..

Strict practitioners, on the other hand, eat a single meal and forgo any type of sustenance after noon.

..

In my experiment this week I've snacked a lot—usually due to social situations. It's odd, but except during those after-school snack hours, I haven't been ravenous. And if I have, three bites of food completely satisfy me. If I were dieting, I wouldn't have such control; but here, now, for this, it's easy, a minor concern.

..

I now understand what Maechi Roongdüan meant the first time I met her when she used eating to illustrate how we misplace our energies. *Dukkha.* Suffering.

..

Already I feel so clean, so free. Sometimes, I think: I don't have to worry about the issue of eating all day! I feel free and full of energy. I have so much more time. I begrudge even the moments spent on the one meal; for if one thinks about eating and concentrates on the actual act of chewing and chewing and chewing, one soon tires of it all.

At last a profusion of vegetable gardens and flowers turning their faces to the east signaled the *wat* entrance. There were none of the usual indicators—the encircling walls of limed stucco, the *wat* name spelled out in flowing, gilded script next to the gate, the manicured grounds with neatly swept cement walkways, the white buildings with triple-tiered roofs. Instead we found ourselves in a cool garden surrounded by bamboo and pastel cages of songbirds.

Panting, we breathed deeply and looked around. To the left of the stone walkway stood a new building with a traditional roof. I assumed it was the *vihara,* where worship services are held. To the right an open-air *sala* of teak with a linoleum floor marked the reception and dining areas. A *bod,* with statues of the Buddha, was tucked in back. We appeared to be alone.

We moved deeper into the interior, this time our mouths dropping. Crossing the tiny footbridge, we entered an ancient Japanese wood carving. There, spread out before us, twinkled a scene of aching beauty. High rock walls stretched up on either side, wedging the temple into a narrow gully between two mountains. The faint sounds of chanting in the caves above wafted down like a cool breeze. Where the mountains met, a waterfall spilled out, cascading into a stream that flowed toward us, slicing the grounds into two camps.

To our right, across another bridge, the monks' side of the stream exploded with color and activity: bare-armed monks bustled about in the bright sunlight, hitching up their saffron robes as they churned the packed earth with brooms or hoisted buckets of water up from the rushing stream. Golden dogs scurried behind, shadowing their every move.

In sharp contrast, the *maechi* quarters directly before us were shielded from the sun. Lush, tangled greenery dominated the landscape; pale butterflies the size of two human hands flitted in and out. Silent women swathed in white drifted slowly through the shade. Others sat meditating in open-air pavilions. At the end of the rows of *guti,* private meditation huts, I glimpsed the entrance to the forest.

As if by magic, Maechi Roongdüan appeared on the walkway, moving so smoothly she appeared to be gliding, that smile of hers like the moon emerging from behind a nighttime cloud. "So you came!" She clasped her hands together and rested them low against her body. I had the impression that she was shaking with delighted mirth, though she stood perfectly still.

We beamed.

She led us to the red-roofed open-air *sala,* and we sat together drinking cool water. "What do you think of my *wat?*" she asked, and we soon learned that it was indeed her *wat.* She was the head *maechi.*

I glanced at Ajarn Boon to gauge his response. Maechi Roongdüan couldn't be more than thirty! The idea of this young woman with perfect posture heading up a famed *wat* in hierarchical Thailand amazed me. I wondered how she negotiated governing women who were older (as most *maechi* were bound to be) and therefore socially superior. She was even more interesting than I had originally thought.

Ajarn Boon was full of his usual questions about *wat* organization, and she offered to explain "the special rules." "We eat a single meal a day, rather than the standard two," she began as I gazed out at the reds and gold of the monks' quarters.

For the first time in months I felt at rest. Real rest, not the momentary contentment of having escaped my troubles at home and disappeared into this *farang* life of exotic diversions and constant movement. True, I loved elaborate wordplay and outrageous jokes with Scott and my Thai friend Chong. I loved nursing a salty limeade over a book in a coffee shop where no one knew me. I loved hearing the tones of Thai trip and soar over my tongue. I loved Thai politeness, in particular the green-voiced evening greetings of my host brother and sister. I loved showering from a barrel of cold rainwater before dinner. I loved piloting my red motor scooter through the silent forest. I loved the Night Market with the crowds of Thai, Chinese, Hmong, and Indian vendors.

Many people are curious about why a woman would want to become a Buddhist nun. They wonder what motivates such a decision. . . . Many imagine that life as a nun is a type of escape and means cutting oneself off from all human contact. . . . There is a mystique and strangeness associated with the idea. . . . The notion seems both attractive and grotesque.

—KARMA LEKSHE TSOMO,
Sakyadhītā: Daughters of the Buddha

January 23
3 Days Before Ordination
··
Jim asked me why I'm ordaining. Now that it's down to the wire, why have I decided to go through with it?

..

I don't know. At first, while planning in the abstract, I thought becoming a *maechi* would be "different." Perhaps even (it's embarrassing to admit) a cocktail party starter. An experience that would benefit both me (developing discipline and peace) and my research (if I presume to explain the lives of those I study). Something to look back on. Something to make me brave.

..

I've been toying with the idea ever since Ajarn Boon said that I can't write about something I haven't experienced. Of course, I can never be a Thai woman—but how can I hope to render the interior life of *maechi* on the page if I don't have a language for it?

..

The vocabulary of spirituality, of Buddhism, is so vague to the Western mind. How will I know what I'm reporting if I haven't felt it?

But these were isolated moments in a landscape of fear. I was afraid. I worried about Scott and Chong doing things without me. I worried about not being special, about being replaced by another *farang* who spoke better Thai or adapted more smoothly. Most of all, I worried about the inevitable return home. Thailand wasn't real. I had nightmares about returning to the West, where once more I would be alone, standing still, stupid.

Within minutes all fear melted away in the dreaming shade of this temple, this territory of ambiguity, this yin and yang of landscape. There was just me, and this green and gold place. So this was peace. This single moment rewarded the bumpy two-hour bus ride from Chiang Mai, jostled between AK-47s and bound chickens, standing upright all the way. Rewarded the thirty-minute hike in the airless jungle heat. Rewarded the months of indecision over whether to ordain. America had never seemed so far away. Suddenly I was ready, clear.

I turned to Maechi Roongdüan and Ajarn Boon, unable to stop myself from interrupting their conversation. "I've finally decided," I blurted out, not even knowing if my plan was possible. "I want to ordain. Here!"

ॐ

AJARN BOON signals the twenty-six people who have come to witness my ordination that we are about to begin. He then beckons me to come greet the abbot, an elderly man with a square face and crop of steel-colored stubble marching across his scalp. A pair of rectangular metal-rimmed glasses completes the geometry of his face.

I *wai*, hands high on my forehead, and thank him for agreeing to honor me with this unprecedented ordination. He nods, his mouth a straight line bisecting the stern quadrant of his jaw.

Flanked by two huge crested serpents carved of white stone, the procession follows him up a staircase. Atop sits the *bod*, its red lacquer facade intricately carved and gilded. A traditional three-tiered

Siamese roof floats down over gold filigree walls. All *wat* roofs are made of overlapping round tiles of orange and green, and finished with fluid, upswept buttresses of gold. Long before I ever considered ordaining, I would feel my heart start to flutter like a bird trapped in a tight space at the unmistakable sight of orange and green and gold.

Preparing for my ordination has reinforced my understanding that everything in Thailand exists in threes. Monks are allowed to own three robes; the canon of Theravada Buddhism consists of three parts *(Tripitaka);* devout practitioners affirm their belief in the Threefold Refuge, or Buddhist Trinity, or Triple Gem.

At the doorway, we take off our shoes and kneel, entering the cool, dim interior on our knees. I bite my lip and shuffle forward, the stone floor cold and hard through the slippery sarong. Behind me, I can hear laces untying, Velcro tearing, the slap of sandals falling to the ground.

Atop the ornate altar, a gold likeness of the Buddha smiles faintly, eyes downcast. Unlike community *wat,* royal monasteries usually house ornamental sacred buildings and artistic works. This statue, called *Phra Singh* (Sri Lankan Buddha), was brought from Sri Lanka circa 1400. According to local lore, its special powers render it one of the three most potent statues in all of Southeast Asia. It's an odd statistic, as if there were an annual contest between statues to see what they can do. Pots of jasmine incense and fresh lotus buds perfume the air. The Sri Lankan Buddha looks modest, as if unaware of its strength.

By now my heart has clawed its way out of my rib cage and into my throat, where it quivers fitfully, planning escape. We pay silent obeisance to the Buddha, foreheads touching the bare stone floor three times. With an expert flick of his saffron robes, the abbot shifts around so that the fifteen-hundred-year-old Buddha hovers behind him. I kneel facing their combined authority, hands in front of me, palms together. It strikes me that I am once again where I always find myself—alone and out there.

..

He said I should at least live in a *wat,* even if I don't ordain.

..

I agreed, because it's a strange place to stand—the black woman anthropologist. I don't want to be a detached scientist reducing Asian women to objects of study; I want to use my ability to enter cultures, my own multiple perspectives, to understand, translate, bridge. Participate.

..

And I've wondered. Most Thais, men in particular, dismiss female spiritual aspirations, but the *maechi* I've met belie their stereotypes. In the face of public ridicule and substandard living conditions, they emanate peace and wisdom, serenity and strength. They seem to draw power out of the very air. So yes, I've wondered.

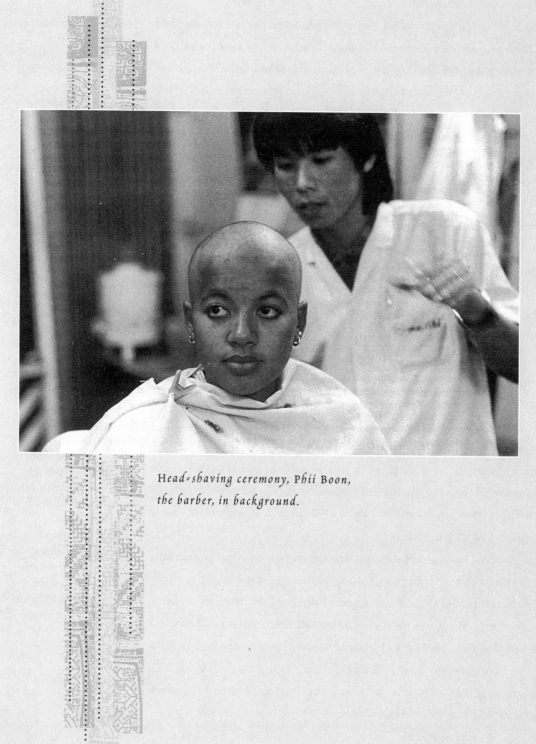

Head-shaving ceremony, Phii Boon,
the barber, in background.

CHAPTER TWO

❧ *Birthing Faith*

AN ACT OF MEDITATION IS ACTUALLY AN ACT OF FAITH—OF FAITH
IN YOUR SPIRIT, IN YOUR OWN POTENTIAL. FAITH IS THE BASIS OF
MEDITATION. NOT OF FAITH IN SOMETHING OUTSIDE YOU—A META-
PHYSICAL BUDDHA, AN UNATTAINABLE IDEAL, OR SOMEONE ELSE'S
WORDS. THE FAITH IS IN YOURSELF, IN YOUR OWN "BUDDHA-NATURE."
YOU TOO CAN BE A BUDDHA, AN AWAKENED BEING THAT LIVES AND
RESPONDS IN A WISE, CREATIVE, AND COMPASSIONATE WAY.

—*Martine Batchelor,*
MEDITATION FOR LIFE

IF I DIDN'T COME from such stubborn ("pigheaded," Old Pappa,
my fiery Swedish grandfather called it) stock, I would have recognized early on the impossibility of ordination. In the months preceding, I spent a great deal of time at a temple near the university
renowned for its lush beauty. It was one of the few *wat* in all of Chiang Mai City that housed *maechi*, so I visited to chat with the eight
resident women and try to imagine myself living among them. So
far nothing had compelled me one way or another.

One afternoon I found another visitor, a thin woman with
impeccable English wearing a hand-tailored lavender silk suit. "She
used to reside here as one of us," one *maechi* explained, at which
point the woman smiled sadly and nodded.

Intrigued by her air of affluence and melancholy, I asked to
interview her. She declined but mentioned that a monk was visiting
from Sri Lanka. "You should speak to him."

"Gladly!" Sri Lankan Buddhism, rumored to be "purer" than Thai, held a certain mystique. The Theravada Buddhism currently practiced in the country had been imported from Sri Lanka in the fourteenth century; the scholarship taught at Thailand's two Buddhist universities originated from Sri Lankan texts; and Pali, the language of scripture and ritual, was an ancient Ceylonese tongue.

The distracted laywoman escorted me to a picnic table beneath a tree where the monk sat reading. A few yards before we reached him, she knelt down, her silk skirt pooling in the red dust, and pressed her hands together.

He glanced over and arched a brow, much like Spock considering some outrageous human behavior. At her request to approach and speak, he invited us to join him at the table, a surprising move. Not only would we be sitting with our heads at the same level as his, but also our proximity increased the danger of accidental touching. It seemed Sri Lankan monks were casual about interacting with women.

"So what do you want to know?" he asked in razor-sharp English. He was young and handsome, with a stare that burned, and I giggled nervously at having no interview questions prepared. "So you're rather silly," he said.

I stiffened, every scripture and sociological study and cultural history I ever read, and every ceremony and ritual I'd observed over the months in Thailand, lining up in my head like a list of annotated sources. Thai women may put up with this *Kneel in the dirt, Giggle behind their hands, Live in the poorest part of the temple* bullshit, my narrowed eyes warned, but not me! Watch out—I'm foreign, a laywoman, way outside anyone's rules!

For a childish, heady moment, I considered reaching across the table and poking him so that he'd have to go through the rigorous purification ritual. My female impurity gave me awesome temporary power!

The monk watched me intently. Before I could do anything

foolish, he launched into a fascinating monologue on the origin of Sri Lankan Buddhism. The laywoman stared sadly into space, her unformed sighs resting as patiently as the hands in her lap.

After a while the monk began to castigate the Thai church for its lax ordination policies. Unlike in Thailand, there is no such thing as temporary ordination in Sri Lanka. Aspiring monks must apprentice as novices, engaging in rigorous Dhamma study for years before they can don the robe. He scoffed at the Thai system, which made ordination accessible to the common man.

"Then why are you here?" I challenged.

"To learn meditation." He confessed that there was no longer any such practice in Sri Lanka. If monks wanted to experience what the Buddha practiced, and not just memorize and interpret his teachings, they needed to go to Burma or Thailand.

I suppressed a smile.

"Why are you here?" he countered.

I explained that I was on a college-year-abroad program, and that in addition to taking classes at Chiang Mai University, I was conducting fieldwork. "Right now I'm in the process of drafting a questionnaire and identifying nuns to interview. When I return to the U.S., this research will form the basis of my senior thesis."

"Are you Buddhist?"

"No. I'm interested in the status of women. In culture."

"Have you meditated before?" he pressed.

"Never. Have you?"

"I'm just beginning. A baby." He flashed a mouthful of bone-white teeth, the open smile of a child not afraid to admit what he does not know.

After we thanked him for his time, the rich laywoman ushered me to the gate. As I stepped outside, she finally let out one of those sighs. "We come here because we think that peace is somewhere in the temple," she said, and I nodded, smiling, *yes*. She continued abruptly. "It's not."

January 24
2 Days Before Ordination

··

Today, all of a sudden, I caught sight of myself in the bathroom mirror and my knees buckled. Why have I agreed to shave my head? Is it to prove my strength of will? Is it out of shame at appearing to care about my hair? Since I'm not Buddhist, why am I doing it?

··

Everyone keeps telling me I can stay in the temple as *upasika*, a devout layperson, dressed in white and following the same rules.

··

Looking in the mirror, I felt my attachment to my hair and fear. Plain fear. I fear future ugliness; I fear that my hair for some reason will not grow back. But I think I am willing to take the chance for this experience.

··

The victory is not that I am brave enough to "deface" myself, but in my release from the fear of ugliness. In a way, I forever free myself.

[*Maechi*] are not suitable fields of merit for the laity. That is, unlike the merit accrued from well-intentioned giving to monks, villagers would receive little merit for providing [*maechi*] with food and the necessities of life.

—PENNY VAN
    ESTERIK,
    "Laywomen in
    Theravada Buddhism"

I stared then at this woman draped in lavender silk and chronic melancholy, not sure I wanted the benefit of her wisdom.

"If the heart is peaceful," she continued, addressing the invisible landscape she seemed to regard constantly, "then you're at peace, whether you're within the temple or without. And if the heart is not," she warned, "you won't find peace here."

I stood like that, one foot inside the temple and one out, for nearly five minutes after she'd returned inside. So in the end it was she, with her quiet comment addressed at the end of an afternoon spent sparring with a scholar-monk, who nearly shook me.

I had spent countless afternoons resting in the shade of *wat* listening to the stories of *maechi*—invalid girls abandoned by starving families, young widows who shaved their heads and relinquished children to their parents, old widows whom no one wanted to feed—each story told generously, with a gentle laugh and always the same authentic smile on a smooth golden face. Peace was here, along with whatever it would take to heal what ailed me.

⟡

INSIDE WAT PHRA SINGH, my host mother kneels to my right, Ajarn Boon to my left. The guests crowd inside the chapel door, forming a half circle behind us. She passes me a footed brass tray with three sticks of incense and three fresh-cut flowers.

Bowing to the abbot, I place the tray before him. He touches the offering, indicating acceptance, and asks the ritual question: *"Maa thammai?" Why have you come?*

I reply in Thai: "I have come to request ordination as *maechi*."

He asks: "Who will sponsor this individual?"

Ajarn Boon gives the ritual response: "I am the one."

The abbot nods, pronouncing to the assembled company: "This is a good thing." Closing his eyes, he laces his fingers in his lap and switches into Pali, an ancient Buddhist language with the hypnotic tonality of Latin. The liquid tones drip off his tongue.

He leads me in a triple recitation of the Threefold Refuge or Triple Gem, holding the *am* syllable of each word and letting it vibrate on the tongue and resonate in the closed mouth:

> *Buddham saranam gacchami*
> I go to the Buddha for refuge
>
> *Dhammam saranam gacchami*
> I go to the Dhamma for refuge
>
> *Sangham saranam gacchami.*
> I go to the *Sangha* for refuge.

I am then instructed to pay homage to the Buddha three times:

> *Namo tassa Bhagavato Arahato Sammä-sambuddhassa*
> Praise to the Blessed One, the Noble One, the Perfectly Enlightened one!

Finally I take the Ten Precepts *(Atthanga-sila)* for novices or *maechi.* Some women now take these vows in Thai, but I've been determined to memorize the traditional Pali. Though I know the ceremony by heart, my voice trembles so much I can hardly speak. The steeple of my hands bobs frantically up and down. I hadn't expected this nervousness. Several times my host mother has to prompt me as I declare my intention to undertake the rule of training:

1. to refrain from killing any living creature
2. to refrain from stealing
3. to refrain from improper sexual contact

January 25
1 Day Before Ordination

..

Today was sunny and still. A faint breeze. Perfect. I wrote letters to Mom and friends in the United States, explaining why they wouldn't be hearing from me, coordinated last-minute arrangements over the phone, had fun with Khun Mae. A long, slow, lizard-green day.

..

Just before I left for the head shaving, Khun Mae called me, and I knelt before her and Khun Pa, holding my palms together in a *wai*. They did the first cut in the living room, with the scent of hibiscus and lemongrass drifting in through the open glass louvers.

..

Afterwards, I completed the *wai*, bringing my hands to my forehead while bowing, so that the merit of what I am about to do will accrue to them.

..

"Sanook, na?" Khun Mae said. *Have fun, okay?*

..

As she said it, I instinctively realized that she felt a big blowout was hardly a suitable way to spend my last night of ordinary life. I lingered in the doorway of our glass garden house, momentarily torn between being the good Thai daughter and the wild American bride.

4. to refrain from lying and false speech

5. to refrain from consuming intoxicants which cloud the senses

6. to refrain from consuming food at inappropriate times

7. to refrain from using scent and makeup

8. to refrain from singing, dancing, and watching entertainment

9. to refrain from sleeping on soft or high surfaces

10. to refrain from touching money

When the ceremony is translated into Thai, several people murmur surprise. The last precept, optional in modern times, is regarded by many as unnecessarily difficult for women, given their lack of social support. Again, a point of pride: I am the first woman to be ordained in Wat Phra Singh; I intend to do it right.

After accepting my vows, the abbot switches into Thai and begins to advise me on monastic life. He points out that the precepts *(sila)* are called "rules of training," indicating that they are guideposts in an ongoing practice, rather than hard-and-fast vows. Unlike Christian vows, designed to ward off sin, Buddhist precepts are meant to clear the mind for contemplative practice. His is the same logic Ajarn Boon used a few nights ago to calm my host mother. It is perhaps the same logic that allows me to think of myself as a visitor to Buddhism—I will keep *sila,* like any good houseguest observes the host's rules, but still be me, untouched, on the inside.

The abbot continues. Besides the Ten Precepts, countless other church strictures govern *maechi* posture, attire, deportment, communal living, and social interaction. This personal attention, in addition to the standard ordination script, is an honor. My host mother perks up at this sign of the abbot's confidence—or at least interest—in me. In my nervousness, her tiny chin jutting upward is the last thing I notice. My senses are shutting down on me. I have no idea what the abbot is saying.

ᏉᏉ

LAST NIGHT, the night before my ordination, I picked up Chong, my closest Thai friend, who was acting strangely quiet and detached, on my red motor scooter and drove to the head-shaving ceremony. The barbershop was a large corner room papered with hundreds of pictures torn from magazines and calendars. Most depicted white models with fluffy, feathered hairstyles no Thai would be caught dead wearing. The barber, a drinking buddy of ours, had been flirting with me for months, despite his recent marriage to his young, pregnant girlfriend, and I was nervous about his insistence on shaving me as his ordination gift.

Everyone was already inside, nearly quivering with excitement, Scott, Eric, and Jim with cameras dangling from neck straps, Angel giggling and swaying, no doubt already stoned, courtesy of Scott's host brother.

"Show Faith!" she urged Jim. He handed over a bag of cookies and a videotape of *An American Werewolf in London*. "Original-language version!" Angel crowed.

"Hey, these are real chocolate!" I ducked just in time as Scott and Eric both lunged for the bag.

"Yeah," Jim explained, "my parents got here yesterday. They send their love. I'll bring them and Keyes tomorrow."

"They're here?" I adored his mother. "With Keyes?" We were reading the work of anthropologist Charles Keyes in Buddhism class.

"Yeah." A lifetime of privilege had dulled Jim. "Keyes is leading the tour. I just had dinner with him."

Scott rolled his eyes.

"And he really wants to come?" I pressed. No pride. Eric took the opportunity to snatch the cookies.

Jim nodded.

"'Before' shot!" Scott cried.

I struck a pose—head thrown back, hip jutting forward, toothy

January 26
Ordination Day

..

I'm still mystified by how, when I went to pick up Chong last night, she insisted on going to buy the sweater she is donating to my ordination—though we were already late for the shaving ceremony.

..

Stunned by her vehemence and poor planning, I sped to the Night Market, whereupon she surveyed row upon row of white sweaters with a strange aimlessness, uncharacteristically silent.

..

Like any good Thai, she claimed to be fine, but she's normally super chatty (in Thai, French, and English) and I wondered if she was upset about my decision to ordain.

smile—beneath a poster of Robert Redford in Christian Dior sunglasses. Everyone seemed to be whirling about except the barber, who stood like a plumb line in the center of the room, the somber cast to his delicate features putting to rest any anxiety I had about his gift. Before I knew it, the five were enfolding me in a group hug, and then tossing me into the chair.

"I need a minute." I shut my eyes.

Scott gestured to the others, who withdrew to clown silently before the mirrors.

Searching for the calmness and conviction I'd had for days, I breathed deeply. *It will grow back.* "Okay, I'm ready," I muttered, "but keep in mind that I haven't ordained yet—if anyone laughs, I may be forced to kill!"

All five sucked in their cheeks and pursed their lips. I was facing a gauntlet of fish.

The barber clipped a pink bib around my neck. "What about the first cut?" he murmured.

Tapping the small plastic bag pinned inside my shirt, I explained that my host mother had done the ritual before I came.

He nodded. "Keep the lock on the upper half of your body for the rest of your life," he reminded me. *"Choke dii ter, kaam dii khao."* *Good luck for you; good karma for her.*

Scott rubbed his long hands together and chuckled. "Okay, Faith. We're going to do it how we decided, right?" He hopped from leg to leg. "Right?"

He explained to the barber: First shave the sides to see what a punk style looks like. Then all the way around, temple to temple. "Slowly," he cautioned, "so she gets used to it. We don't do the whole thing until she's ready."

The barber nodded. After adjusting the bib, he did a quick assessment of his tools, tucking a yellow comb into his palm. He then selected a razor and attached a clipper. The three men palmed their cameras. His thumb twitched and the razor buzzed to life. The five witnesses leaned forward.

My heart crashed around inside my chest, a work elephant run amok in the teak forests. "Scott, I think I need a beer."

Scott stared into the mirror. "Wow! This is great!"

The razor touched my scalp, just above the ear. The sound reverberated through my head. "Scott, could you go get some beer?"

"Yeah, okay, okay." He waved a vague hand in my direction.

"Scott!" I addressed his reflection. "I—NEED—A—BEER."

"Oh Christ!" he blurted before running out the door, limbs flying in all directions. Minutes later he returned with six large bottles of Singha dangling from his long fingers.

Grabbing an icy brown neck, I gulped. Jim snapped a picture. Bitter lager poured down my throat and tore off after the rampaging elephant. My last beer.

As my vertebrae began to loosen, the hair tufted off like down, whispering past my ears, drifting down my neck, tumbling into my lap. Quickly it fell away, leaving me light and vulnerable.

We took a break at the punk stage, sides bare, a tail of hair at the back. "You look like Siouxsie from Siouxsie and the Banshees," Angel chirped, clapping her hands and smacking into a wall. Eric, who was turning brighter red with each drink, his Japanese ancestry declaring itself with a vengeance, doubled over, hooting.

"Let's try something more radical," Scott suggested.

I took another swig and nodded.

Once the sides were gone, leaving me with just a skullcap of curls, we started clowning for the camera. Scott inspected from all sides. Jim and Eric snapped and snapped. Chong clutched my hand with her own tiny Thai one.

I touched places on my head never before revealed, held my entire scalp in the palm of my hands.

The barber's little wife crept down from their upstairs apart-

We speak of the four groups of Buddhist followers— *bhikkhu* [ordained male], *bhikkhuni* [ordained female], layman, and laywoman— but the *maeji* are none of these. They are poised midway between the *Sangha* and the laity, and a double standard is applied to them. For example, *maeji* cannot vote because they are ordained, yet have to pay full fare when traveling by train because they are not considered ordained.

—DR. CHATSUMARN KABILSINGH, "Nuns of Thailand"

*W*hile individual
mae chi may be
admired for their
good acts or medita-
tion skills, as a cate-
gory they are not
particularly admired
or respected. . . .
These women in
white have the poten-
tial for negative evalu-
ation, since their
identity is at best
ambiguous and often
contradictory.

—PENNY VAN
    ESTERIK,
    "Laywomen in Ther-
    avada Buddhism"

ment and darted shyly around the room, her belly huge. "You look
the same," she whispered. "Even without hair, you're beautiful."

"Do it!" Scott directed. The barber shaved a road down the middle of my head and shouted, his first sound. I was Groucho Marx.
We cheered. "More!" I metamorphosed into a Chinese schoolboy
with two tiny horns of hair. "Ohmigod!" We were choking, practically peeing in our pants.

"Let me touch, let me touch!" Scott begged, palming my scalp.
The barber, despite his profession, smiled uneasily. It's an immense
liberty, verging on insult, to touch someone's sacred point.

"Oh boy, Fate!" Scott said, mimicking the Thai pronunciation of
Faith. "So you're really doing it, are you?"

I smiled and smiled, and then suddenly I was bald. The room fell
silent.

The rest of the evening was a blur. I know that Scott's host
brother came sauntering into the room, drunk and cocky, and
blurted out, "Fate! Where did your hair go?" I know that we made
it a real American Night, gorging on chocolate chip cookies, smoking Thai stick, watching the Jiffy Pop from my Christmas care package rise, rewinding the video's mild sex scene and playing it back not
once but twice. I know that everyone, including me, kept forgetting
I was bald and then suddenly remembered, gently fingering my
head.

I know all this, but the last thing I remember clearly was holding my breath while the barber, silent and serious, cleaned the stubble off my head with a glittering, old-fashioned hand razor, the kind
you sharpen with a strop. He then lay me down on a vinyl table,
cradling my head softly in the curve of his palm. With a delicate
thumb pressing against my temple, he scraped away my eyebrows
with the razor like a caress.

I remember sitting up and gazing shyly in the mirror. The person peering back was almost as calm and sleepy-looking as a *maechi*,
finally unlike my previous self.

૭૯

AS SOON AS I emerge, squinting, out of the dim ordination *bod* and into the overwhelming brightness of day, I know that everything has changed. It's not simply that the heat of midday has arrived in our absence or that my legs fell asleep during the ceremony and I can no longer feel them. It's more. I expected what little change there would be to come gradually, through monastic living, over time. I didn't expect to feel so instantly changed inside. I stare at the brass tray in my hands, and it's as if I'm watching myself from a great distance, as if I have left my body and float suspended above it.

"Put these on." My host mother crouches at my feet, a pair of new sandals in her hands. "You're no longer human," she explains. "You can't wear your old shoes."

I hover above the cool stone, unable to tell if I'm walking or standing. I've never heard this said before with regard to *maechi*. I blink repeatedly, frightened at the sight of a Thai elder kneeling before me, her hands near my profane feet. Despite the commonly held prejudice against *maechi,* it seems that being one suddenly means something. This single moment, the flutter of her pale fingers near my dark toes, indicates just how far things have shifted in thirty minutes.

I glance at Scott, Eric, Jim, and Angel. Their faces shimmer like the horizon in heat, distorted and distant. From their odd, nervous glances, I realize that in their eyes too I have become a stranger, something strange. I look away.

Then I see an amazing sight: Ajarn Supatra, my counselor during the year I spent as a high school exchange student, has come! Ever since returning to Thailand, I've been looking for her. People told me that she married late in life and moved to an undeveloped township in the northernmost province. No one at my old school knew where to find her (though they eagerly confided her difficulty conceiving a child). A few weeks ago I mailed her one last letter telling her of my ordination. I had given up hope of ever seeing her again.

She stands at the foot of the *wat* steps. She must have driven hours to get here by morning. My heart shoots off tiny spurts of joy. A small girl peeks shyly from behind her skirts, her eyes huge. She is beautiful. I have not seen Ajarn Supatra in five years. I have never seen her child.

Speechless with appreciation and too many questions to know even where to begin, I move to embrace them both. Quickly Ajarn Supatra raises her hands, the respect of her *wai* reminding me of the distance between us. I see myself in slow motion warded off, bald Dracula staggering back in the face of a cross. There is nothing I can do; someone else controls my actions. I watch myself nodding to her, pleasant, detached, touching her gift, turning away.

༄༅

THAIS LOVE PHOTOS. At every special event, not less than an hour of photo taking satisfies them. I am arranged like a still-life apple with my host family. With the other foreign students. With university staff and unknown well-wishers. With some French tourists who stumble onto the scene. They line up eagerly, shoulders and fanny packs knocking against each other, while their guide improvises frantically about what they're witnessing. Ignoring him, they shove their pointed noses into my face and gawk as if recording the moment.

I don't know whether to smile like my friends or stand stern and detached like the abbot. I feel suspended somewhere between laypeople and the ordained. I will soon learn that this is indeed the reality of all *maechi,* women in white who do not speak, who are neither inside nor outside society. They are no longer ordinary women, engaged in life, but they will never be considered the holy creatures monks are. I feel alone and yet part of them. Simply uneasy, with one new sandal and one old.

Finally it is time to leave for Wat Thamtong. Those not accompanying the send-off party say their good-byes, though I hardly notice. I am exhausted. I want this new life to begin.

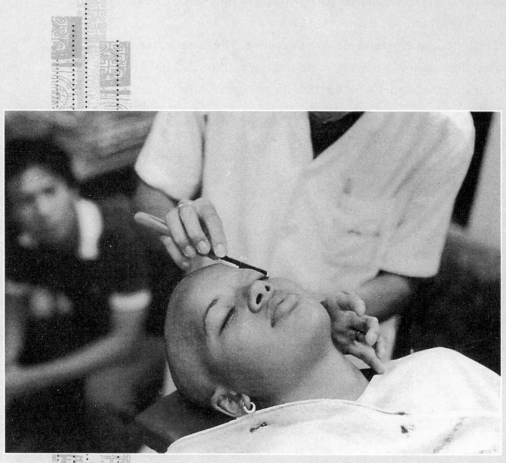

Phii Boon, the barber, shaves Faith's eyebrows.

CHAPTER THREE

❧ The Edge of the Forest

THERE IS NO LONGER ANYTHING OR ANYONE TO LEAN ON.
ESSENTIALLY THE ORDAINED LIFE MEANS RELYING ON THE INNER
EXPERIENCE OF THE TEACHINGS WITHOUT EXTERNAL PROPS....
WESTERN PEOPLE WHO HAVE BEEN RAISED TO FUNCTION INDEPEND-
ENTLY MAY FIND IT EASIER TO ADJUST TO SUCH A LIFE.... [THEIR]
PROBLEMS ... MORE OFTEN RELATE TO DISCIPLINE, EMOTIONAL
CONFLICTS, AND PHYSICAL CIRCUMSTANCES.

—*Karma Lekshe Tsomo,*
SAKYADHĪTĀ: DAUGHTERS OF THE BUDDHA

WAT THAMTONG IS just as beautiful as I remembered from my first
and only visit. Inwardly I rejoice; so I am not completely insane! The
green-and-gold landscape, echoing the colors of the traditional
Siamese roof, is one solace. Maechi Roongdüan is another. During
my registration she stands round-faced and smiling, as she has on
our previous two meetings, emanating that stolid dignity like a
shade I want to rest beneath.

After the ordination ceremony and photo session, guests piled
into two white minivans the department rented for the occasion, picnic baskets in tow. In contrast, I spent the entire eighty-kilometer drive
wedged between my host mother and the car door. As I was now
banned from physical contact with males, Ajarn Boon had to drive so
that Khun Mae could sit between us. Suddenly Ajarn Boon, my partner in Buddhist crime, was lost to me. We had started down this path
of Adventures in Buddhism together, but only I would continue.

WAT THAMTONG
SCHEDULE

3:30 a.m.
Bell rings for first
meditation

4:00–5:00 a.m.
Communal prayers,
seated meditation,
and Dhamma teach-
ing in caves

7:00–8:00 a.m.
Communal sweeping
of grounds

8:30–10:00 a.m.
Communal meal

Day
Individual chores
(e.g., laundry, clean
bathroom and *guti*)
Pay respect to the
Buddha in cave
Walking and seated
meditation

4:30 p.m.
Put out glass for
flower water

6:00 p.m.
Individual lesson with
Maechi Roongdüan

Evening
Walking and seated
meditation
Write in journal
Wash contact lenses

11:00 p.m.
Sleep

He piloted my host family's pickup with customary wildness, chattering away to my host mother, who giggled and exuded clouds of jasmine perfume and rose powder and tried not to watch his driving too closely. I sulked against the cold metal door. I was supposed to be the star! I was the one, after all, who had ordained, stammering my vows perfectly and prostrating myself beautifully before the abbot (I heard the appreciative murmurs from the Thai women in the crowd), and yet here they were ignoring me.

We reached the turnoff to the dirt path, and the Nissan jolted along four more kilometers, my head bobbing up and down against the window like one of those dashboard dogs. By the time we reached the flowering gates, Khun Mae gasping with pleasure, I felt mildly concussive.

It's hardly a surprise, then, that I remember little of my reception and registry. Photographs of the event show my ordination gifts spread across a table. Ajarn Boon and the Professor Grim confer with Maechi Roongdüan and an elderly *maechi* with betel-stained teeth. I stand at the periphery, pale in my unyielding white robes, eyes wide as the camera lens. Bouquets of fresh flowers wrapped in cones of newspaper form a mound on the table next to bags of oranges and bananas and mangosteen—all donations made to the *wat* on my behalf. Maechi Roongdüan thumbs a pencil, entering my belongings in an oversized leather register, a bald Asian Bartleby.

In one photograph the Americans—Scott, Angel, Eric, Jim, and Professor Keyes—peel oranges next to the stream. As usual, they joke and roughhouse, caught in blurry mid-action. I sit alone, uneasy in the shadow of their rowdiness.

Another photograph is populated with people I don't remember having been there—Scott's host brother, random university staff and professors, even someone's elderly mother. Perhaps it's the static nature of photography, but everyone seems to be waiting. Scott watches me with odd, sharp eyes. The air hovers, flat and carved around each image.

"Take your friends to see the caves," Maechi Roongdüan suggests, and I lead the way. Thais and Americans alike gape slack-jawed at the rock walls above us. The Thai, who love nothing more than to *bai thiow* (go on tour), especially if photo opportunities are forthcoming, clamber up the stone stairs carved into the rock face. *"Bai thiow!"* they shout, zigzagging back and forth.

The caves themselves are underwhelming—small, scooped-out pockets filled with second-rate Buddha sculptures—nothing like the soaring, dramatic formations of Thailand's southern islands or the narrow, brilliantly colored crevasses farther north. The Americans glance around, puzzled.

I gesture back over my shoulder. The real reason for the climb is what we left behind—the view: an aerial sweep back over the grounds, a sliver of green-and-gold community curved into purple rock, bisected by glistening water.

Finally we're ready. I follow Maechi Roongdüan into the interior of the *wat*. She walks with slow purpose. The send-off party trails behind, voices low. She halts at the last building before the forest entrance. It resembles a long dorm, a row of attached rooms sharing a common veranda. My heart sinks at the sight of such pedestrian architecture. I had imagined myself (doing what, wasn't clear) in a picturesque teak cottage with flowers on the path.

She opens the first door. "This is temporary; tomorrow you move into your own *guti*."

Just like a real *maechi*! I try not to let relief animate my features.

I step inside, resolved not to pay the place much mind. It's a simple bare box with wooden shutters, precariously perched over the rushing stream. Despite the forest setting, it reminds me of the housing projects of my early childhood, boxed-in and isolated. So much for my experiment with natural, communal living! I blink, calculating just how lonely this new life might be.

Suddenly, as if on cue, everyone in the send-off party snatches up his or her picnic basket and hurries away.

FOREST HERMITAGE TEMPLES

Temples following the Forest Tradition are removed from secular communities and focus on the pursuit of personal liberation via mental development. These *wat* emphasize isolation, yogic practices, discipline, and austerity. The vast majority of rural and urban *wat* do not teach meditation, and therefore, the monks . . . do not practice it either. . . . There are, however, a few genuine forest hermitages, composed of a limited number of monks, novices, and nuns who devote themselves primarily to meditation in the classic tradition of *arannavasi* (forest-dwelling meditating monks) and who in pursuance of the contemplative life have minimal transactions with the laity.

—S. J. TAMBIAH,
World Conqueror,
World Renouncer

Day 1 Assignment
..
Walking Meditation 1
Standing
Wanting to walk
Right foot
Left foot
Wanting to stop

Sitting Meditation 1
Sitting
In (Breath)
Out (Breath)
Wanting to open eyes

There are two types of meditation in Buddhism. One is Samatha meditation; the other is Vipassana meditation. Samatha here means concentration. Vipassana here means insight or experiential knowledge of bodily and mental phenomena. Of these two types of mental training Samatha meditation is practised to attain higher concentration of the mind, peaceful and blissful living and the cessation of suffering. Vipassana meditation is practised to attain not only deep concentration of the mind but also liberation from all kinds of mental and physical dukkha

Openmouthed, I watch them go.

Scott lurches off on gangly legs and glances back over his shoulder, signaling some unspoken message.

I try to hold his gaze and breathe, but my eyes stray to Pōng, my Thai brother. He's a smooth-faced, self-contained fourteen-year-old with the heavy lids and amused smile of a much older boy. Dressed in khaki schoolboy shorts, he scuffs along the path, his long oval face framed by a yellow-green turtleneck of nuclear intensity.

Though we're not particularly close, I fight the urge to grab him and hold on. I ball my hands into fists and press them against my robes.

Pōng sees my look and returns it, eyes shining and wide. That private Buddha smile flickers across his golden face. Finally he detaches himself and stumbles down the path, his chartreuse sweater shrinking like the sun before my eyes.

And so I am left alone in a dim room at the edge of the forest.

୧୨

ONCE MAECHI ROONGDÜAN sees the visitors off, she asks me to join her on the path overlooking the stream. Lowering herself onto a stone bench, straight-backed as always, robes pooling around her, she pats the seat next to her and smiles.

Trying to mimic her slow grace, I feel myself plop into place.

After searching my face, she raises her brows and gives me a look as if to say, *So here we are! Now what?*

I grin.

She announces in English: "Wat Thamtong is not a *wat*."

Somehow I have the sense not to show how much this rattles me. What does she mean, "not a *wat*"? I'm here to study *wat*! Perhaps she means it's not like Wat Phra Singh, a fancy royal temple and tourist destination. That's fine. I want a working congregation precisely in order to observe the famed reciprocal relationship between temple and community. Since Thamtong *maechi* are so well known, I hope to see how much of the standard ceremonial, counseling, and educational functions they provide to laypeople in exchange for donations of food and money.

"This is a retreat center for intensive meditation practice," Maechi Roongdüan elaborates. Pōng smiles, his figure getting smaller on the path. My brain clicks. This is what she was trying to explain the day Ajarn Boon and I visited, only I wasn't listening.

"Intensive meditation?" I ask tentatively. Inside I'm screaming. I've never meditated in my life!

She nods, a gentle, fluid bending forward, exposing a crop of dark stubble against an ivory neck. "We practice the Forest Tradition."

I nearly bolt from my seat and dart down the path. Maybe I can still catch the minivans as they tear up the trail! A Forest Temple! The rigorous Forest Tradition, a return to the Buddha's original ascetic practice, is the stuff of legend, the obsession of bony hermits in the drought-ridden northeast—not the territory of beaming, robust women in Chiang Mai Province.

In all the *wat* I visited in the months preceding my ordination, monks lived relatively comfortable, albeit disciplined, lives. They consumed two moderate meals a day. They divided their time between religious study, temple chores, and ministry. They came and went freely, accompanied by young novices or laymen who handled their money for them; the streets and roads teemed with saffron robes.

Of course I don't expect to live this exact life. I know that *maechi* are often relegated to the *wat* ghetto, cooking and cleaning and serving monks to earn their keep. Religious study is generally not open to them, certainly not at the two Dhamma universities in Bangkok, and travel is restricted. However, as Thamtong is known for its equitable and enlightened treatment of *maechi,* I expect to experience as full a monastic life as is possible for women.

"This is one of the few places that allows women to practice the

or suffering, through realisation of our body-mind processes and their true nature.

—CHANMYAY SAYADAW, "A Vipassana Meditation Course"

..

I begin my first walking meditation at 3:40, determined to last the twenty minutes assigned. Immediately I feel peaceful, nothing on my mind other than my breathing and walking. This disappears as my steps and breathing slow, and there is more time to think. I don't know *how* to think only about walking. I space out, coming to a standstill, numbly droning the litany, *standing, standing, standing . . .* and I have to jolt myself into awareness.

An itch develops on the left side of my face. Maechi Roongdüan said that if I focus on distractions (rather than giving in to them), they will fade away. As I focus, the itch becomes so painful that my entire face twitches violently. I come to a halt, clench my fists, and clamp my mouth tight to keep from crying out. Eventually the pain subsides. The few incidents that follow are much less intense.

..

I become obsessed with knowing the time. I'm terrified that only a few minutes have passed. Fear and desire nag over and over. I resolve not to stop walking until the urge to stop has passed. How much of one's mind can be occupied with the actual act of walking?

..

Maechi Roongdüan said that being overly serious the first day could lead to headaches and stiffness. Already my shoulders are very sore.

Forest Tradition," Maechi Roongdüan says, nodding firmly, a move I recognize from childhood, my mother announcing a new family policy of great morality and equal inconvenience. "Monks and *maechi* come from all over the country for temporary residence."

And of course this news bite does it, as she might—and my mother certainly would—have guessed! Always the cultural ambassador, I plump in the wake of her words. I've stumbled (albeit through no skill of my own) into the situation of the century—a Forest Temple for women. Even better, I am the sole Westerner and first black resident!

"The day," she explains, "is devoted to intensive meditation practice and mindful chores." Fair enough. She continues, "We rise at three-thirty in the morning and do not sleep before eleven at night."

My eyelashes flutter like the butterflies darting around us. "Pardon?" Three-thirty! And I was worried about getting up at four-thirty or five, standard *wat* rising time. My inability to function before 8:00 a.m. is legendary. And furthermore, how is it possible not to sleep before eleven? Are we really expected to function on four and a half hours of sleep? To devote nineteen hours to meditation and mindfulness? Surely there must be a siesta!

"There is no lying down permitted during waking hours," Maechi Roongdüan volunteers smoothly, as if she can read my little mind's feverish calculations. "We eat a single meal, and only liquids are allowed after noon."

I feel like I've jumped off the triple-tiered roof and landed on my back, the wind knocked out of me. For weeks everyone has worried about my ability to subsist on two meals a day. I'm not sure whether this concern is an extension of the Thai preoccupation with *farang* eating habits or a veiled reference to my weight. Whatever the motivation, it's moot now. I have bigger problems.

I'm digesting this new situation when Maechi Roongdüan hits me again: "Most communication is forbidden. That means no speaking, reading, or writing except when absolutely necessary. Our mail is censored and our contact with lay society limited. Ajarn Boon and I agreed that yours would be nonexistent."

My eyes threaten to flood. I've never heard of contemporary monastics taking vows of silence. This is the stuff of myth. I understand the decision to restrict my visitors and letters, given the relative brevity of my ordination, but how can I be me and do what I came to do if I can't read or write? My *purpose* is research. Besides, a major portion of ordained life is Dhamma study, so how can reading and writing be forbidden?

Again, Maechi Roongdüan anticipates my objections in the approximate time it takes me to formulate them. "This will be hard for you," she allows. "So perhaps you should keep a journal. I only ask you to restrict the time you spend writing in it. I also ask you to focus on the practice as if you were any other *maechi*. Then, at the end of your stay, you can interview any woman who agrees to participate in your study."

She widens her eyes, indentations like thumbs in clay where the eyebrows should be. "Is that fair?"

How can I argue with her logic? I did, after all, indicate a desire to replicate the *maechi* experience for myself, and she opened her *wat* to me, accepting me without question. The least I can do is abide by her schedule.

I nod, and she continues her description of life at Thamtong, most likely a repeat of what she told us the day I turned off my ears and brain and decided with some unfamiliar part of me that I needed to ordain.

Scheduled daily activities consist of three things only: communal prayer and Dhamma study from 4:00 to 5:00 a.m., sweeping the temple grounds from 7:00 to 8:00 a.m., and mealtime at 8:30 a.m.

She points to the caves like dark eyes watching us from above. "You may remain in your room during Dhamma study."

I stiffen my features to remain impassive. Unsure of how I feel

..

Eventually I calm down, though thoughts still flit through my head: people's reactions upon my return to lay life, whether my face will glow with peace and wisdom like other *maechi*, the color of my Thai brother's sweater this morning, the look on Scott's face as he left.

..

I become aware of the sensation as one foot descends and the weight shifts onto that leg, and the other foot rises, poised to move ahead. It's wonderful, smooth. I am suffused with happiness. I can do this "boring" activity indefinitely!

..

I go inside to check the time—forty-five minutes! Though proud and eager to do more, I feel drained.

INSTRUCTIONS
FOR SITTING
MEDITATION

Settle into a comfort-
able, upright balanced
posture. Then on the
basis of working from
the gross to the sub-
tle, from the body to
the mind, feel the
touch sensations of
hardness or softness
from the body's con-
tact (earth element).
This anchors the
attention to the body,
especially when
assisted by the mental
label of "touching,"
"touching."

Then tune into the
natural rise and fall
movement of the
lower abdomen, mak-
ing a mental note or
label of "rising," "ris-
ing" concurrent with
the upward move-
ment, and "falling,"
"falling" with the
downward move-
ment. This gives you
a reference point or
primary object to
establish the attention
on.

Having established
the movement of the
abdomen as a base, be
wary of clinging to it.
When secondary
object arises, such as

about this decision, I don't want to sway her one way or another. Yes,
the thought of trying to present myself as a proper Thai woman,
contained body language and all, at 4:00 a.m. is certainly terrifying,
knowing how closely Thai women study *farang,* a giggle at the
ready; nonetheless, Dhamma study seems like one of the few opportunities for communal interaction. Do I really want to forgo it?

"I will come to teach you privately each evening at six o'clock."

It is settled. I cannot refuse such an honor. My presence obviously complicates her life, adding another duty to her personal
schedule. She appears not to mind, however, continuing her smooth
delivery. "*Maechi* behavior must comply with the regulations published by the National Maechi Institute."

I'm in the midst of translating this very same publication. It
seems primarily to be a reworking of the precepts governing monks
to apply to *maechi.* The discrepancy between the number of precepts
followed by each group is a common justification for the difference
in status. *Maechi* only live by eight or ten rules, the Thai are always
saying, so they are clearly spiritually inferior to monks who observe
227. Which merit field would you support? Both the National
Maechi Institute and Maechi Roongdüan herself, it appears, plan to
counter that argument. I grin.

Maechi Roongdüan explains, "The permanent residents live by
the strictest regulations. Most are vegetarian and have taken vows
not to wear shoes nor to use money." Though there's no trace of
pride in her voice, I'm impressed. "We do not expect the same of
visitors."

Regardless of this policy of accommodation, my heart begins
throbbing so hard I can feel it in my ears. Perhaps it's a delayed reaction to the cumulative impact of the rules. My breath bottoms out,
quick and shallow, just as on the rare occasion when I am talked into
riding an elevator and dig my nails into my palms to keep myself in
pain and therefore upright during the interminable, elephantine
lurch from floor to floor. If, when at last we reach my floor, the ele-

vator settles, sits, pauses, the steel doors frozen, impenetrable, that's the moment my body betrays me, that instant of complete, pure panic as I wait for the doors to decide to open.

Maechi Roongdüan, the head of my new home, speaks, and I don't know whether to cry or to scream. I am completely unprepared for this life. What was I thinking?

∞

BEFORE LEAVING, Maechi Roongdüan gives me a brief lesson in the simplest levels of walking and seated meditation. I try my best to focus. For seated meditation, I'm supposed to clear my mind and concentrate only on my breath, inwardly noting the rising and falling of my diaphragm. Distractions—internal or external—are to be noted as they arise. For walking meditation, I should break down each step in walking and make internal "note" of it before proceeding. Every desire, such as wanting to stop, should be noted prior to taking action.

"Eventually you will progress to higher levels," she assures me. I must look skeptical. She explains that for seated meditation, it means focusing on an increasing number of key points on the body. For walking meditation, it entails noting each tiny movement involved in walking, such as raising the heel, lifting the arch, swinging the foot, touching the ground.

"Do walking meditation for twenty to thirty minutes at a time, and sitting for fifteen to twenty. I'll return in a few hours."

Back in my room, I stare at the walls, shoulders shaking with the effort to keep from screaming. As a child, no matter how hard life became, I always had books. And even in college, where I seemed to have lost everything else, I had the distractions of television and sleep. These very things are now forbidden. All I have are the contents of my own mind.

My body and mind feel thick, as cottony as my stubborn robes. I've been dazed, perhaps even concussive, for hours, Maechi

thinking, sensations or mind-states, they too must be noted until they disappear. Only then, if nothing else takes your attention, return to noting the rising and falling movement of the abdomen as your primary object; but always be prepared to attend to secondary objects (sensations, feelings, mind-states and thinking) as they arise.

TECHNIQUE IN WALKING MEDITATION

While meditation is usually associated with the sitting posture, insight meditation exercises can be practised while walking. Walking in insight meditation is essentially about the awareness of movement as you note the component parts of the steps. When walking meditation alternates with sitting meditation it helps to keep the practice in balance.

Walking meditation is also a skilful way to energise the practice if the calming effect of sitting is making you dull or you are becoming over-concentrated. Actually, it can be the preferred mode in insight meditation as it is meditation in action.

—VEN. PANNYAVARO, "Insight Meditation Workshop"

‥

It turns out that I did walking meditation a bit incorrectly: I must feel the steps; noting the feeling should correspond to my breath. *Standing. Wanting to turn* (always turn to the right). *Standing. Wanting to walk. Right foot stepping. Landing. Left foot stepping. Landing.* My eyes should be on the path in front of me.

‥

When I am sitting, my back should be relaxed but straight, one palm atop the other, tips of the thumbs touching, right leg crossed on top of the left or both flat. I should note *sitting, sitting, sitting,*

Roongdüan's terrifying announcements just one more in a series of strange occurrences beginning the instant I stumbled out of the darkened sanctum of Wat Phra Singh and slipped on new shoes.

    ∞

WHEN SHE RETURNS in the afternoon, Maechi Roongdüan stands on the path outside my room and calls: "Maechi Faith!"

"Yes?" I come to the doorway. I feel like a silly Thai girl, perpetually teetering on a giggle. How is that I, who have been *maechi* for all of one afternoon, am called by the same title as she?

I stand aside for her to enter, but she says, "Come," and turns toward the path. Perhaps there is a rule of deportment banning us from entering each other's sleeping quarters.

We walk to the *sala*, where Ajarn Boon and I drank water that first visit, to practice sitting and walking postures. Maechi Roongdüan says, "At first you will be bored. Everyone in their *guti*. No one to talk to. All day and nothing to do. You'll have to 'note': to focus on all that you do and all that you intend to do. And when you become bored, note it. You will see that it rises and falls, comes into being and fades—just like everything else. You have to live in the present, be aware only of the present. If you see this, you see the Dhamma."

She cautions me to work gently into "mindful life," sleeping and eating little. I should be aware in all four postures: standing, walking, sitting, and even sleeping. Kneeling down, touching the mat, spreading out the body. The rise and fall of the abdomen as I wait for sleep. Upon waking, I should take a deep breath and note, *knowing, knowing, knowing,* thereby becoming aware of my body and myself at the instant of awakening.

"Meditation is simply training the mind to become alert and aware," she explains. "At first it seems difficult and picayune." (She *actually* uses the English word "picayune"!) "Soon it will become automatic. Until then, note everything, gently. You do not need to try to think of 'truth.' Truth comes on its own once the mind is cleared."

Despite my first experience with meditation not an hour ago, this discourages me. How I can spend hours each day just blanking out my mind? When can I rest? And what's the point? How much calm does one person possibly need? How will all this time pass if I'm always slow, precise, aware? Going to the bathroom is an ideological act! I long for sleep, some mental respite.

With a smile, Maechi Roongdüan hands me two books written in English and gathers her robes in a dimpled hand. "If I tell you the truth," she said, "you will forget it. But if you experience it, touch it for yourself, you will never forget." She stands, and I see the doors to my old life slamming shut. "You are here to prove the truth of the Buddha's Dhamma yourself."

I stare at her back, erect and graceful as it recedes. Somewhere in the deepest recesses of my mind, I've been clinging to the idea that this is only research, that despite shaving my head and eyebrows, despite taking the precepts, despite leaving friends and family behind to move into the forest, I didn't *really* have to change my life. Now I see it—I'm not here to observe women's monastic lives; rather, she intends to make a nun out of me!

and take three to five deep breaths. Then become aware of my breathing: *In, Out.* Notice the length of the breaths. Concentrate on the abdomen's movement. If something distracts me, an itch or desire, just note it.

..

Maechi Roongdüan says this is how to stop the mind from wandering—by simply noting that it has. Discipline is not about forcing the mind. By itself the mind will soon tire of having to stop to note *wandering, wandering, wandering,* and stay in place. If I want to shift my position, I must note that as well.

..

What is she talking about? I don't expect to sit for more than fifteen minutes, period!

..

I read one of the English books Maechi Roongdüan brought me. I don't understand all of the phrases that intrigue me, and at times I scoff at the Hallmark-greeting-card approach, yet I have to admit that much sounds compelling and applies to me.

We live our lives fearfully to such an extent that we live dishonestly.

We progress according to honest wisdom (realizing what we feel, knowing what we think, opening our attention to all).

She says it's easiest to meditate in early morning and at night. During the daytime after the meal, I'll feel sleepy (as it's the single time I'll be full in the twenty-four-hour cycle), so I shouldn't expect to sit for more than fifteen minutes.

"Detached" includes loving kindness, compassion, sympathetic joy, equanimity.

Anger is most dangerous. It destroys you, the person next to you, and the place where you live.

When he walks, he walks; when he talks, he talks.

If we accept everything in life as our teacher, we will soon be free from the pain of unnecessary resistance and unnecessary desire.

We run here and there trying to be successful, correct and right, when the goal of life is learning.

Thoughts are not necessarily connected with reality. That is why the Buddha taught us to be aware of them before we are influenced by them.

Nothing is gained without effort. To train your mind, you have to work every minute.

Karma means intention. Then action.

Neurotics depend on holidays, weekends, and days off; those who cultivate their appreciation celebrate daily.

Impeccable means: making conscious choice of what we eat, where we live, our friends, our clothes. Forget helplessness and "but."

Every day you are responsible for how you feel; no one can make you unhappy or nervous.

The untrained mind is so vulnerable to circumstances: something good happens and it is happy . . . something bad happens and it is in pain.

Irritation is natural. Don't deny anger—understand it.

An immense amount of fear is created as we spend our lives dodging pain.

Our relationships are unfree to the extent that we demand things of others.

Afterwards, I do some sit-ups and then walking meditation for twenty minutes. I like it, finding it much easier than seated meditation, fewer itches. I stop when I feel trancelike. I'm so very tired today.

..

Night. Can't sleep at all. Mind wild with thoughts and the fear that 3:30 a.m. will sneak up and find me asleep.

Moths crawling up my sarong. Finally can't stand one that flutters over my face, into my shirt. Grab at it, trying to brush it away, perhaps killing it. First sin of my new life.

When I open my eyes, it's as if they were still closed: it's that dark. No city lights. The absolute blackness of night in the forest of a country halfway around the world from home. I'm quite alone.

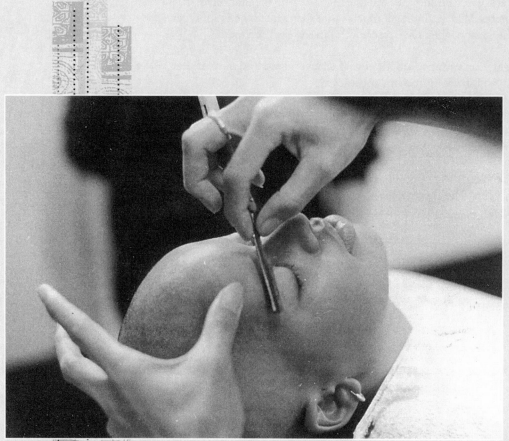

Upon ordaining, women shave their hair and eyebrows,
the sign of having forsaken householder life.

CHAPTER FOUR

The Anthropology of Place

IF I TOLD MY FRIENDS AND COLLEAGUES THAT I WAS NOT ONLY
ATTENDING, THE REPORTER SECRETLY TAKING NOTES IN THE MEN'S
ROOM, BUT BUYING INTO [A BUDDHIST RETREAT], FEELING REAL
SPIRITUAL CHANGE, I WOULD PROBABLY FIND MYSELF DROPPED FROM
A NUMBER OF INVITATION LISTS.

> —*Dinty W. Moore,*
> THE ACCIDENTAL BUDDHIST

MY TERROR ABOUT being able to wake with the three-thirty temple bell turns out to be unfounded (if only because I didn't sleep a
wink in the first place). Sometime before three-thirty I hear the
maechi next door rise and flick on the light. No sounds follow other
than the roar of the waterfall and the steady rush of the stream. She
must be meditating. I rise in the blurry cool of predawn, fix some
orange juice from a bottle of concentrate, and go to the basin to
wash my face.

There in the murky light floats a large, brilliant green beetle. A
flash of panic slices through me. Am I responsible for the death? Is
this an omen regarding my career as *maechi*? A second pain, equally
sharp: sudden insight. I have taken these precepts, such as the
refusal to kill, but have no idea how to keep them.

I stare at the jeweled segments of black and emerald bobbing
atop the water. The whole setup feels like a test. The beetle is so big
I can't imagine it scuttling across my floor unnoticed, and so vividly

Day 2
..
Level 1 Walking,
twenty-to-thirty-
minute stints
Level 1 Sitting, fif-
teen-to-twenty-
minute stints
Level 1 Eating
Level 1 Sleeping

..

As I sit in meditation, my body is plagued by itches, shooting back pain, a sleeping foot. I realize that I am forcing my breathing, keeping it slow so that I can accommodate my internal notation.

At a loss, I concentrate on the pains, hoping the breaths will even themselves out. They do, and when I return the focus on my breathing, the result is instantaneous.

Until this moment, every other time I closed my eyes, I saw light and dark splotches of red and felt my eyeballs twitching beneath the lids.

Now, for the first time, there is smooth, even darkness. I exist inside a large, empty, peaceful dark space. I have become part of my breathing, its ripples so shallow as to barely call attention to itself. The landscape is foreign, perhaps a different existence entirely. I can scarce believe the

colored it doesn't seem dead. I fish the glittery body out with my spoon and slink to the window to dispose of the evidence.

Then I remember: I forgot to wake mindfully.

❧

THIRTY MINUTES into meditation, I finally relax from my sleepless night, tipping over onto the mat and falling into sleep. I'm out from 4:10 to 5:00, then from 5:00 to 6:00, finally from 6:00 to 7:00. Each time I wake with a start, realize I need more, and return seamlessly to the same deep, refreshing sleep.

Upon my final awakening, my stomach complains, sour with acids. At the very same moment, my eyes catch sight of a tangerine across the room. Somehow one from the bag Khun Mae brought as an offering to the *wat* has ended up among my belongings. I nearly drool, anticipating the clean bite of citrus.

I avoid touching the fruit, eyeing it atop my box of belongings. May I eat it? Running through my ordination preparation in my mind, I know that eating after the sun reaches its zenith is forbidden. But what about eating in the morning before the meal? Is the issue the time of day or the number of meals? How strict is the single daily meal policy?

I reach for the fruit. I have no idea whether I'm going to rip it open and consume it on the spot or toss it out the window after the beetle. As my fingers heft unfamiliar weight, I nearly drop it. The tangerine is uncommonly hard. I hold it close. Several deep gouges pock a surface as thick and firm as an uglifruit. I sniff: no citrus, no smell of any kind. It is no longer a tangerine.

Relieved and a bit frightened, I nudge open the wooden shutters and lob the orange ball into the rushing stream.

❧

WHEN THE BELL sounds at eight-thirty, *maechi* emerge from their *guti*, moving in that strange, slow way of theirs, and line up according to what I will later learn is ordination seniority. The longest-ordained *maechi,* the elderly woman who participated in my registration yesterday, heads the line. She flashes a row of red-brown tooth nubs ravaged by betel, and I return a grateful smile. Everyone else seems to be studiously ignoring me.

I perk up to see Maechi Roongdüan, but she appears preoccupied, giving me a perfunctory nod after a quick, frowning assessment of my success (or distinct lack thereof) with the over-robe.

She leans toward me and I turn to catch her whisper: "Go get your thermos."

Though she is the head *maechi,* she tails me, nudging me into line before her, forming a physical barrier between the pair of resident laywomen and me. The two women are *upasika,* ordinary women on temporary retreat from their normal duties as wife, mother, grandmother, career woman, worker. Like *maechi,* they adhere to eight or ten precepts and wear white. Unlike *maechi,* they keep their hair, and their shorter sarongs are topped with only a tunic and sash.

Once the procession of monks crosses the bridge to our side of the stream and reaches the path before us, the women begin to proceed toward the front of the *wat.* Again this slowed movement, as though they're all perpetually practicing tai chi. Each woman walks deliberately, stepping in the footsteps of the one before her, her mind apparently only on the progress of feet.

Upon reaching the *bod,* they place their thermoses in a row on the ground and dip first one foot, then the other, in the stream. As we enter the open, red-roofed pavilion, Maechi Roongdüan pulls me aside down a flight of stairs. Suddenly we're in a warm, cheery room—the kitchen populated by ruddy-faced *maechi* hard at work. I stare: it's like tripping over a hillock and landing in *Brigadoon* or Alice tumbling down the rabbit hole.

Maechi Roongdüan begins tugging on me. Apparently I have the over-robe on backwards, the left shoulder exposed instead of the

transformation happened so quickly. I'm terrified the experience will evaporate. Immediately I concentrate on my thoughts, on this fear. Then a light blue drips down my vision like a top coat of thick paint. This happens several times, several layers. Something important is happening.

Mindful Activities
..

Eating 1
Seeing food
Taking spoonful
Lifting spoon

Prostrating
Touching (hands)
Lifting (to face)
Lowering (to mat)

Sleeping 1
Touching (mat)
Lying (down)
In (breath)
Out (breath)

Waking
Knowing (self)
Wanting to open eyes
Wanting to get up

right. As she wrestles with my stubborn body and cloak, the kitchen *maechi* stop their work to grin. I hold my face still, resisting the urge to ham it up for my audience.

Back upstairs, the monks finish seating themselves inside the *bod,* facing the statue of the Buddha. A waist-high partition separates them from the *maechi,* who kneel and walk on their knees to places on three long mats. They sit according to rank, each *maechi* two feet behind the woman in front of her, all of us facing the Buddha. This time Maechi Roongdüan is third; the two laywomen are directly behind me.

When all the *maechi* are kneeling, our over-robes tucked around our legs and over our feet, thus shielding the profane from the person behind us, the smiling senior *maechi* rings a small bell. A tinkling replies from the monks' side, and two monks scoot forward on their knees toward the Buddha. Everyone else puts her or his hands together in a *wai* as the two light three joss sticks each, bring them to their foreheads in a salute, and place the incense in an urn of sand before the altar. A beautiful harmonizing commences, male and female voices together reciting in Pali.

It takes two verses for me to realize that I know the words. It is the most basic of Buddhist chants honoring the Triple Gem, but I've never known the intonation of the consonants or the length of the vowels. No one taught me how to hold the words, allowing them to thrum in the throat, to quiver on the tongue. It's tantamount to knowing the lyrics of a song but not the melody. Keeping my palms flattened together, I move my lips and watch, memorizing every detail. At the appropriate moments I join the others in prostrating myself three times to the Buddha.

With a rustle of cloth, the monks stand and file past us to the tables outside. Slowly, slowly, they ladle food into the black-and-gold alms bowls nestled in the crook of their arms. During this long process, the *maechi* relax, sliding off their knees and tucking their legs to one side. A not-quite-voiced sigh stills the room. Some reach

THE TRIPLE GEM

The Exalted One, far from defilements, perfectly enlightened by Himself
I bow low before the Buddha, the Exalted One

(Prostrate selves to mat)

The Dhamma, well expounded by the Exalted One
I bow low before the Dhamma

(Prostrate selves to mat)

The *Sangha* of disciples, who have practiced well
I bow low before the *Sangha*

(Prostrate selves to mat)

for the round metal trays next to the mats and pour water from teakettles into yellow plastic glasses; others tear sections from toilet paper rolls and fold them into neat thirds to use as napkins. Maechi Roongdüan and a few others immediately shift into full lotus, backs straight, and begin to meditate.

My eyes rove as freely as I can manage without drawing attention to myself. I catch several *maechi* eyeing me, but their dark glances slide away so quickly, returning to the thick ritual of waiting, that I wonder if I've imagined it. I become aware of a recurring cough coming from the row of senior *maechi*. The woman hunches over, covering her mouth. Her limbs are mottled with the dark purplish lesions of some severe burn or skin disease. No one else seems to pay her any attention.

After the monks finish, the *maechi* serve themselves according to seniority. As soon as a woman reaches the doorway leading outside to the food table, the next one puts her hands together in a *wai* and salutes the Buddha. Raising herself to her knees, she crawls off the mat. Safely off the mat, she stands and turns to face the door. She then arranges her robes neatly before beginning to walk. Throughout all this, Maechi Roongdüan remains immobile, still meditating.

When my turn comes, I try my best to imitate what I've observed, though I can't manage to slow my movements to match theirs. I can't imagine what takes them so long. Praying I won't be my usual clumsy self and overturn a stack of glasses and metal trays with a great clatter, I teeter toward the doorway on cramped legs.

The sight of the long tables groaning with Thai delicacies nearly makes me cry out. Vegetarian food is rare in Thailand, and I had pictured a battered tin cup of white rice, perhaps some steamed lotus pods. But here are giant bowls of fragrant jasmine rice; a pilaf of brown rice, peanuts, beans, and tofu; mounds of steaming sticky rice (the staple of northern Thailand and my personal favorite); the choice of two raw vegetables that look like tree leaves; spicy chilies;

..

I waste the rest of the day trying to reconstruct the meditation experience I had this morning. Trying to force it, I get impatient. Help! You have to try hard but not too hard. Your mind always has to watch itself.

My back hurts so much that it's difficult to maintain concentration during meditation. The only thing that helps is to lie down, which is forbidden during the day. The monastic way of life is not so terribly different from the military: regulated sleep, the careful maintenance of greenery and walkways, control, habit, ritualized eating, rank, summons by bells, early rising, an abhorrence of sloth.

I think that the army targets the body, monastics the mind. Which has more freedom?

I now see what *maechi* mean when they say that, outside of their many restrictions and chores, they have all the freedom in the world. Freedom of movement in lay life is merely a way to compensate for the lack of freedom while standing alone with oneself.

In a sense, these *maechi* have such restricted, sleepy lives, but in another sense, it is freedom, freedom, freedom.

VERSE OF
EXCELLENT
BLESSING

May there be for you
     all blessings,
May all the *devas*
     guard you well,
By the power of all
     the Buddhas,
Ever in safety may
     you be.

three side dishes, one with what looks to be meat; green oranges and finger-sized bananas; even dessert—glossy black glutinous rice.

Following the lead of the *maechi* in front of me, I pile the entire meal into a large white enameled bowl, the oversized serving spoons clinking against the sides as I try to scoop out a space for each dish. Ah, if only my family could see me now—I who for years traveled from cookout to cookout with my own supply of those paper plates with the dividers so the different foods wouldn't touch! Though everything looks and smells tempting, I take small portions, remembering my oft-regretted tendency toward buffet-line madness. The bowls of the women in front of me tower with food, Himalayas to my tiny Mount Rushmore.

Behind me comes Maechi Roongdüan and, putting considerable respectful distance between themselves and her, the two laywomen. Once we return to our seats, placing our bowls on the mat before us, the two bells sound again. A short recitation I will later recognize as the Verse of Excellent Blessing is spoken three times.

My eagerness to try the meal dissipates completely when a monk—very old, to judge by the creaky timbre of his voice—begins chanting the *Anumodana*, a prayer of blessing and thanks. The other monks and *maechi* join in, surrounding the first monk's call with an exquisite wall of sound. The hairs on my neck quiver as the women harmonize with the men, their liquid notes weaving intricately in and out of the melody, sometimes an octave higher, sometimes lower. I feel pricked and tearful, as when the impossibly beautiful, aria-like chords of the two solo violins in Bach's Double Concerto in D Minor tug at my heart and spine. There are musical moments I don't understand, when the experience is wholly visceral, an emotional reminder that we are all sinew pulled taut between poles, skin stretched tight on a drum. Heart. Breath.

My pulse flutters in my throat. I ache to join the voices as they meet, male and female lowering in unison to the passionate, guttural drone of Islamic song. Suddenly I'm on the sun-baked streets of Penang, the air vibrating with the wild cry of a Malaysian muezzin, wishing for just an instant that someone would close his eyes and lean out a tall spire to call for my soul with such intensity, such devotion. I'm falling upward, out of my body. This is why I am in this gully of northern Thai rock, is it not? To fall out of this body and into another.

I sense (though I will only know how very true this is later, when I read the actual translation) that I'm surrounded by wise, dedicated individuals who wish me no distress, no danger, only happiness, long life.

A line ends, the long Pali words still humming in the air, and my heart plummets. The monks and *maechi* take deep, ragged breaths, creating a polyphonic texture nearly as gorgeous as their chanting, and lean into the next line. Again the room swells with sound.

When the *Anumodana* ends, I feel that I might cry. Suddenly I am alone again, returned to this body I can barely manage, earthbound. I sit glumly through the next chant, the *Tankhanikapaccavekkhana,* Reflection at the Moment of Using, which is called upon when receiving gifts of any of the four basics—clothing, lodging, food, or medicine.

The room lapses into silence. I can hear the kitchen-duty *maechi* chanting downstairs, someone filling our thermoses. One by one, each *maechi* salutes the Buddha at what appears to be her own leisure, assumes a more comfortable sitting posture, rearranging her robes about her, and begins to eat.

I pick up my fork and large spoon, the traditional Thai utensils, and check the large clock on the wall. From 9:15 to 9:45 we eat mindfully, according to five steps of increasing complexity posted on the wall. Though the food is delicious, there's little pleasure involved in the actual act of eating, so preoccupied is my mind. My eating slows, as it's too difficult to note *chewing, chewing, chewing* if already starting to *take a spoonful, take a spoonful, take a spoonful.*

I eat until the act of eating bores me, something that's never

ANUMODANA

Just as the rivers full
  of water
Fill the ocean full,
Even so does that
  here given
Benefit the dead.
Whatever by you
  wished or wanted
May it quickly be,
May all your wishes
  be fulfilled,
As the moon upon
  the fifteenth day
Or as the wish-fulfill-
  ing gem,
May all distress be
  averted,
May all diseases be
  destroyed,
May no danger be for
  you,
May you be happy,
  living long.
He of respectful
  nature who
Ever the elders hon-
  oring,
Four qualities for him
  increase:
Long life and beauty,
  happiness and
  strength.

REFLECTION AT THE MOMENT OF USING

Properly considering
    alms food I use it:
Not playfully, not for
    intoxication,
Nor for fattening, nor
    for beautification,
Only for the continu-
    ation and nourish-
    ment
Of this body, for
    keeping it
    unharmed,
For helping with the
    brahmacariya
    (virtue),
(Thinking) I shall
    destroy old feeling
    (of hunger)
And not produce new
    feeling (of overeat-
    ing, etc.).
Thus there will be for
    me freedom from
    (bodily) troubles
and living at ease.

..

I awake carelessly at
4:45, then scrub the
toilet, impatiently
cleaning up some
black gnats in the
process. Two sins,
Day 3 begins.

This landscape has a
life of its own. Every
hour I can feel it
changing. I'm not
Nature Girl, but every
time I step out of my

happened before. Though I took one of the smallest portions, I'm the only one with food left. When later I see them scraping my bowl, guilt over my wastefulness burns my cheeks. I try to console myself: how was I to know how much food to take for my first single meal in a twenty-four-hour period?

Like most Thai, the *maechi* wait until they've finished the entire meal before drinking water. This is followed by a series of cleaning rituals, their execution as precise as in an assembly line. Each *maechi* dribbles the last sip of water from her yellow cup onto her silverware and wipes it and her bare bowl with her used napkin. She then passes her bowl to the woman behind her, who in turn stacks them with the utensils inside. The trays and water kettles are passed to the last row—mine—and the glasses stacked. Several *maechi* have special treats, extra vegetables or spices, which they wrap up and tuck into their robes. Still we continue sitting. My legs feel as if they had long since snapped off.

Finally the two bells sound, and once more we take refuge in the Three Gems. The monks then leave quietly, one by one, and when approximately half are gone, the *maechi* salute one last time and begin rolling up the mats and piling the trays and kettles on a table in the corner. It is precisely ten o'clock. I balance on rubbery legs, feeling useless, the room now straightened, until Maechi Roongdüan tells me to get in line. Only then do I notice that the *maechi* have retrieved their thermoses and stand waiting for me. How did I miss this?

We return to the *wat* interior, moving as slowly as before. My mind wanders. I realize that outside of the chanting and the whispered instructions to me, not a word of conversation was uttered the entire time. I'm not entirely bothered. An introvert and only child, I'm well used to silence. Much of my life I've been an observer, the witness on the bridge reporting back to two warring fronts—black and white, African and American, welfare mothers and Ivy Leaguers, rural westerners and urban easterners. In the absence of speech, surely this observer role will only be heightened, communication flowering instead from my ears and eyes and fingertips. But to whom will I report?

☉☉

AFTER THE MEAL, Maechi Roongdüan moves me into my real *guti*. Hefting my luggage herself—two of the square red-and-blue-striped totes ubiquitous throughout Asia's markets—she leads me to a hut on stilts in the center of the women's row. Flowering plants hedge the walkway. A meditation bench encircles a shade tree out front. Attached is a private stone bathroom, its entrance outside, with a square recessed area for standing while showering, a built-in stone trough of water, and a stone dais with a squat toilet inset. Water pipes in from the small stream running out back. Both the *guti* and the bathroom have electricity, testament to Thamtong's modernity and funding.

It is the very *guti* I would've chosen if given a choice. Midway in the row suits me; any nearer the bridge in front or the forest in back, I would have felt excluded. Now I am in the heart of the *wat*, the thick vegetation cool and green, silent *maechi* in their clouds of cotton drifting slowly through the shade.

The *guti* faces the monks' side, and I'm struck once again by how much theirs differs from ours. The *wat* interior receives limited hours of sunlight as it is, but given the way the mountains are positioned, the sun misses us completely, storming instead onto the monks' side, where soil stains huts, trees, the mountain wall all the color of brick the height of a man.

Maechi Roongdüan heads up the steps. There is absolute quiet around us, save for the two streams tripping over stone and the *whisk-whisk* of sweeping across the water. Tunics sashed at the waist and over-robes thrown over their heads, the monks work, saffron intense against the cinnamon-colored *guti*.

Inside I find a dim wooden interior constructed for life without

guti I'm overtaken by admiration. Each time of day is different and, in its own way, more intriguing than the last.

The monks are all tall, dark, and young, or at least they appear so, viewed always from across the river in sunlight. They never look at us.

The dogs are always where the monks are. If you see a dog or two on our side, lying in wait on the path, it means that a monk has come over to take visitors up to the cave.

··

I think the monks just discovered me. This morning when they were waiting in their line on the bridge and we on ours, it felt like two of them were looking at us, which never happens. Then at the meal I thought I heard a male voice say *chi farang* (foreign nun).

Is it really Day 4? Time moves so quickly and yet so slowly. One week, which seems like a mere fraction of time on the outside, is forever in the *wat* (especially if you're awake nineteen hours a day).

I'm learning an incredible amount. And yet, the time speeds by. I can't *imagine* being here months, years, and yet I see myself drifting into it. I'm filling my journal at the rate of ten pages per day!

furniture: five shuttered windows low to the floor. White gauzy mosquito netting floating in the open door. Moths and grasshoppers fluttering through. Dying to measure the place and sketch a floor plan, I unzip my bags instead. Once she leaves, I will pace out the dimensions: ten of my feet in one direction, fourteen in the other. I estimate that's somewhere around eight feet four by eleven feet eight.

At night, it will be even more fantastic—bright with fluorescent light, the whirring of cicadas. I will flick on the golden light to my little stone bathroom and take a shower in cold spring water. The white towels will be soft, velvety, sweet-smelling. Without hair, my body will be easier to clean. Then I will put on my simple cotton robes and go barefoot into the night.

It takes four minutes to unpack. On a wooden crate I line up my four books about Buddhism, my journal, the bottle of orange juice concentrate and jar of instant coffee, and a spoon and glass. I fold my two extra sets of robes and fluffy lavender blanket and two towels and put them in the corner atop my sleeping mat. I arrange the pair of pens and three candles on the windowsill. I hang the flashlight and plastic bag of toiletries on nails in the ceiling beam. Lastly, I put my blue plastic bucket in the bathroom and my bath sandals on the step. Done! Moved in.

"Hmm," Maechi Roongdüan remarks, "so much stuff."

My lip quivers. It's impossible to read her tone, to know if this is a rebuke or merely an observation, but instantly my pride at never before having traveled so light and set up house so quickly fizzles. I'm like a child reading the rules wrong; whenever I allow myself some confidence, I blunder.

I scan the nearly bare room, trying to take pride in its neat order. What could I have pared down? What is inessential or frivolous? One towel instead of two? Two candles, not three? What limits does spiritual quest require?

All my rooted life I've surrounded myself with visual stimuli.

I'm a pack rat, a collector of photographs and postcards and trinket boxes and colorful wall hangings. In order to write, I need a room cluttered with personal treasures. All my traveling life, however, I've been terrified of carrying too much luggage. Always the lightest traveler in any group, I live in perpetual fear of being shamed by some truly rugged backpacker who needs absolutely nothing. The night before any trip, I toss and turn, dreaming about arriving at my destination and seeing my host's eyes widen in alarm, the size of my bags a clear indication that I plan to overstay my welcome. The Ugly American.

Arriving at Wat Phra Singh, the Royal
Temple of the North, the morning of the
ordination, dressed in the white sarong,
tunic, and scarf of maechi.

CHAPTER FIVE

☯ Orchids:
Half Sacred, Half Profane

[BANGKOK'S] TWO MOST COMMON AND APPEALING SIGHTS ... WERE
ITS HOLY MEN, IN SPOTLESS SAFFRON ROBES, AND ITS SCARLET LADIES.
BY DAY, THE MONKS EVOKED A VISION OF PURITY ... BY NIGHT,
THE WHOLE GRIMY CITY FELT ... TRANSFORMED AS SEQUINED GIRLS
SANG THE BODY ELECTRIC. AT LEAST, SO I THOUGHT, THIS DAY=AND=
NIGHT DIVISION WOULD ENSURE THAT GOOD WAS GOOD, AND EVIL EVIL,
AND NEVER THE TWAIN SHOULD MEET.

> *—Pico Iyer,*
> VIDEO NIGHT IN KATHMANDU

THAILAND HAS OVER A QUARTER OF A MILLION MONKS
AND TWICE AS MANY PROSTITUTES.

> *—Rudolph Wurlitzer,*
> HARD TRAVEL TO SACRED PLACES

INVARIABLY EVERY ASIAN advertisement serves up a graceful, gracious, smiling, pliable woman, the embodiment of the West's Ori-
entalist desires. Often she is characterized as a flower—the delicate
lotus and exotic orchid bending to your will like a green willow or
bamboo reed; heady, aromatic jasmine; the slightly titillating cherry
blossom you pluck. The images are nearly as powerful as a drug,
and it is difficult not to drift into a fantasy of perfumed air, brilliant
landscape, bouquets of hothouse flowers. As I ordain, moving out
of the West and into the East, I am torn. I want the empowerment

..

The walk to the meal is marvelous. Cool, our feet firm, soundless, as we move along the pathway. Blind to all but the spot on the path six feet in front of me, I can feel the beauty. Far below, streams slice the vegetation—tangled greenery ranging from fragile celadon to black pine, from iced orchid to glossy crimson. Long bugs skim water. Suddenly we run into sunshine on the path, the sun still low in the hills. The path glows red-gold, warming our feet.

..

Our numbers increase: five laywomen in line behind me, even more new *maechi* ahead. I am still less mindful than the others, so move more quickly. This makes me appear lost and without purpose, as if dog-paddling in the air to kill time.

..

Also, I sleep too much, perhaps a way of avoiding mindfulness.

of a *maechi* without the subservience of a Thai woman. I want the privileges of Americans without the empty soul. I want beauty without danger. In this landscape, who will I be?

> [PHOTO] Li — Shy as a flower
>
> [PHOTO] Jiap — Untouched beauty
>
> These girls are not seeking marriage
>
> or any similar relationship.

—Phuket Girls Web page

Sacred Lotus

SHE IS LOTUS. *Nelumbo nucifera*. A distinctive, fragrant water lily associated with the Buddha. She is sacred yet edible (though there is truly nothing sacred about her taste). Stir her bitter rootstocks and leaves into soup, grind her stamens into tea. But her body, her body! Her flower inspires religious carvings and paintings, lends her name to the most important teaching in Mahayana Buddhism—*Lotus Sutra*. Upon stumbling across a pond, who could fail to be humbled at the sight of her? A cluster of glistening green pads shining atop a pond's mirrored surface, large white-and-rose blossoms unfolding like perfectly sculpted sheaves of wisdom.

She awakes. Don't touch!

WHEN A WOMAN wants to hand a monk something, she kneels on the ground before him and spreads a handkerchief in the space between. She then places the object on the handkerchief so that the monk may retrieve it himself without fear of touching or being touched by her.

Even as a *maechi*, I am not clear about what will happen if a man accidentally touches one of us, that is, where does impurity reside? I learn that we are not allowed to speak more than six words to a man in the absence of another *maechi*: not another monk, not another laywoman—another *maechi*. At a monthly meeting, one *maechi* tells of seeing a crazy man weaving toward her, arms outstretched, and worrying that, not understanding the significance of her robe, he would embrace her. He turned off the path before reaching her, fortunately for her but unfortunately for me, as her story ends and I never find out what would have happened had they collided.

Earlier, while preparing my research project, I had surveyed the scriptures and discourses in both Theravada and Mahayana Buddhism that deal with women, searching for historical and scriptural precedents for female transcendence. Though there was debate over whether women could become Buddhas in female form (without first being reborn as male and ordaining as monks), it was generally accepted that, upon being pressed to ordain women, the Buddha had admitted they were equally capable of living the Life of the Robe and becoming *arahants* (often translated as "saint" or "worthy one," a pure person no longer destined for rebirth).

Just before the day I met Maechi Roongdüan, I had decided that painstaking academic research was not my interest. Women as subjects of study, words on the page, the observer role of the anthropologist, were all losing their allure. To be honest, I was seeking strategies for living, for participating in life.

Prior to my ordination, I was constantly being drawn into debate—at the university, in the marketplace, in *wat*. Thai men and some women were eager to dismiss the spiritual aspirations of women. Their first strategy was to cite scriptural precedent, the Buddha's apparent disinclination to ordain women.

"After achieving enlightenment, He established the order of monks, *bhikkhus*," my host father announced over toast and eggs

I notice that the *maechi*'s feet in front of me are beautiful. I can just see her heels and a hint of the side when she lifts them up and places them firmly down, arched and turned slightly outward. When she leans forward, poised to take a step, her heel rises gracefully, clean white robes skimming her ankles. When she descends the steps, the robe hovers centimeters above the moss-covered stone. This soft white pooling then quickly lifts to reveal strong ankles, the determined foot!

And the different colors and textures of white! Thick, rough, slightly wrinkled off-white. Crisp, glowing, smoothly woven white. Bluish gauzy, floating cheesecloth.

After we cross the wooden bridge we come to the gravel. The leader falters a bit and we think about the pain, crunching our way across the bits of stone.

I meditate during the serving, fascinated by the rich sounds all around me. The stately ticking of the grandfather clock. One of the owls whooping. A faint cough, muffled in white cotton. The clear call of swallows in the trees. Someone scrubbing white cloth with handfuls of soap. Another filling all of the hot water thermoses. Plastic lids being screwed on and off, picked up and put down, as if there were no hands involved.

Later I do walking in the cave. It doesn't delight me as it often does, but upon stopping I feel calm and mentally refreshed. I descend to the mid-level ledge and perch on one of the stone benches. Perfect! If I sit bolt upright with both feet on the ground, the stone railing supports my throbbing back. Fanned by cool mountain breezes, I try the "sitting in a chair" meditation posture.

sunny-side up. I grimaced at the garish yolk. "It was only after his cousin Ananda pleaded on behalf of women that he agreed—*very reluctantly*"—he stressed, emphasizing with a wave of toast—"to ordain women as *bhikkhuni*." She Who Has Received Higher Ordination, almswoman, female monk.

I dipped the ball of rice I'd been working into *nam prik ong*, staining it red with the spiced meat, and pointed out that this supposed hesitation (if we could even believe it came from Him and not the generations of monk editors) could have been for any number of reasons. He was an Indian man, after all, living within a particular social and historical context. Perhaps He envisaged problems with the monks, who were supposed to be celibate, or with the laypeople they relied on for donations, who might now lose wives and daughters to the order.

"He also hesitated when first asked to preach." My sticky rice ball waved at his toast. "Should we now question the wisdom of the Dhamma?"

Khun Mae stepped in with a tray of dried and fried things that she'd arranged around a cup of black, pulpy chili paste. "The important thing," she trilled, "is that he *did* ordain women, giving them the exact same title as men, and that his own aunt became the first *bhikkhuni*."

"But their status was not equal," my host sibling's favorite fried banana vendor later reminded me. "A hundred-year-old *bhikkhuni* was required to bow down before a newly ordained *bhikkhu*, and the conditions of their ordination were very strict."

With a flip of her wrist, she ran a wire ladle through her wok and dumped a mass of crispy fritters into two bags fashioned from her daughter's old homework. "Read the *Bhikkhuni-Patimokkha*, the strictures governing how *bhikkhuni* travel and live!"

I dropped six coins into her palm and handed the bags to Pōng and Nuan-wan, who grinned and crinkled their noses like hamsters. "Oh, the *Patimokkha* is simply proof of the Buddha's concern for the safety of women!" I gave an airy wave, acknowledging both the kids' *wai* of thanks and the vendor's point. "Every rule was established in response to an actual incident, such as the *bhikkhuni* who was raped by a forest-dwelling *bhikkhu*. Furthermore, it confirms women's inferior social status in ancient India—not their inferior spiritual capabilities."

"Well, anyway," my Thai literature professor said, moving on to the logistical part of the night's program, "the order of *bhikkhuni* has died out in Southeast Asia."

He shrugged.

"There may be *bhikkhuni* in China or Japan or even Sri Lanka, but there can be no higher ordination for women in Thailand, since only a *bhikkhuni* can ordain another *bhikkhuni*."

Suddenly historical precedents didn't matter; it was all about current social realities. Someone misplaced the last female saffron robe, so we're stuck with something called "nuns," glorified laywomen in white. I countered that the ordination lineage for men has also died throughout Southeast Asia periodically, and that only by traveling to other countries to revive it has the tradition lasted this long.

I pressed on. "What makes Thai ordination so special, so different from ordination in east Asia or on the subcontinent?"

He pinched the Dunhill hanging from the corner of his mouth and tossed it out the window, an Asian James Dean. If it weren't rude in Thai society to stand arms akimbo, we'd be doing it.

Ajarn Boon advised me to avoid such arguments. Historical precedents were not the issue. Women have the power to change current reality. As he saw it, the Buddha was a radical, a social revolutionary who liberated women and attacked the excesses of Hinduism: "In a single gesture, He erased the entire caste system," he enthused, the shock of gray hair in the middle of his forehead bobbing up and down like a confirming second opinion.

As usual, he was motoring back dreamily from another *wat*

Not sure if I am meditating or dreaming (how can one tell really?), I have a vision. The bottom half of a woman's torso appears: tall, slender, clothed in a billowing sarong of glowing pure white. The cloth is soaking wet, though not transparent, and thousands of water droplets sparkle in the blinding sunlight. The woman is being spun slowly in a large beam of light, as if caught in slow motion. The sarong covers her immobile feet, twisting round and round, wrapping her ankles until her torso resembles an Art Nouveau vase. It's impossible to tell front from back, but when the sarong finally stops spinning, I feel that her back is to me. The whole vision has the artificial, muffled, waiting feel of a silent movie, a scene out of Fellini.

No sooner have I noted the strangeness of the vision than another follows. This one is like a sequel—similar actors, same location, but without the fresh beauty of the original. This time the sarong is a normal bluish white. This torso is skinny and graceless, its wetness ordinary. This woman stands with her back and right side exposed, legs slightly parted. She is walking in place, her legs moving back and forth, feet planted on the ground, as if she is trying to dry the soaking cloth or free her thin legs from its clinging embrace.

Unlike the first vision's slow, dreamlike pace, this one's pace is quick and realistic. Whether it is the same woman, I cannot tell. A lesson?

visit, one wheel dragging the shoulder, his pale eyes contemplating the temple we'd left instead of the road.

I gripped my seat and tried not to be so attached to life.

"Buddha said, 'Out of My Mouth there are born four groups.'" Ajarn Boon held up his right hand, four fingers outstretched, and the Peugeot swerved into the right lane, narrowly missing a water-buffalo-drawn cart. He righted the car, exchanging a friendly wave with the farmer atop the cart, and the fingers descended, one at a time. "'Ordained man, householder man, ordained woman, householder woman.'"

I finally let go my breath, and mistaking my audible relief for amazement, he nodded, "Exactly!"

His eyes crinkled to nothingness. "See? Each group is equal, their worth determined simply by performance to their respective duty."

This is one of the moments I fall in love with the Buddha. There are many, in the beginning masquerading as a grudging respect for intellect. As a Unitarian Universalist and my mother's daughter, I appreciate Buddhism's tolerance toward other religions, its respect for individual intelligence, its reliance on rational, scientific inquiry: the practitioner as scientist conducting the experiment of Dhamma in the lab of her body.

Other moments in our love affair fall into the breathless, magical realm of spirituality, the unspoken hunger that's fed when I sit in meditation, when I see the Buddha's face in Ajarn Boon's amused, detached goodwill (metta) as he chats with abbots and children alike, in his unfaltering equanimity (upekkha) as he nearly kills us, in Maechi Roongdüan's fierce compassion (karuna) as she greets dangerous animals, in her glowing, sympathetic joy (mudita) at my bumbling attempts to be a lotus.

But I am certain to fall in love with a privileged prince turned revolutionary. *Each group is equal, their worth determined simply by performance to their respective duty.* From childhood I have been addicted to fairness and equality, holding them in esteem over nearly every other value. When in middle school I was caught talking in class to a known troublemaker and he was given detention while I, the top student (and a teacher's daughter to boot), was not, I rushed home hot with indignation. The next day, I insisted that my mother deliver my demand: equal sentences! Punish him less or me more.

And when our seventh-grade science teacher started letting students gamble their semester points—double or nothing—in a move clearly designed to raise the grades of star athletes, I bet and bet until I lost my straight A's.

"If the gambling counts for a single person, it counts for us all," I declared from my perch on Mount Self-righteous as poor Mr. Green puffed and blinked behind his Coke-bottle glasses like a blowfish. "If anyone's grade improves, I expect to flunk this class."

If morality was my mother's religion, equality was mine. And if Buddhism was grounded in equality, then I would certainly give up money, my voice, and regular meals for it, yes. I was well familiar with performance and duty. Some strong (albeit unfocused) sense of it is what lifts me from my straw pallet each morning at three-thirty and propels me into the foreign landscape of spiritual sojourn.

What I can't accept in these conversations is the inherent impurity attributed to this body. I imagined that the female-body problematic was Western, stemming from Eve's loss of innocence and the Madonna-whore dichotomy of Christianity. Why must Buddhist female salvation be tied to purity? Why is a female devotee making an offering to the Robe a potential source of impurity? Why am I forever reminded of my own cultural dilemma—two opposing identities residing in a single body?

I fled the West precisely because of this, because of dichotomous thinking, the crushing pressure to be either-or, to exist in black or white. This pressure has led me, like any respectable American girl, to hate my body a bit. It is, after all, the site of a tiresome external identity: the blackness that will get you tossed before a sub-

I meet Pranee my third day. Maechi Roongdüan finds me reading outdoors, which, while not forbidden, is a waste of daylight better spent meditating, and suggests I go meditate. I am on my way up to the caves when I see two young *maechi* gazing over the railing. The younger, only a girl, shiny and eager-faced, grins and waves me up. On the wide stone landing outside the cave, she asks if I speak Thai. At my nod, she tells me her name is Pranee and she's seventeen years old.

We beam at each other, delighted—me at having discovered my first teenage *maechi*, she at having discovered we can communicate. It feels that at any moment someone should drop in to dispense candy and bonbons.

As the elder, the other—a twenty-one-year-old with a delicate, swanlike neck—does most of the talking, asking the standard questions: *Where are you from? How do you like Thailand? Can you eat Thai food?* She then asks what "level" I am at and whether I can "practice" a lot yet. Though the literal meaning of her words is clear, I have no idea how to answer. What is "a lot"? Am I being graded, passed on or held back?

It is my first time speaking to another human being in three days, except for my daily thirty-minute lesson with Maechi Roongdüan. The Thai words feel runny and disobedient in my mouth.

The girls peer over the wall, monitoring the underbrush with obvious distraction. The newest resident, a young *upasika* in whose vow-taking I participated the previous night, stands nearby, staring at the mountains surrounding us. Four mats lay

way train, the femaleness that will get you felt up or held down. The biracialness, a lack of clarity, which never fails to unsettle. The East, famously, romantically, tolerant of ambivalence, of a both-and world, is supposed to be my salvation.

I hadn't imagined that I would take it this far, that I would shave away my hair and eyebrows and hide my body. But why not? The body stood outside our house. My mother, being naturally clumsy and unnaturally bookish, abhorred physical activity. Her ideal day was camping on the sofa with a stack of history books, a box of crackers, and a paperback mystery chaser. And though I grew up with my knees perpetually skinned, once puberty hit and we moved into town, I moved into my head. Too middle-class to work the farm and not middle-class enough for the world of health clubs and varsity sports and costly uniforms and lessons, we ignored the life of the body completely. So here I am, on a year's hiatus from Western thought—a year of transcendence in the spiritual sense, of passing in the physical. Thailand reminds me that the body doesn't matter; it is just, as Maechi Roongdüan has said, a "skin sack" getting in the way of our work.

Nearly every girl had a tale to tell, and nearly always it was the same one. She grew up in a village in a family of twelve. A local man came along when she was in her early teens and promised to make her rich. He said she would make her fortune, but she ended up making his. He said she would be "a maid," then forced her to become a slave. She bore him a child, she returned alone to her village, she worked without joy or profit in the fields. Now she could support her offspring only by coming to Bangkok. Who looked after her child? "Ma-má." Did her still devoted parents know what she was doing? "No, I tell them I work in a boutique. They know I work in a bar, they kill me."

—PICO IYER,
Video Night in Kathmandu

Profane Poppy

SHE IS POPPY. Genus *Papaver somniferum*, named for sleep. With nodding buds, four crumpled petals, and milky juice. Her papery blossoms signal the beginning of opium season with white or sometimes vivid red hysteria. A Thai girlfriend and I heeded the call. We trekked a muddy road high up the side of a mountain, through narrow crevasses and mossy caves, emerging into a secret field, not a government-sanctioned and -monitored one. There she was, her brilliant bursts of red everywhere, tiny flags of blood on a green body. It was hallucinatory, and we nearly stumbled in the gaze of the thousand black-beaded eyes staring at us.

Later came the harvest, the sticky white sap oozing thick from gray-green pods. And then the smoking—a dab of brick-colored opium hissing in the pan, the sickly-sweet stench pluming the air.

"Where are all the women?" it occurred to me to ask. We were curled beneath a roofed platform with the village men.

"They're in the poppy fields," my friend muttered, "doing all the work."

We lay on our sides like babies, mouths suckling long bamboo pipes. But it was the opposite of nursing, this place of blackened teeth and no women, as life drained from our bodies. Slow death. Profane milky poppies.

Asian girls at the wildest place on earth! Bangkok girls? Thailand girls? Asian girls? Philippine girls? Oriental girls? Sexy girls! Wild girls! Beautiful girls! Here you will find real information on travel to Asia's most exotic locations in the world. You will find girls for fun, girls for sex, Asian girls to entertain you like nowhere else in the world!

—WWW.WILDPLACE.COM/GIRLS

at her feet, suggesting that she awaits group instruction.

All of a sudden, Pranee notices that I'm standing with one foot up on the lower rung of the bench.

"Goodness!" she cries, grabbing my leg and straightening it. "*Maechi* have to stand up straight!"

Her laughter tinkles. "Being Thai, being *maechi*—there are many rules!"

Just then Maechi Roongdüan appears on the landing, as if from the sky, and with a fierce look rebukes Pranee for wasting time. Just as quickly, she joins the laywoman.

As I descend the stairs, feeling sheepish, Pranee smiles sunnily, her mood undimmed. "Time's up," she whispers behind her hand, and I realize that she is the one always turning around and grinning at the swan-necked one during meals. What's this high-spirited thing doing as a *maechi*?

..

The young *maechi* who sits in front of me at mealtime looks a bit like Barbra Streisand. She lives somewhere else in the *wat;* her group arrives at the meal from another direction, after ours. The day before yesterday I saw her staring at me, more intently than the others do. Her eyes flickered away when I turned and caught her but returned after a beat, darting butterflies in a landscape trying to decide whether to settle on me, the strange, bedraggled *maechi*. I smiled and that clinched it; she returned a beautiful, friendly grin.

..

Today she takes every opportunity to catch my eye and beam. Maybe if I were staying forever, she'd even speak to me!

..

I'm convinced there's talking going on somewhere. Last night in my *guti,* I distinctly heard voices in the forest. Streisand probably thinks I

∞

LET'S BE HONEST! Danger was partly what drew me to Thailand. I watched myself pass through the countryside, traversing towns owned by bandit kings, climbing up to drug lords' lairs, jumping off trains in the middle of the night, and felt powerful. My physical body was more at risk, but my mind was infinitely more at ease. I believed I understood what was unsafe about Thailand in a way I didn't understand violence in America. Here crime followed a simple equation, its laws as causal as the Dhamma's: Obvious Wealth + Obvious Poverty = Risk of Robbery. There is solace in that. It's a hunger that can be fed, not an American-sized pain that requires an automatic weapon and a roomful of innocent people to accompany you on your journey. Every American with a gun it seems is a potential Chinese emperor or Egyptian pharaoh, in dire need of company even in death.

We Westerners make much of Thailand's so-called contradictions. Imagine—a country with so many monks and prostitutes! We shake our heads. Raised on dichotomy, we craft tension-filled narratives that make for a fine holiday: we visit jeweled temples by day and opium dens/sex bars by night. In our narrative, it is the Thai who are delightfully hypocritical, who can't seem to reconcile themselves. Male travel writers (dedicated journalists all, who never fail to cover Thailand's flesh trade) are downright dismayed to see bar girls give alms or wear Buddhist amulets. Look at that— prostitutes with spiritual lives! In our narrative, the global economy and local pimps and johns (Think Globally, Act Locally) have nothing to do with employment; profanity resides deep within the female body.

What we don't see is the constant battle Thais wage against the profanity threatening to overtake their women. They too believe (a strain of thought traceable through Buddhist texts back to ancient

India) that female sexual appetite is uncontrollable (and therefore destructive). The primary concern for girls and young women is to appear *rieb roi,* proper. *Rieb roi* girls never touch boys, not even a playful slap or poke, without an instrument, such as a rolled-up notebook, between them. *Rieb roi* girls know that dating will get them kicked out of school. *Rieb roi* girls stand with both feet flat on the ground and sit with their legs tucked beneath them. *Rieb roi* girls sleep with their brassieres on and keep a sarong around their bodies while changing, the edges held between their teeth, so that no one (they themselves included) ever sees their naked bodies. *Rieb roi* girls speak softly and *wai* beautifully and behave in a supple manner that makes Western men begin to sweat.

Before and after my ordination, I spend a great deal of my time trying to mimic this proper behavior so that stereotypes about American and black women won't put me at the kind of risk from Thai men that Asian stereotypes put Thai women at risk from Western men. It doesn't work. There is no safety for any color body. The country is filled with brown women chained to beds in exclusive beach resorts, eight-year-old girls behind glass on Patpong Road, former farmers and students who've trained their vaginas to smoke cigarettes and blow out matches and draw pictures and eat bananas. Perhaps that is the nature of the world. We lock up our own women and go out looking for theirs.

Much as I detest acting like a *rieb roi* Thai girl, it is woven into the fabric of ordination. *Maechi* are Proper Thai Girls squared. I'm not quite sure if *rieb roi* is supposed to jump-start us on the expressway to *Nibbana* or if it's simply contextual residue. The payoff, however, is clear—freedom from the emphasis on physical attributes, freedom from the gaze of men. For now I hide in white robes; later I will cloak myself in fat. Thailand teaches me that the body does matter. It teaches me the power of desire, which at times is just another word for hatred.

can't speak Thai. I don't know anymore; can I? I wonder where her group goes; after the meal, they seem to disperse in all directions. Is where they go as beautiful as where we stay?

..

Just as I finish writing this, two *maechi* walk by, heading toward the forest and speaking out loud as if they were normal women. They're really going at it in central Thai dialect. One looks like Barbra. Both carry baskets of laundry, and as they pass by my *guti*, Not-Barbra says, "This one, with the blue sandals."

..

Barbra looks at my bathroom sandals on the step and laughs. "Oh-*ho!*" she exclaims. "*Rongtàuw yaayyaay!*" What huge shoes!

Since 1971 the Queen's Foundation for Thai Maechi has addressed *maechi* affairs through the Thai Institute.

A private organization affiliated with the official church hierarchy, the Institute receives no government funding and is dedicated to the stability and progress of *maechi,* increasing faith in *maechi* among the people and training *maechi* to help lay society.

Its programs include an annual national convention, rural development training programs, a monthly magazine, and self-sufficient, all-female centers for *maechi.*

The institute also publishes a popular pamphlet with suggestions for ordination procedures and rules governing daily life and practice. The pamphlet attempts to debunk negative *maechi* stereotypes and discourage social rather than spiritual motivations for ordaining.

In addition, it regulates family ties and

Some species of orchids are pollinated by bees that are attracted by means of deception. . . . The most exciting and unusual examples of deceit, traps, and manipulation of pollinators are to be found in those orchids that are pollinated by male euglossine bees.

—*Encyclopaedia Britannica*

Exotic Orchid

THAILAND IS WHERE I learn to be beautiful again. After the great hoopla in the delivery room and a childhood spent receiving treats from strangers on the streets of Seattle, there was a lull in the tribute to my beauty. I was Sunnyside's only black girl, and the one boy who liked me in junior high was so ridiculed once our romance went public that he sent an emissary to break up with me the next day; the next boy—years later in high school—didn't make the same mistake. Beyond these stolen kisses, the only other encouragement I received was an anonymous request in the school newspaper to be someone's valentine, "because she's cute and smart." And though I suspected the handiwork of my longtime pal Cheryl, dispensing a Christian charity that even I couldn't fault, I glowed for a day.

In college, black tastes ran to more overtly girly types with permed hair. I did discover an exotic currency, however, in being dusky enough to spark white men's fantasies, while still behaving and speaking white enough to not scare. (It took a few parties before I got what a Liberal Education really meant.) Even better, my blackness was not American blackness; it was Special Blackness, straight from Africa! *You're half Scandinavian-American and half Nigerian?* began the eager inquiry, revving up for the inevitable refrain: *How interesting!* Isn't it?

Exotic is a tightrope to walk. If you keep moving, eyes toward the sky, you reap admiration from a distance. But if ever you slow down, lock eyes, listen to what someone is telling you, then you tumble into the mud of the erotic. So quick the fall from sacred to profane!

After I leave the *wat*, my curls still *maechi*-short, I will wander Southeast Asia, free, oh-so-mysteriously quiet, wrapped in a colorful sarong, my bag light. One night I will find myself at a long table on a private white-sand beach seated between the drummer from one of my favorite British bands and an explorer who'd been speared in the thigh while rafting on an isolated island whose inhabitants had never before seen a white man. Bamboo torches ring the table, throwing flickering gold light on the imported proscuitto and pasta.

The men at the table will be expatriates from Australia and England, the women travelers drawn like satellites to their social systems. Each of us will be claimed during the time she is in town.

When the explorer places his hand on my thigh under the linen tablecloth, at about the same place the skin puckers, hard and shiny, on his own leg, I will stand up and walk back to my guest house and start to pack for the north. Keep moving.

ᏃᎬ

SHE IS ORCHID. *Orchidales.* Inscrutable Oriental. Her thick, waxy flowers improbably shaped and spotted like sexual organs. Esoteric, exotic, erotic. She straddles the distinction between the sacred and the profane.

Chiang Mai, dubbed "the Garden of Thailand" by enterprising tour guides, was home to both us and the orchid. Scott and I visited the famed orchid gardens, which boast ten thousand species. We learned that the business of orchids is attracting "suitors" to pollinate, through deceit and traps if necessary.

We chuckled uneasily. Everything in Thailand is titillating, full of suggestion. Brochures about the zoo and local handicrafts read

encourages *maechi* to transfer allegiance to the monastic community.

With Maechi Roongdüan away, the atmosphere during the meal is distinctly relaxed, except for the prissy-looking *maechi* who still sits up perfectly straight with a proper, pleased smile. She is always the last to finish eating. There's a great deal to be said for iron determination, devotion, and stamina, I'm sure, but she's too much! She makes me wanna slap her. (Lucky for her, I'm a *maechi* and we frown on that sort of thing.)

After the meal there's actual talking. A worried-looking *maechi* calls me back from the procession. She says something that sounds like, "You have a letter." I frown. Letters are forbidden me.

"Oh, can she speak Thai?" Barbra interjects, looking from Worried One to me. "She can speak Thai!"

I step back. Up close she looks like a short, creepy version of Streisand with bad teeth and no hair. The second vision.

The two exchange some words in a dialect I don't understand, and then Worried One snorts and takes my arm, pulling me to the line. The letter issue is over. If ever there were a day to talk to *maechi*, today is it. Strangely, I no longer think I'm up to the task.

..

That new *maechi* in the *guti* next door has been here five days, each day worse than the previous. I can't meditate on the path or beneath the tree we share without her coming to her doorway and glaring at me. And I dare not go outside if she's already there. She'll stop what she's doing and stare at me, the black stubble glinting in the sunlight around her head like a demonic halo.

..

I think she might be crazy. She actually spits on the ground

like pornography, everything bending like pliant willows, dripping with fruit and perfume. The glistening pseudonectaries on Thai orchids imitate the eyes of a female bee; their stigmas reflect sunlight, just like the genital orifice of the female fly. *Aren't Thai women beautiful?* Every Thai we meet chants this mantra, as if pimping around the clock.

Most tourists dive right in. Men fly halfway around the world on three-week package deals that include airfare, hotel, and a "wife"/tour guide. The deal is clinched by a staged "marriage ceremony" after which the Thai woman—invariably a dark-skinned ethnic Lao from the drought-stricken farmlands of the northeast, or a preadolescent from the factory slums of Bangkok—refers to her client as "my husband."

The "husbands" we met at the Night Market were eager to share the sheer beauty of the situation with us. "Ya see," Graphic Designer Mark from London explained, looking brightly from Scott to me (perhaps assuming we had a similar arrangement), "sex is not a sin in Buddhism!" This is a popular statement among *farang,* almost as common as *Mai pen rai* for a Thai.

"Well, that's certainly convenient." I accepted a rose from one of my favorite child vendors. "I mean, for the prostitution and all that."

Associate professor Charles from New York knelt to adjust his Tevas. "Besides, she tells me that we treat them better than the Thai men do." His dark, earnest eyes widened. "They're actually better off!"

"Is that so?" Scott asked, with a worried glance at me.

"Well, that must be quite a relief for you." I patted my pockets for coins as the small flower girl watched, doe-eyed.

Seeing Dr. Steve from Cleveland's blank expression, I explained. "To be able to help out both the economy and the social fabric this way—while getting your rocks off."

He was just starting to shout, "American women like you are why we have to!" when Scott dragged me away.

We ducked into a quiet bar frequented by off-duty bar girls and shared a few with pals. As we chatted, I grew intrigued by the idea of temporary marriage. The travel writer in me was tempted to make a grand sidebar statement about how any arrangement is available temporarily in Thailand—from marriage to ordination. And given the similarities between the two ceremonies, am I perhaps guilty of the same sort of disingenuous, self-serving pact with the Buddha?

But there is something more to these pseudomarriages, this desire to create a sacred space within a profane arrangement. Again two realities in the same body, but simply binary this time, not opposed. Woman as pure and impure. Like man. The john, the pimp, the monk.

৪৹

BACK ON THE ole orchid farm, Scott and I learned that night-flying moths are drawn to light-colored, strong-smelling flowers. Butterflies follow bright color. Birds choose primary colors. Flies, annoying as they are, have to be tricked.

Relegated to a separate wing of the greenhouse, far from the good flowers, these trickster orchids are the most interesting. They resemble tropical fish with their blotchy, rich colors. *Beware of smell*, a sign warned us, listing the times of day that the trickster orchids attract, releasing a particular stench.

We circled them warily, morbidly, like passersby to a car wreck, noting their underwater markings of olive and aubergine. We kept fingers near our noses, trying to identify the smell.

"Uh, that's definitely shit," Scott concluded with a brisk nod and step back. "Oh yeah, that should bring in a fly boyfriend or two."

"Mine's carrion!" I complained, seeing the sign and preparing to bolt. "I don't want to smell a corpse."

"That's the price of looking," he mock-rebuked me. "Beauty has its costs, baby."

like a layperson and giggles! I heard her say that she hates it here and wants to go to Bangkok. Fine, go!

..

When she returns, Maechi Roongdüan stops by my *guti* with a magazine published by a Buddhist reform group. I've become obsessed with visiting the places described in the publications she brings me. When I leave the *wat*, I want to go to Burma, to Mahasi Sayadaw's center in Rangoon where Maechi Roongdüan studied Burmese *Satipatthana Vipassana* techniques. He's written the best handbooks on meditation I've found. Then I want to go to Ratchaburi in southern Thailand, where there's supposed to be a center solely for *maechi* and laywomen, and the National Maechi Center near Bangkok, which is rumored to have two hundred to three hundred resident *maechi*. I also want to visit Woramai Kabilsingh, the only Thai *bhikkhuni*, and her Asoke movement.

I thank Maechi Roongdüan for the magazine, and we stroll to the front of the *wat*, Maechi Roongdüan pointing out the different plants and trees in Thai and English.

"This is a *bodhi* tree, the type of tree the Buddha was sitting beneath when He became enlightened. Every temple must have one."

I remark that it's so peaceful here, and she sighs. She tells me that in Thailand, women with problems either run to the temple for a while or kill themselves. "There is no other alternative."

..

The evil *maechi* leaves her door open and I see inside her *guti*. It makes mine look like a frivolous palace. The sum total of her worldly belongings are: a straw mat, a thin pillow, a thermos, one cup, two blankets, a book, a pair of spectacles, a flashlight, a windup clock, and a second set of robes. The walls are bare.

We are known for our gracious service. This includes personal attention to passenger needs, with special treats (like gift orchids for all female passengers).

THAI's distinctive livery incorporates the colours associated with Thailand: the shining gold found in its temples, the magenta of its shimmering silks and the rich purples of its orchids. Our logo has been likened to an orchid but is simply a symbol meant to convey the essence of Thailand; its soft, curving lines combined with a speed line suggest effortless flight.

Similarly, our slogan "Smooth as Silk" derives from the texture and luxurious look of Thailand's most famous creation: silk. It suggests both the way we fly our aircraft and the way we hope passengers feel when they fly with us, wrapped in comfort and pleasure.

—THAI AIRWAYS ROYAL ORCHID SERVICE

☙❧

AT TIMES IT is hard not to get caught up. When we leave the country to rejoin the ranks of Americans trawling for the most authentic Thai takeout, we will be swept into the luxury of Thai Airways. We will dazzle the flight attendants with casually dropped Thai phrases and feel honored, along with all the other travelers, to find a fresh purple orchid on our meal tray.

Far below us, the Thai woman is pale, almost white, but infinitely more touchable. Anglo women are white lilies and blushing roses who must be protected (well, at least in terms of rhetoric and literature). Snow White, Rose Red. Peach blossoms and magnolia rising high above the dark soil.

Who are the African flowers? Black women are sweet, I gather, but in a way that makes you lick your lips, rub up against her in public, take that which wasn't offered, deflower her. In a way that dispenses with the need for even the fake marriage ceremony before-hand. Brown Sugar, Mocha Delight, Chocolate Love. When do we get to be flowers? Beautiful? Untouched?

And high above the clouds, enfolded in a curve of gracious service and headed for home, we will remember how some species of orchid grow without soil, in the air—like magic!

This is her life. I am ashamed for harboring ill thoughts toward her.

Receiving ordination gifts from a Thai professor,
while friends look on. Cathy is on the far right.

CHAPTER SIX

∞ *American Girls*

1 SHOULD HAVE TOLD [MY TIBETAN BUDDHIST TEACHER] THE TRUTH
WHEN HE'D FIRST ASKED; SHOULD HAVE BLURTED OUT THAT 1 SUF⸗
FERED; THAT 1 WAS OFTEN FRUSTRATED AND ANGRY; THAT SLAVERY
AND ITS LEGACY OF RACISM HAD TAKEN THEIR TOLLS ON ME; 1 HAD
COME SEEKING HELP IN COPING WITH FEELINGS OF INADEQUACY,
UNWORTHINESS, AND SHAME.

　　　—*Jan Willis,*

　　　　ÐREAMING ME: AN AFRICAN AMERICAN WOMAN'S SPIRITUAL JOURNEY

CATHY, ONE OF the St. Olafers, is here at Wat Thamtong. The month before my ordination we'd been sitting in the food commissary at Chiang Mai University, an open-air patio ringed with flame trees and vendors working steaming woks, when the crowd from St. Olaf's arrived. All year every time we met a Thai student, he or she invariably asked, "St. Olaf?" and we had to explain that, no, we're not part of the St. Olaf program. Soon we learned to add that, yes, we *can* speak Thai, and no, we'll be here the *entire* year. We're the serious ones!

Scott, himself from the Twin Cities, explained that St. Olaf was a small Minnesota college known for its ability to shelter midwestern farm kids from the secular evils of college.

Immediately the Christian school in my hometown (so named to distinguish it from the Catholic school and pretender to the throne of Christianity) surfaced in my mind like an LSD flashback. Its primary function seemed to be the protection of the fair-haired

..

During the mealtime chanting, two owls weep in liquid tones at each other, louder than us, louder than the grandfather clock downstairs. I feel clean, physically clean, though I haven't yet showered.

It's Pranee, the seven-teen-year-old, who has that startling voice like a muezzin calling Muslims to prayer—deep, pas-sionate, nasal. Eyes closed, she gives her-self over completely. Her thin shoulders rise and fall with the swelling and collaps-ing of her diaphragm.

··

At two-thirty I make the long climb up to the caves to do walk-ing meditation on the stone balcony. A group of tourists shows up to view the caves. They're dis-tracting until I find the correct posture, and then walking feels glorious. Eyes six feet in front of me, the smooth rise and fall of my steps. I think I am smiling.

Maechi Roongdüan says that walking meditation generates thoughts while sitting meditation calms the mind, but I find walk-ing calming. After thirty minutes, I'm relaxed enough to sit. The only problem is that I keep hunching my back, which is sore, and overcom-

daughters of Dutch dairy owners and German cattle barons. What they required protection from was vague and varied, ranging from crazy evolution talk to the smoldering attentions of the sons of Mexican field hands.

The sons of Christian farmers, however, were allowed to attend public school with the rest of us. Apparently they were made of stronger stuff, or perhaps the absence of state-ranked varsity sports at the Christian school played a role. The sons engaged in real sports, football and basketball, that required European bulk and diets of milk and beef—not wrestling, where even a tiny mestizo could triumph within his own weight class.

One of the Thai administrators told us that St. Olaf sponsored a semester abroad program. A classroom of students traveled the world, with our very own Chiang Mai University as their final and longest stop. Most knew nothing about Thailand, the administrator explained, puffing up a little on our behalf, and few learned any Thai.

Our chests plumped too. Scott, Angel, and I had all lived in Thai-land before, and the other three spent the summer before our arrival doing intensive language study in Wisconsin and planning fieldwork.

The Thai administrator munched on the fat finger bananas we brought and continued to tell us what we wanted to hear about our American rivals. The St. Olafers spend all their time together in a big cluster, moving around—she paused for effect—"like tourists."

Gasping, we recoiled. Tourists! (This display aside, secretly we couldn't have been happier.) Dedicated to the art of Real Travel, we considered ourselves reborn onto a higher plane. Let the lowly tourists inhabit the bottom realms of vacation hell, relegated to staged cultural shows and superficial encounters in hotel lobbies. We were Travelers!

And so I find myself eagerly awaiting the arrival of a St. Olafer to my new home in the Thai forest, a situation not without irony. Cathy, distinguished by her pleasant, intelligent face and interest in something other than partying every minute out of Minnesota, had attended my ordination and mentioned something about being inspired by my example and wanting to stay as a laywoman for a few weeks. Ajarn Boon had agreed to make the arrangements.

I spend all day telling myself that I'm not really looking forward to a visitor. *I have to get over my notion of this being summer camp!* I berate myself in my journal.

Midmorning I meet her moving into the *guti* next to mine, already dressed in the white robes of a laywoman—shorter sarong, standard button-down tunic, shoulder sash instead of the over-robe. Her hair distinguishes her from *maechi* and *upasika* alike—dirty blonde, tucked behind her ears.

Having received permission from Maechi Roongdüan to speak with her ("You will need to help Cathy with the transition, but take care not to harm your own practice"), I greet her with guarded delight. I get a wide-eyed look of panic in response.

"What's wrong?"

She gives me a list: she feels unprepared; the *wat* seems harsh; yesterday she fell in love with that long-haired artist in the humanities department.

"Wow." I'm impressed and not a little envious. I like the guy. He's thirty, one of the radicals who fled to the jungle during the anti-Communist crackdown on student activists.

They spent the entire day together. She describes one of those perfect days charged with intellectual and sexual attraction. In the morning he and Ajarn Boon drove her out here.

Now full-fledged jealousy kicks in. As Cathy whispers, tortured, I fume to myself. I can't believe that Ajarn Boon came and went without asking to see me. When Cathy asks how in the world I manage to be mindful, it's like a glass of water to the face. Startled, blinking, I stammer. I remember that together Ajarn Boon and I agreed I would have no letters or visitors. A rule is a rule, controlling even its maker.

I smile, trying to convey calmness and sympathy. I know exactly

pensating on my left. It's a struggle at first to breathe unself-consciously; for a while, I just concentrate on the rising and falling of the abdomen, then I internally verbalize "up" and "down" without the points.

Finally the space behind my eyes becomes dark, my breathing shallows, and I realize that concentration already exists in my mind—it's not a precarious, accidental state, which will shatter if I admit, for example, that a large insect is buzzing overhead.

I feel the breathing motion expanding to enfold me, though my breaths are gentler than ever. Everything becomes increasingly dark, though not reaching the perfection of yesterday morning. My back aches, but my concentration does not break. After thirty minutes I descend, happy, from the cave.

At dusk I walk along the upper stream next to the open-air pavilion. Definitely worth the bug bites. Then I sit beneath the tree outside my *guti* until it's dark.

*D*esigned for its appeal to the laity, who lack formal training in doctrine, *Vipassana* affords women, most of whom similarly lack religious access, the unique opportunity to practice—and perhaps eventually teach—their religion. The revival of meditation accompanies a return to a personal involvement in Buddhist practices, as opposed to the pursuit of salvation via monks and their teachings. Meditation makes it possible for women to achieve spiritual expertise and social legitimacy independent of the formal church hierarchy.

what she is feeling. Temple life is so far from ordinary life. This is not the place to be if you have second thoughts.

I head back to my *guti*, telling myself that Ajarn Boon is magnificent but this time he goes too far. I can see the panic in her face and it calls for the same in me.

ᏸᏋ

MY MOTHER wouldn't let Barbie in the house. It wasn't just that she wouldn't be caught dead spending money on a Barbie doll—no gift Barbies were permitted either. "Horrible, sexist creatures," she would shudder when questioned. "Lord knows it's hard enough to raise a healthy girl without constant propaganda from the toy box!" Barbie's blondeness didn't help.

Eventually I did get a Skipper, chest flat as a board, with a cloud of blonde hair and dusting of brown freckles across her pert nose. I suspect this semi-shift in policy was due to Skipper's size—perfect for the log cabin my uncle built me. Someone had to stoke the wrought-iron stove, after all, and sleep in the painted Dutch bed. Besides, she resembled Cousin Heidi on the Swedish side.

When I was five and Diahann Carroll became the first black American woman to star in her own television show, my mother broke down—wasp waist, torpedo breasts, and permanently high-heeled feet be damned—and got me a Julia doll. It didn't escape me that Julia was just Barbie with milk chocolate skin, a white nurse's uniform, and a short cap of straightened hair. Instead of learning to love myself, I suspect that I learned a complicated equation: Flat Chest (Skipper) > Blonde (Barbie); Brown Skin (Julia) > Unrealistic Body Type (Barbie).

Mornings I waited for the school bus at my grandparents' house, and if she had time, Mummi sat me down before her large round vanity mirror, surrounded by tubs of blue and pink Dippity-Do, and set my hair in ringlets à la Cindy Brady or Buffy from *Family Affair*. I quivered with anticipation as she wrapped my soft black curls into large spiky rollers set vertically around my head like shells in an ammo belt. The resulting cylinders were wispy and short-lived.

"I wish you wouldn't do that," I heard my mother whisper one morning on her way to work.

"She begged," my grandmother whispered back, her blue eyes soft, pink plastic hairpins poking out of the side of her mouth. "She's just a little girl."

My mother sighed and hugged me good-bye. Her hair, long then, fell in a curtain around us. "Who's my beautiful pun'kin?" she said, peppering my nose with kisses. She liked to tell the story of how all the nurses oohed and aahed when I was born. I had such big brown eyes, a perfect rosebud mouth, a full head of curls! Then there were the strangers who stopped us on the street whenever we went out and plied me with gifts—shiny coins and candy. Biracial babies were rare in 1960s Seattle. Everyone wanted to touch me!

Junior high society in Sunnyside, however, required the impossible: Farrah Fawcett hair, a tousled mane of blonde highlights, and a curling iron. My grandfather bought me the iron—a sleek lavender rod that I heated up lovingly and snapped in anticipation—but there wasn't much we could do with it until my mother (after much pleading on everyone's part) finally relented and let me straighten my hair, just this once! Racial self-loathing surely couldn't take root in a single incident.

Instead of falling to my shoulders in bone-straight, shining tresses (as the photo on the box had led us to believe), my hair poofed around me, thick and unruly as shrubbery. I looked like the biracial kids I would later hear black students talking about in college:

"You can always tell who has a white mother," a girl bemoaned freshman year, as an interracial graduate student couple and their two kids entered the dining room. The little boy had a close natural, but the girl's hair billowed out in a wiry, chaotic cloud caught at the end with a rubber band. "They have no *idea* what to do with their children's hair."

In the thin light of three-thirty I open my eyes, then remember I should be mindful. When the bell rings a minute later I'm able to note *knowing* . . . and *wanting to rise.* . . .

I tidy up, wash my face and dishes, make coffee. Meditating feels supremely calming, but I'm so sleepy I can't remember to watch my breathing, which makes meditation no more than sleeping upright.

Cathy and I help with sweeping the grounds, attacking the forest floor with a curved straw broom. The entire *wat* resounds with the rhythmic *whisk-whisk* of both communities on either side of the stream. It's odd, though invigorating, to be sweeping dirt and leaves.

Maechi Roongdüan passes by, saying, "Do it slowly, not as if you wanted to finish it. The leaves fall; it is natural. Every day they will fall, and every day we will sweep them. Our work is for the meditation."

Next I scrub the bathroom and clean my *guti,* moving deliberately, feeling the meditation in the acts. The meditator doesn't need to do exciting things—the ordinary acts of survival are wonderful enough.

The table *mmm-hmmed* its agreement, and a second girl protested, "You think they'd *ask* someone! Even *they* must notice that you don't see kids with black parents running around all wild and bushy-haired like that."

A third girl sounded mournful. "It hurts. I just want to go over there and say, 'Please, can I just braid your poor child's hair?' "

In the freshman dining hall, I'd been overcome by shame and sadness. Shame that I still didn't know how to work my hair, that my own body was foreign to me; and sadness to learn that as a black baby, I had indeed come with an instruction manual—only it was missing!

No one in my family, no one in the entire town, knew what to do with my straightened hair. My uncle's girlfriend spent hours shaping and curling it, but each time I turned to see my uncle's face, his pursed, painted smile, I started to cry.

Later, when I negotiated full authority over my body from my mother, when haircuts and makeup and clothes came entirely within my jurisdiction, I shaved an upside-down V into my hairline and fired up the curling iron, creating two little wings above my brows like fat black caterpillar larvae.

Despite the fact that nearly every black woman straightened (or, as they called it, permed) her hair—then slicked it back into a bun fastened with scrunchies, bobby pins, and barrettes, a veritable ammo belt of accessories—college turned out to be less about looks and more about class, along with academic or extracurricular specialization. And so I scraped by. I was the traveler, the cultural chameleon, the adventuress, the empath. I could advocate on behalf of Southeast Asian refugees and homeless Americans, interview Latino immigrants, teach English to the illiterate. I could pass through the inner city unscathed, dress for black-tie affairs, ramble from Burma to the tip of Singapore, crossing borders with a single bag and no reservations. I passed, I passed. I was the tiny wrestler in a school of would-be quarterbacks. My ability to Go Native carried me over the occasional bump, such as a knot of corn-fed Minnesotan students come to enjoy the travel-poster version of Thailand we wouldn't allow ourselves.

ᢒᢗ

AS WE WATCHED from our tables in the food commissary, the St. Olafers were herded down the covered walkway through the center of Chiang Mai University. Tall as trees, they moved with the speed of foreigners, impossible to miss. There were roughly two dozen of them, nearly all female, nearly all blonde. Of course, I reminded myself, the Midwest! The Scandinavian half of me taken root in tropical soil.

As they galumphed along, churning the air, the entire commissary looked up. From the tables on all sides of us, Thai phrases crackled. *St. Olaf's is here! This year's St. Olaf's have come!* Male students laughed and gestured with their chins. A few sycophantic girls who'd tried to use their English on us grabbed up their books and scrambled after them, bobby socks flashing.

Uncharacteristically silent, we pushed *pad see eiuw* around our plates and eyed the interlopers. For those of us in the advanced class—Scott, Angel, and I—our reign as exotic, special birds was surely over. After all this work, we would be reduced to nothing more than part of an easily discernible group of outsiders, clumping around on big feet, making oversized arm gestures.

Eric grinned, thrilled at the possibility of finding someone to sleep with (harmless flirtations with *rieb roi* Thai girls weren't cutting it). Jim and Francis (the latter of whom we suspected of shopping for a cut-rate Thai wife) considered the new possibilities. They had been bumped up the food chain, now relative experts in Thai language and culture. Clearly Angel and I, the American girls, had the most to lose.

In a flash of blonde, the St. Olafers were gone, leaving me with the memory of my first nightclub. When I was sixteen, the spring

I encounter two monks (a tall, pale, young one with a smaller, older, dark one leading) on our side. When they have to pass by me, they hug their side of the path, going single file.

I wonder if there is indeed no interaction between monks and *maechi*. Of course, the whole point is that we're not supposed to be interacting with each other, but the monk-*maechi* schism seems particularly acute in this place. There's little interaction beyond meals and ceremonies, and then the sexes are segregated.

A Thai woman, Woramai Kabilsingh, has ordained as a *bhikkhuni* (a female monk as recognized by the Mahayana Buddhism practiced in northeast Asia). Though the Thai church does not recognize her status, she has considerable lay support, which has allowed her to build a large temple in central Thailand. Her female followers (she has males as well) look like *maechi* but have taken fifty additional precepts and refer to themselves as Boddhisattvas.

Her daughter, Dr. Chatsumarn Kabilsingh, the editor of the *Newsletter on International Buddhist Women's Activities* and active in the international women's Buddhist movement, is a vocal advocate for the reinstatement of the order of *bhikkhuni*.

before I came to Thailand as a high school exchange student, I took a study trip to Mexico. One night all the students went to a nightclub, my first. As we walked in the door, a hush fell over the entire club. In the silence, we made our way to a collection of sofas just off the dance floor and ordered drinks.

Suddenly there was a shout and a stampede in our direction, a collective surge of bravery. The music started, and when the dust settled, every single one of the American girls was on the dance floor with a Mexican partner. Everyone, that is, except Mrs. Allen, our fifty-something chaperone—and me.

It took Mrs. Allen, clearly still stunned by the rush, a few minutes to see me huddled in the corner of the sofa, choking with adolescent humiliation. Her mouth dropped, though only for an instant, recovering to a bright smile. We stared at each other, wondering how we would play out the rest of the night together, the white grandmother and the sixteen-year-old black girl who had just learned that her undesirability was so wide it spanned the borders of nations.

What would we say to each other during the two hours the tall, angular white girls and the short, busty white girls spun and shuffled on the dance floor? How would we pretend not to see the elephant—ugliness, Blackness, Blackness, ugliness—in the center of the room?

Later in the trip we would grow even closer. When on a crowded Metro a man kept rubbing against me, despite my attempts to shift away, despite repeatedly turning around to glare at him and hiss, *"Vámonos! Déjame en paz!"* until I felt his belt buckle, cold metal, against my left buttock and got off at our stop to find a circle of liquid, cold and white, soaking through my pants, not a belt buckle at all, she would be the one to hold me as I wept in a knot of stunned American girls.

Perhaps it was her prior impotence at the nightclub that drove her with such fury, or the irony of the situation, that this was the kind of desirability I was discovering at sixteen. Not the desirability of someone you ask to dance, but the desirability of someone you take from behind, standing up, not caring who sees, like a slave. She would organize us into a protective phalanx every time we rode the Metro, boys on the outside, but for all her ferocity, there was nothing left to protect me from.

Five years later, at Chiang Mai University, the girls from St. Olaf's, the promise of America, arrived in an aura of solicitous care, and it all returned. I could see them, beautiful, swaying on the dance floor, and him, eyes wide open, grinning and undulating, grinning and undulating behind me.

ඬ

IN THE EVENING after my shower I take Cathy my bottle of orange juice concentrate. As I walk the short distance between our *gutis*, my heart bounces with my steps. I feel giddy as an adolescent, like I'm hosting a slumber party. Is it so wrong to enjoy companionship?

Cathy thanks me for the juice and asks, "What do you usually do in the evening?" as if evening differed from morning or day. I have no answer. The creatures come out; we go in. It's strange to realize that in her eyes, I'm the expert.

She looks miserable. I envy her the man she pines for. Here I've been in Thailand for months and months; I read and write Thai; I'm well versed in Thai culture and politics, but I can't get a date. She drops in for a two-month visit and gets the pick of the crop: a political intellectual, a principled artist, a kind revolutionary. Someone who has really lived but is humble about it. One of the few with the bravery to act on his beliefs.

Is life for some women really this simple?

ඬ

RIGHT BEFORE COMING to Thailand this second time, I found myself in a basement classroom at the University of Wisconsin

I see what Cathy means. This place is too intense, a summer camp gone berserk. It's not an ordinary *wat*, a walled community existing side by side with the real world. It's über-temple!

One nice thing, however, is that if I stay near my *guti*, it's good (whereas at summer camp such behavior would be labeled anti-social).

Sure, meditation is an effective way of achieving goals, but there are other ways. I think someone like Maechi Roongdüan may have discarded the ends for the means, so in love is she with the actual act of training the mind. But summer camp teaches us skills to use the other three seasons of the year, doesn't it?

Isn't the peace I feel as a *maechi* the same kind of peace I experience after spending a day at a *wat* as a layperson? At first I felt I had freedom here, but as a *maechi*, there's so much I can't do. The simple act of reading, for example. As a layperson, it's calming to read at a *wat;* for *maechi,* it's generally forbidden. A former *maechi* once warned me that we think peace is somewhere in the temple, but we are wrong.

Cathy's sadness here makes me unsure, sad.

Moments I'm a bit impatient with *wat* life. What *am* I doing here? Chiang Mai City, with all my friends and clubs, is only an hour away. But when I slow down, breathe, I'm fine.

watching a tall blonde at the front of the room refuse to be seduced. It was a summer spent in the language lab and library preparing for the year ahead at Chiang Mai University. In the evenings we joined students preparing to go to India for joint cultural workshops.

On this particular evening, Scott and I had been separated; Bob, the director of the Thailand program, having discovered that stern glares were not enough to kill our high spirits, had resorted to placing his sobering bulk between us.

"I would like to take you on a picnic," the man at the front of the room said to the girl, an India-bound student who'd volunteered from the audience for this part, "to thank you for kindness to my family." They placed two chairs side by side and commenced to drive out to the Indian countryside. How delightful!

"Where are the other members of our party?" the girl asked, tall and confident, surveying the imaginary scenery.

"Well, I needed to see you alone," the man, an administrator in the long-running College Year in India program, confessed. Apparently they were now at the picnic spot, perhaps next to a waterfall. He patted the ground next to him. "Please sit. I have something important to say."

She sat.

"I think that I'm in love with you." He leaned forward.

Immediately she stood up, calmly smoothing her skirt, though she certainly had no idea he was going to say that. How was it that she, having just volunteered on the spot, had the self-possession to see through his words, to know that he didn't love her, couldn't love her, stuck as she was in a foreign landscape alone with him?

The girl turned and walked back to the imaginary car. "I think we should go back. I don't feel comfortable with this conversation."

He cut her off, making a move to sweep her into his arms. "Please, I feel so close to you. You're so mature, so understanding. The way you've learned about our culture is astounding. In fact, in time I would like to send—"

"—My children to join you in America," I finished the sentence with him.

Scott and Bob glanced at me, and I was well aware of the fact that I was sitting on the edge of my seat, as precarious as Humpty-Dumpty in my thin shell at the role-play being enacted in front of me, while the audience laughed at the would-be suitor's weak lines that wouldn't fool any twenty-two-year-old! The basement room was hot, cold, hot again, and I had to remind myself that I was in Madison, Wisconsin, that I was in my twenties, no longer seventeen, that I hadn't known, hadn't known, hadn't known.

I saw the man signal for Mekong whiskey, which appeared like magic out of the darkness of the secluded restaurant, and heard him explain why no one was at my farewell party, heard him thank me for tutoring his children in English. *In fact,* he says, *in fact . . .*

I remembered climbing on the back of his motorcycle, giddy with whiskey and the sense of danger. I remembered roaring along country roads, the air black and cold, feeling free for an instant, then flying into a garage, a boy rushing out to close a billowing curtain behind us. I remembered staggering off the motorcycle and asking, *Where are we? This isn't home,* and the man pulling me into a lit room off the curtained garage, and my seeing the bed, just a room with a bed, and saying *No!* and turning to the door and the man throwing his arms around me, pleading, *Please don't be scared, Faith, I love you, please wait, we'll just talk, please, you can go anytime, we'll just talk.*

I remembered feeling a spurt of power in all that pleading and allowing myself to be talked down, sat down, grabbed, kissed, undressed, broken. *"Mai khoey, mai khoey,"* I remembered saying in time with his rhythm. *I've never done this before. Never.*

Five years later in a classroom basement during my first visit to the Midwest, I found out what really happened to me. What I had excused to myself as passion, an exotic first time, turned out to be something else entirely, so trite it was in the manual, word for word. Which was worse—getting fucked or learning that you've been fucked?

"Are you okay?" Bob asked, and I couldn't even pretend.

"That happened to me," I whispered, still mesmerized by the girl at the front of the room, who was insisting on being driven back to town. So easy for her! "Everything, down to the last word."

"Whew!" Bob shook his head, looking sympathetic. "How did you get out of it?"

For the first time, I looked away from the tableau unfolding before me and stared at him, stunned again, this time by his assumption. Perhaps it was having to admit you were fucked that's worse, having to become the victim. I was a Resourceful American Girl, after all! The one who rose above the world's expectations and stereotypes, the one who avoided disasters in a single bound! The savvy traveler. The Junior Ambassador. The one who had a different answer from: "I didn't."

With these two words I tipped, slid, cracked on the floor. And Bob, for all his degrees and experience sending students abroad, despite his Thai wife and the mixed-race child they will have, despite weathering his own demons, had nothing to say to put me back together again.

Taking her vows inside the *bod*, the ordination hall of
Wat Phra Singh. Ajarn Boon in the background.

CHAPTER SEVEN

✂ Going to Hell

HUMAN EXISTENCE IS ONE OF MIXED PLEASURE AND PAIN. BELOW
MAN, IN DESCENDING ORDER AND INCREASING PAIN OF PUNISHMENT,
ARE THE DEMONS, THE [SPIRITS OF THE DEAD UNDERGOING PUNISH-
MENT], THE ANIMALS, AND THE INHABITANTS OF THE HELLS....MEN
WHO LIVE DOMINATED BY ANGER, HATE, AND VIOLENCE WILL BE
PUNISHED IN THE HELLS.

—Robert C. Lester,
THERAVADA BUDDHISM IN SOUTHEAST ASIA

AT SEVEN O'CLOCK in the morning there's a knock on the door of my *guti*. Though I've been up since four studying Buddhist texts, it feels like a surprise spot check at camp. No one has ever knocked. Is my sarong at regulation height? Does my straw mat have proper army corners?

Maechi Vilawam, the cute little *maechi* who's always to the right or left of Maechi Roongdüan, stands grinning on my stoop.

I *wai*, bowing. *"Sawasdee kha, maechi."*

She returns the greeting, and then gestures toward the front of the *wat*, where the sun is just coming up in the direction of the road to Chiang Mai City.

"Will *maechi* join Cat-tee to go see *phra*?" She flashes that big grin of hers, full of crooked teeth.

Other than the fact that I'm needed to accompany Cathy, I'm not sure what she means. *Phra* (capital *P*) refers to the historic Buddha, while *phra* (small *p*) can be both Buddha statues and Buddhist

..

When she comes to "check my mood," as they call the evening lesson, Maechi Roongdüan carries a loaf of bread. It's one of those perfectly rectangular loaves that tastes like white cardboard and must have been invented by a Thai baker watching British television.

..

My high school host families were always trying to foist such bread on me, along with fried eggs, for breakfast. As soon as they left the kitchen, the servants and I would drag out the chili paste and sticky rice.

After her teaching on mindfulness, Maechi Roongdüan asks if I'm having any problems with the food. Surprised, I say, "Of course not!"

She then tries to give me the bread. I refuse. She tells me to take it and keep it in my *guti* "just in case." She holds out the loaf.

Horrified, I shake my head. It's bad enough to require special Western food, but to break the precept on eating after noon? "Thank you," I say, keeping my hands firmly in my lap, "but I don't want it and I don't need it."

monks. Nonetheless, I figure I'd be happy to see any *phra,* so I nod and snatch off my stocking cap.

After I wrestle my breasts and over-robe into some semblance of respectability, I step outside. Cathy stands on the path in lay-women's white, her look screaming, *What's up?*

We walk east to the *sala* tracking the arcing sun. No wonder we never see it, stuck back in our narrow western gully. What a pity! The sky is the softest, purest shade of pink imaginable, neither garish nor faint. A darker pink sun, ringed with gold, hangs low in a soft blue sky. The colors hover, separate and distinct, in the still morning air.

At the *sala,* we follow Maechi Vilawam downstairs. The kitchen is the proverbial hive of activity, the kitchen-duty *maechi* all talking at regular volume and moving at normal speed. It's like the shock of ducking out of a bright summer day into one of those dim underground pubs in Boston. My eyes and ears blur.

Everyone greets Maechi Vilawam, probably the most popular *maechi*. The older laywoman who sits behind me at mealtime and treats me with such overt respect that I'm tempted to believe I might actually carry off this ordination thing, appears in civilian clothing. Maechi Vilawam explains that the woman is returning home today.

Prostrating herself to us beautifully, the woman serves us a tray with small glasses of hot Ovaltine and a plate heaped with tinned biscuits. Is this the traditional transition breakfast, or do they still believe Cathy's dissatisfaction comes from not being able to eat the food?

Yesterday Cathy said she had mentioned not being happy, and Maechi Roongdüan sent someone to her *guti* with a can of sweetened condensed milk and a loaf of white bread.

We had chuckled quietly. The Thai seem convinced that (1) Westerners can't eat spicy food and (2) the root of all unhappiness stems from gustatory distress.

I bow my head and decline. I can't eat this early; besides, I detest Ovaltine.

YESTERDAY AFTER THE milk and bread, Cathy knocked on my door and announced that she'd decided to leave. "I can't concentrate, Faith," she said, squinting in at me as if she were the one emerging from a dim *guti* to find a blonde standing in sunlight on her steps. Hands behind her back, she cocked her head. "Can you tell me the best way to break the news to Maechi Roongdüan?"

I couldn't have been more surprised if she had kicked in my *guti* door and come in shooting. My mouth swung open. "But I thought you were getting used to being here!"

She shook her head. "I'm wasting everyone's time."

I peered back at her, stunned that someone could walk away so easily from a commitment, from a challenge. Behind her the stream rushed by. How to do that? Then a darker unvoiced feeling fluttered around my chest, a songbird intent on escape. Slowly I recognized its colored markings, its name: panic, the heart beginning to crumble in the face of abandonment. It's a lover mouthing *I've been thinking,* a friend sighing *You expect so much,* an aunt or uncle storming away from the table, a father slipping away before birth.

"Why not wait a day or two?" I advised, not entirely sure which one of us I was addressing. "Any change is initially difficult. It's only been a day. Give yourself enough time."

Again she shook her head, a blonde halo of determination. "I have a limited amount of time in Thailand," she explained. She owed it to herself to see if this relationship could work. She wanted to visit all the places they had talked about together.

AFTER OVALTINE TIME, Cathy and I follow Maechi Vilawam outside and up some cement steps set recently into the ground. She unlocks the door of a building that resembles a schoolhouse and we enter the *vihara,* where they must hold services for the occasional

She looks relieved and rises to leave. She tells me that I have only "a few days in this life" to practice meditation, but I could live to be eighty years old, so there will be plenty of time to go shopping, see friends, get married, buy a car.

I like this: Get Married, Buy a Car!

I *wai,* thanking her for the teaching, and go inside. Obviously Cathy's unhappiness has upset her. It upsets me too, but it's obvious Cathy should go. Anyone can read the panic on her face. It will only get worse.

I light a candle and brood a bit. Maechi Roongdüan's fanaticism is admirable— but with other people's lives? I have always distrusted proselytizing. She needs to understand that meditation must be internally motivated.

"Maechi Faith!" a voice calls softly.

When I step outside, Maechi Roongdüan is sitting in the same exact place I left her. She asks me, please, to explain what Cathy needs. "Is the *wat* too strict? Do *you* require anything?"

"No," I assure her, touched. "The *wat* is fine; I'm fine. This is simply about what Cathy needs from the external world right now."

"Yes," she agrees, "Cathy's mind-set is such that she should go home." She promises to send Cathy tomorrow in the car that is returning another *maechi*. She stands up, scooping up the bread and regarding it with regret. "I was just afraid that Ajarn Boon would be disappointed with me."

I have misunderstood her. Shame waters my eyes.

visitor. The inside is small and breathtakingly ugly. Even the three painted *phra* on the altar are mediocre. Garish murals cover the walls—scenes from the *Phra's* life, the history of the temple, hell.

These last are truly amazing: grotesque, leering men hack naked bodies in half. The round blades of table saws fly through the air, lopping off unsuspecting heads. Lynched humans hang from trees. A large cauldron fueled by burning skulls boils up a stew of screaming bodies. Dogs devour their own legs. There's an immortal—a headless man with a face on his naked torso—eyes on the breasts, mouth on the stomach. Out from his open neck emerges the skewered and bleeding figure of a second man.

"Oh!" Cathy exclaims, startled. "It's looks like Christian hell."

I nod, speechless. I've been certain that Buddhism eschewed literal manifestations of heaven and hell.

Maechi Vilawam beams.

৩৫

WE CHAT—with me acting as translator—with Maechi Vilawam, who's been ordained four years. She's thirty-six, a widow with one child and four years of primary schooling behind her. This last bit of information surprises me, given how close she and the intellectual Roongdüan are ("I call her mother, sister, friend," Maechi Roongdüan says when I ask about her smiling shadow).

I ask how many monks are permanent residents, and Maechi Vilawam admits sheepishly that she has no idea. "They come and go, sometimes many, sometimes hardly any. Just like *maechi*—sometimes thirty or forty, sometimes seven or eight." She herself came to live here three years ago because she was curious about "*maechi* who don't use money and who eat leaves." She chuckles at her own naïveté, her open face inviting us to do the same.

She reports that the *wat* itself is thirty to forty years old, though the lovely *vihara* isn't yet ten. (They were better off without it, I say.) "Look." She points a tiny callused finger at the landscape painted behind the main *Phra* figure, a stilted jungle of *bodhi* trees and stylized palms, India as imagined by Rousseau or a seventh-grade cartoonist. Sacred lotus curl about the meditating Buddha, oversized stalks undulating menace.

Laughing ruefully, she tells us that once many birds flew into the *vihara,* thought that the painted trees were real, and crashed into the wall, falling dead at the foot of the Buddha.

After a surprised silence, Cathy inquires about her child.

Maechi Vilawam smiles. "My parents raise."

&

WE WAIT FOR whatever it is we're waiting for, and soon the tall, light-skinned *phra* I've seen on our side of the stream creeps in, shoulders hunched, eyes on the ground. (I've never seen such humble-looking monks in my life.) He climbs onto the platform, and we wait for him to prostrate himself to the *Phra* before prostrating ourselves to him.

Close-up, I can see that he's very young, with a pale moon face. As my forehead touches the straw mat before me, it occurs to me that as *maechi,* no matter her chronological or ordination age, Maechi Roongdüan has to bow before this child. Anger flashes in me on her behalf, a hot telegram, but is it really on her behalf if she herself doesn't mind?

Sounding as if he has too many teeth in his mouth, he asks Cathy in English why she is going and whether she will have achieved her purpose in coming to Thailand if she gives up her search for the Dhamma so soon.

I stifle the urge to laugh.

He then requests quite sweetly that she say what knowledge she has gleaned from life over the past twenty-one years.

"Well," she begins politely, "that's a little difficult to put into so many words."

"I think it would be better if you left tomorrow," he states,

··

The next morning, after Cathy's departure, I hide out in the bathroom. During my absence, someone, probably Maechi Vilawam, leaves a bowl of food inside the door of my *guti.* There's a huge mound of sticky rice and side dishes, covered with slices of watermelon, dried bananas, and this morning's biscuits. Enough to choke a mindful horse.

I try to be mindful, eat about half, and go to sleep, feeling very depressed and sorry for myself.

At ten o'clock, Maechi Vilawam brings my thermos and washcloth, which someone had taken to breakfast for me, and a mini-can of Ovaltine, which I firmly decline.

She takes my bowl, and I go back to sleep until two-thirty. When I awake, my stomach and throat ache, and I shudder with chills, though my flesh is hot. I'm not sure whether my bad mood has made me sick or whether being sick has put me in a bad mood.

I drink some coffee and water, then wash up and sit beneath the tree to meditate.

Sitting meditation is so difficult; the conditions have to be just perfect. I drape my thin, gauzy sash over my head like a veil to ward off mosquitoes and last barely thirty minutes. I want to cry.

Maechi Roongdüan calls me for my daily instruction. I am now supposed to be mindful of *everything I touch* and *every desire.*

"Be aware of every time you want to open a door, stand up, pour water—every common desire. We note common desire as practice, because it is easy, because it is difficult to note our emotions. Like anger—you cannot touch it. But eventually we will be able to note it, and then we can deal with it."

I wonder why she chose anger as her

"since Ajarn Suchin and I have to go to the airport. We have some business in Bangkok."

He leaves, and Cathy's eyes start to get that wild, wide look.

We wait.

The second-most-senior *maechi*, the one who stands ahead of Maechi Roongdüan, enters. She too is leaving today for her home temple. It was she who got up to meditate at three my first day here. A dark, frail woman, she lists a little to the left, her body seeming perpetually on the verge of collapse, a visual illustration of that Laurie Anderson song about walking and falling.

But what a face! Large round ears protrude from her head, flanking a full, plum-colored mouth. At first glance she gives the impression of being old, though upon closer inspection, I wouldn't bet money on her age. Her skin is flawless—smooth, delicate, glowingly translucent—tight yet without lines. Her eyes—long, liquid, dark—are shaped like inverted tears, oval at the top, then drooping down to the side in a long tail. I can't see the whites, only long darkness.

Looking at her, I get the impression that she's a woman who has achieved incredible peace, whose face has grown continually younger until even the normal lines of life have been erased.

The temple she comes from is near Bangkok and has thirty *maechi*. "Is it a 'supporting *wat*'?" Maechi Vilawam asks, and I think she answers wanly, no, *maechi* have to find their own food.

She answers these questions shyly, long eyes downcast, only occasionally raising her head with the ghost of a smile.

The monk returns as cautiously as he left and says that it's fine if Cathy leaves today, but he would like to try to talk her into staying. With that, he launches into an hour-long monologue on something (life, pain, the nature of the universe? I don't know!). At first I'm pleased to be sitting like a proper *maechi*, that is, made of stone. After a while I try to understand what he's saying but can't decipher his lisping monotone.

Then I begin to wonder what I'm doing here. Why do I have to endure this torture? The *maechi* look like they're meditating, but they could be asleep, who knows? My leg and back ache so much I want to scream. Every three minutes I consider shifting my position, but something always stops me: momentary relief, a great surge of interesting pain, the urge to cry, but mainly pride. Oh, and let us not forget the desire to maintain the pain and thus my anger.

Finally, when we can hear the mealtime chanting, the monk realizes how late it is. "Time to end," he lisps, launching into yet another story.

He tells us that he studied one year in England and one in the United States. His parents wanted him to return to help with the family business, but he "has found the real happiness without problems" as a monk.

Good for you! I want to shout. I envision clapping him on the shoulder and bolting out the door.

"People who travel," he mumbles, "that's not real happiness. It's just chance, luck, that they have the opportunity to go around."

I'm willing to concede this much, remembering the doomed, deluded birds circling the *vihara*. Yes, travel is a question of chance and luck, though I don't quite see why it isn't a valid form of happiness for that particular lucky person?

Or is he referring to someone like me, who derives pleasure in the actual act of movement because it fills the senses and provides goals and things to think about that transcend the mundane? (Or are the thoughts still mundane and simply the landscape that's transcendent?) Yes, for me, it is easier to be happy in a new landscape. If I fail, it's culture shock; when I don't, the scenery's breathtaking.

Okay, I'm not that much on the run! I guess that, despite the lessons to be learned, travel is not real, pure, down-home happiness at its foundation. It's superficial delight, dependent on locale. If this moon-faced boy were a mother, he might say: "Go back to America; deal with life." But he's a monk, so he says, "Give up the world and be mindful."

example. Then I think back on today and how I deliberately held on to anger during the monk's monologue against the backdrop of hell. I could easily have relieved some of my pain or started to meditate—both would have calmed me. But I chose instead to cling to anger, thus wearing myself out and ruining my entire day. Ill feeling actually led to an ill body.

I held on so that I could say, "I was fine until that inconsiderate monk did thus-and-such." Everyone is always doing things to make me sad or angry, so that (1) I'm absolved of the sin of anger and therefore not a Bitch or—horrors!—the Angry Black Woman (instead I'm a Righteous Avenger!), and (2) I don't have to deal with what's *really* got me angry, the injustices that should be struck down with the righteous sword of anger. Sure, each petty grievance feels legitimate, but it doesn't need to be.

I think that I don't like to be mindful because I like to live my inner life without discipline, to allow the private me to be meaner, less ethical, more emotional, less successful than the self I present to the world. For example, I know I am too easily angered, but instead of dealing with the root of this anger, I deny it or, alternately, look for petty, tangible excuses for it. This means I can't let people get to know me because I'm a fraud. I'm "passing."

Does this explain my constant low-grade guilt and obsessiveness about privacy? There are two MEs, the private one always spilling over onto the public one. If both were content, perhaps there would be only one.

Suddenly the Hallmark platitudes I read my first night come to me: *Every day you are responsible for how you feel. No one can make you unhappy or nervous. The untrained mind is so vulnerable to circumstances. Some-*

After one more attempt to make Cathy wait until tomorrow, he says it has been a "pleasure" (his voice still a sweet, concerned monotone) "discussing the Dhamma" with her.

Again, I have to stop myself from cackling loudly. Then he apologizes for running over into our mealtime and creeps away, moon face heavy on its stalk.

As we get up, staggering on rubbery legs like newborn foals, I ask Maechi Vilawam if I can skip the meal. My body can endure only so much motionless ritual; besides, I'm improperly dressed.

No problem, she promptly replies. My food will be brought to me.

We leave, the two *maechi* heading toward the reception area, Cathy and I giggling quietly behind. "Well," she whispers, "it's hard but not impossible to Escape from a Buddhist Temple!"

I imagine the scene: the two of us at night in our white robes, scaling the *wat* walls and leaping from roof to roof, while in the watchtower the abbot trains a blinding searchlight on us, his amplified voice rising above the sirens. "We've got you covered," he blares. "Now get down, go to your rooms, and meditate!"

AS WE PASS the kitchen area, a monk emerges. He's small and dark, with a face so alive, so pleasant, it radiates. Seeing him, I get the same feeling I got the first time I visited Wat Thamtong—trust, and something stronger.

Smiling and pointing to the *bod* where the rest of the community is gathered, he says, "Partake of the meal." He speaks in formal monastic dialect.

Embarrassed, I nod. "Please never mind," I say in regular Thai, and scurry on.

"That was Ajarn Suchin," Maechi Vilawam says gently. The abbot.

I'm stunned. Not just by my inappropriately casual and dismissive behavior but by the fact that this handsome, very young-looking monk is the abbot.

I am also struck again by the difference between monks and *maechi*. These *maechi* are always gentle, friendly, and kind, but they seem somehow otherworldly. The older ones are good and wise. The dynamic ones, like Maechi Roongdüan, seem in a way taut—as if their core had turned to steel from years of restraint and determination. But none seem as vital and steeped in the present as the abbot. He clearly loves striding around the *wat*, fetching water from the stream and feeding the dogs.

Why are the good monks like this? Is it that ordination offers men a full life where they can cultivate all their talents and energies—meditating, studying Dhamma, traveling, teaching, speaking, gardening, building, administrating—whereas it only offers women an escape from life, where they spend their energies cultivating their minds and erasing the rest?

As I turn to enter my *guti*, I see the abbot burning down the path toward me, the English-speaking monk drifting along behind, arms encircling an alms bowl. I realize that the two monks who passed me the other day had to have been these two. I had wandered right by the abbot himself! No wonder they had gotten out of the way, practically jumping off the path. It must have been obvious that I was adrift, possessed, with no intention of prostrating myself to anyone!

Embarrassed, I quickly duck inside.

No such luck! The abbot stops on the path before my *guti* and softly calls, *"Maechi ja, maechi ja." Ja,* the particle used as an endearment by elders, social superiors, or lovers, has never sounded so sweet.

I emerge timidly, by now too confused to know up from down, and stand blinking like a half-wit—once again neglecting to prostrate myself. The abbot smiles gently. We regard each other, I obviously at a loss as to why he has called me, he at a loss as to whether we can communicate.

thing good happens and it is happy. Something bad happens and it is in pain.

And I understand how I work. In my anger, I become the headless immortal out of whose open neck emerges the bleeding figure of another. Like the birds, I've become distracted by the wrong destination and fallen dead at the very foot of the Buddha.

In Thai the young monk tells the abbot that he should speak English to me. The abbot nods and then addresses me in Thai: "Join the partaking of food; they wait."

I hesitate, touched by his use of Thai, his apparent belief in me, and tempted just to return to eat with the others. At least I avoid the possible impropriety of offering my explanation—and the difficulty of speaking the special formal language used for addressing monks.

"Well," I begin in Thai, "Maechi Vilawam said that I could eat— I mean, partake—here."

"Oh!" He understands. "Then," he reconfirms in a patient, sweet voice, "they will bring it to you, *na?*"

"*Kha.*" I smile sheepishly. *Yes.*

He nods to himself, pleased, and then nods at me, since again I am staring blankly, clearly unable to prostrate. He picks up his plastic bucket and the two of them stride on, surefooted, leaving me blinking on my steps a few feet off the path.

Faith in the courtyard of Lowell House,
her Harvard dorm.

CHAPTER EIGHT

﹇ Harvard Rules

ANYONE, ACCORDING TO THAI FOLK CUSTOM, CAN LOSE THEIR [SIC]
KHWAN [LIFE SPIRIT]. IT HAPPENS WHEN SOME GREAT SHOCK OCCURS
TO THE PSYCHE, SUCH AS A DEATH OR A BETRAYAL OF ONE'S INTEGRITY,
THAT PUTS A DENT IN YOUR IMMUNE SYSTEM OR THE CENTER OF YOUR
BEING.... IN THE WEST IT'S CALLED DEPRESSION OR MELANCHOLIA.

—*Rudolph Wurlitzer,*
HARD TRAVEL TO SACRED PLACES

I HAD NO IDEA that whenever I piloted my red motor scooter out
of the sanctuary of my host family's teak and glass house and onto
the Thai highway, I was joining the ranks of kin of a sort—the walking dead. Unaware, I motored happily along, dry paddies of golden
rice blurring along either side, waving to truckloads of grinning,
sinewy workers perched atop mountains of bagged rice. If I did
happen to notice the cluster of small white flags and white string
with chalk lines etched in the dirt on the road shoulder every few
miles or so, I assumed they were traffic markers. It wasn't until I had
visited a few spirit mediums, along with entire families laden with
offerings, and read about the indigenous, pre-Buddhist rituals of the
north, that I realized what I was seeing/not seeing, who was marking time along the side of the road with me as I sped.

Each intricate display marked not traffic but the site where a
traffic victim had perished and been lain to rest by a spirit medium.
The highways were crowded with them. Thai motorists, it seemed,
were dying at an alarming rate. The thin white string, *khwan,* which

THE THREE
CHARACTERISTICS
OF EXISTENCE

dukkha—All things
are unsatisfactory
(often inaccurately
translated as "suf-
fering")

anicca—All things are
impermanent

anatta—All things are
nonsubstantial
(often translated as
"no self")

..

Much of Buddhism doesn't concern me. I don't care about finding out the Truth. I just want to set realistic goals and follow through. What I need right now to be happy out in the world is to honor those who have helped me (Ajarn Boon, Maechi Roongdüan, Ajarn Supatra) by following the precepts well and trying to realize my meditation goals.

THE FOUR NOBLE TRUTHS

1. The truth of *dukkha*— Human existence is unsatisfactory, imperfect, anxiety-ridden, based on a cycle of cravings for permanent happiness derived from impermanent things.

2. The truth of the arising of *dukkha*— Desires, thirsts, cravings cause *dukkha*.

3. The truth of the cessation of *dukkha*— There is liberation, freedom from *dukkha*, which is *Nibbana* (Nirvana), enlightenment, the ultimate goal of

I had noticed wrapped around wrists at wedding and ordination ceremonies, had been tied by mourning family members hoping to bind the dead to earth until the soul's issues could be resolved. The chalk lines showed just how delicate the boundary between our two worlds—corporeal and spirit—is. Every day I was motoring pleasantly through a map of death.

When I move to Wat Thamtong with its quiet, bowing graces and endless landscapes of time, this realization deepens. Just as meditation clarifies my understanding of rebirth, showing regeneration of the self as a figurative psychic condition, I AM, so too I realize that there is more than one way to die. As I sit, eyes closed, my diagnosis presents itself. Like the souls wandering the side of the road, I too have lost my *khwan*. My integrity has certainly been betrayed; there is a dent in the very center of my being. Somewhere on the road to adulthood, rather than finding a lily pad upon which to stand while I grew, I found instead a great shock that knocked my *khwan* clear out of my body.

Sitting on the tree bench outside my *guti*, I feel a bit like the Buddha groping for Enlightenment beneath the *bodhi* tree. I'm not sure where and when *khwan* fled, and the prospect of revisiting the scene of the accident on my hands and knees to look for bloody clues terrifies me. Do I really want to stare into the maw of death, relive the screech of tires and grinding of metal? I nonetheless have a sneaking suspicion that such an investigation may be necessary. If I don't know what truck smashed through my psyche and where, scattering my *khwan* like grains of rice burst from a brown burlap bag, the turbaned field hands dazed and barefoot by the side of the northern Thai road, then how in the world can I go about getting it back?

සිෆ

I SET MYSELF up in the cave, the place in the *wat* I like least of all, in preparation for visiting my foolish, most vulnerable self. It's a bit like biting the bullet. The first clue comes easily, the proverbial vision. Sitting in Thailand, I watch myself at age seventeen get the mail and change my life.

The year following my exchange to Thailand, I took the usual round of pre-college standardized tests and soon crisp ivory packets with gold-embossed seals began to fill our rickety mailbox. The first time this happened, I shouted and ran inside the house.

I found my mother at her desk engaged in her favorite pastime—reading and underlining two books at once. Bursting through the doorway, I blurted, "I thought that Harvard and Yale didn't exist anymore! Aren't they historic places for people long ago or characters in books?"

My mother laughed, lowering her ruler and fistful of colored pens. From my vantage point in Thailand, I can see her, clear as day—the wild cowlicks, the mad dash to cap markers. Hands free, she wriggled her fingers. "Give, give!"

I handed over my treasures, my creamy, heavy-bond passport to a charmed circle of New England privilege, and peered over her shoulder to read along about fencing and crew and lacrosse teams (glamorous-sounding sports I couldn't imagine anyone my age knowing how to play), day trips to sophisticated cities like Boston and Philadelphia and New York, courses in Arabic and Chinese (languages I imagined I would study before circling the globe).

"Imagine!" my mother breathed, already planning her first visit back East. I knew her eyes were glittering at the sight of photos of wood-paneled libraries with their soaring ceilings, sparkling sunburst windows, and leather-bound collections to rival that of the Library of Congress.

"Yeah," I sighed back, tracing my finger over the images of fresh-faced black and Asian and white students sprawled reading on velvety lawns before turreted, ivy-covered brick buildings, or communing in harmonious clusters with day packs slung over one shoulder of their hand-knit sweaters. It was exactly the world I'd imagined awaited me outside my small town.

all Buddhist endeavors, the complete extinction of and freedom from thirsts.

4. The truth of the path leading to cessation of *dukkha*— The Middle Path is a way of self-discipline toward the end of cravings and development of insight.

..

Even though I am still bloody from America, I don't agree that life is suffering. Some of it definitely is (the number of people lacking the basic rights to food, shelter, work, and safety prove that), but I don't expect to be deliriously happy one hundred percent of the time anyway.

I don't believe that joy is impermanent, but even if it is, I see nothing wrong with that! Impermanence is part of joy itself, what makes it so precious. (Oh, I just contradicted myself and conceded one of the basic Buddhist tenets!) What I need right now is to be pleased with my personality—secure and not lonely.

I don't agree with detachment, with not needing people. I need and enjoy friends. I guess it's natural to be hurt by them at times. Just don't be unaware or overly dependent. What I need right now is to have reliable friends with whom I feel comfortable.

I don't agree (or don't want to agree) that anger is bad. Anger is a bad thing to *hold on to,* but I have to be careful not to walk away from this experience with a complex. I'm always made to feel guilty—as a woman, a black person, the daughter of High Moralists—for being angry, and so I try not to feel anger. I only end up letting it fester in my subconscious until it explodes.

Besides, much anger is necessary—at oppression, poverty, disrespect—and can be channeled in healthy ways—for social change or for getting out of unhealthy relationships. I simply need a better way.

Though I'd always been the top student in school, my ambition was unfocused. My exchange year had confirmed that once and for all I had to escape eastern Washington, with its born-again Christian and country western radio stations, and that once again escape would require winning—this time a scholarship to a "good" college. Now, suddenly, there it was—a worthy goal, my hunger to be the best transformed into an actual location: the Ivy League. The stiff, crackling papers and full-color booklets suggested possibility: that an ordinary person could simply request an application and try her hand at leaving behind the world of teenage pregnancies and marriages, farm accidents and jobs at the local convenience store, keg parties and souped-up Camaros.

In the cool dimness of the cave, I smile at the memory. For all the questioning of authority my mother taught me, she and I were still descendants of the American immigrant dream. It took only a mailing blitz to convince us that college admission was the last frontier, where a nobody could be discovered, could rise to glory on the basis of merit alone. America at work!

In the America of memory, my mother jabbed a finger at the financial aid FAQs. "These private schools have so much aid money," she marveled, "that it might actually be *more* affordable to go to the most expensive." Our eyes met.

So here it is—the first lesson I now need to breathe out in a shallow cave—the price of success. The seventeen-year-old me learned paradox, that being poor might actually work to my advantage. Later that year, once the luster of recruitment letters had dulled a bit, I learned the price of leveraging (or appearing to leverage) this disadvantage. My success would always be questioned, ascribed to social circumstances. But I would have pursued it anyway. How could I stop the deep hunger sparked that day? I wanted a better life. Buddhism knows. Open your mouth and start the cycle of *dukkha,* unfulfilled craving that leads to life's dissatisfaction.

Through academic contests and political organizations and

writing conferences, I began to make a group of friends on the other side of the mountains: glossy, ambitious, upper-middle-class students who used SAT vocabulary words in everyday conversation, inhabited the geometric glass houses I gazed at through the windows of the Greyhound bus as it motored through Seattle's lake districts, and attended private schools (another institution that for some reason I thought no longer existed outside of teen movies and British novels).

Pastel sweaters knotted carefully over their shoulders, my new friends taught me that all the things I'd been doing—volunteer work and travel and college prep courses and publishing poems—could and should be packaged in a way that would gain me entrance into the Ivy League. At first it seemed harmless enough: I was simply highlighting things I was already doing, marketing my strengths, putting my best foot forward, being American. Nothing wrong with a little external validation.

And what's wrong with wanting a "good school"? the cave me asks, particularly if good means a four-year world populated with people who also cared about books and politics and travel. Together we would, as my parents' friends had in the sixties, form brave new alliances and stay up all night, cigarettes dangling forgotten from our fingers, Mason jars of red wine staining the coffee table, arguing passionately about how to make the world a better place.

☙❧

MY SECOND VISION also happens in the cave, like a vacation slide presenting itself on the screen of my memory. I open my eyes and there it is, in full color against the rippled cave wall. The golden Buddha figures and I watch me navigate a party for Barney Frank supporters on my very first night in Cambridge, Massachusetts.

Alan Dershowitz spun through a doorway, calling back at someone on the crowded dance floor, and slammed into me, upending his drink down the front of my second-best dress. As the celebrity

I don't agree with the concept of *kamma* (karma). *Kamma*, as I understand it (which is not at all well), and rebirth seem to encourage passivity and apathy. What I need is to feel in control of my life— where I live, what I do, how I survive, my education, my political commitments, my art.

I don't agree with the rejection of the body, and I'm certainly not interested in overcoming sensual desires. The senses are what keep us alive! True, an incredible amount of evil in the world can be attributed to sexual desire (take the flesh trade in this country for one), but it's not sex itself that's responsible so much as the evil ways desire manifests itself. What I need right now with regard to the body is to have no back pain and be the right weight.

..

Despite what Maechi Roongdüan or any books say, I have my own goals for my ordination:

- to develop my concentration
- to overcome the suffering that comes of emotions and desire
- to recognize and understand my emotions
- to think and know before I act
- to overcome fear and anger
- to be content with myself
- to interact constructively with people
- to maximize my mind's full potential
- to take control of my life
- to be able to accept failure
- to demand less from relationships
- to be able to find relaxation and solace within myself
- to be less attached to food and sleep
- to judge others and myself less harshly
- to understand people better.

And, ironically enough: to set and attain realistic goals

lawyer pawed at my skirt with a cocktail napkin, my friend Chris, a volunteer on Frank's congressional campaign, stepped in to introduce us.

Dershowitz nodded gamely and gave my hand a firm shake. "Nice to meet you, Faith."

Fresh off the farm, I had only the faintest idea who this man with the wispy red Afro was. It was years before the Claus von Bülow or Leona Helmsley or Mike Tyson or Woody Allen trials that would catapult him to notoriety, overshadowing his previous work in human rights.

As Chris disappeared in search of a sponge, Dershowitz said, "So you've just arrived. Which school?"

I blinked and answered, "Harvard." Hadn't Chris just said so?

"I know, but which school?"

I stared at him. This guy was supposed to be a famous defense attorney and Harvard professor? "Harvard," I repeated.

He leaned in closer against the noise of the party, hungrily scanning his empty glass, and tried yet again. "But which school?" His stamina was amazing.

Chris returned, laughing, to rescue my dress and the conversation. "She's a freshman in the college," she explained to a much relieved-looking Dershowitz before dragging me away. Safely out of earshot, she daubed me with soda water and explained that "Harvard" consisted of numerous "schools": the Law School, the Business or B-School, the Medical or Med School, the College of Arts and Sciences. The undergraduate college was just one of *many* Harvards, each famous and desirable in its own right.

Her tone was gentle, only serving to underscore the enormity of my ignorance about this institution I had worked so hard to enter. I couldn't lay claim to this new Harvard identity I'd hoped would erase my dusty, dissatisfying Sunnyside one. I didn't even know where I was!

Though of course I eventually figured out where I was and even how to work the Harvard identity, I would remain the quintessential scholarship student, torn between the values I was raised on and the cold reason and individual ambition around me. With our dazed smiles and shaky legs, we scholarship students staggered around like astronauts whose bodies haven't depressurized after space travel.

I complete my meditation and open my eyes: exactly an hour, the goal I set upon closing my eyes. It's odd, but this quiet accomplishment feels like the first real thing I've ever done. Meditation and mindfulness are the only accomplishments that aren't about how I package or present or sell myself, about how I jump through burning hoops or work the system or get smashed upside the head by the system. They are real precisely because they can't be celebrated or résuméd or measured by anyone else. It is me, all me, all real. Only I know if I'm able to control my mind's wild rampages, if I'm able to wake from sleep mindfully, if I can meditate for the hour-long goal I set for myself. Either I sit in meditation or I don't. Either I overcome weakness or it overcomes me. There is no way to package or spin it into something more.

Meditation forces me to be brutally honest with myself. If I'm impatient to note my twenty-eight points, in a hurry to be somewhere else, and neglect to take the time to note all my thoughts, I don't get results. If I see that the goal is in the process itself, I will do it skillfully, I won't forget the points, and concentration will deepen and deepen. There's no reason to try to fool anyone or take shortcuts. The goal is in the practice. The good is in the practice. The god is in the practice.

෨෨

MY THIRD VIEW of the accident takes place during the ordination of a new *maechi*. I sit in the *sala* surrounded by bald, beaming women of various shapes and sizes and wonder how in the world I came to be here, the only Westerner, the only black. On the surface,

and values. Are these Buddhist goals?

Simple, bourgeois, impossible, romantic, egocentric, and hopelessly social! Will meditation help me realize these hopes, or simply show me that they're improbable, perhaps foolish? And where do my own personal beliefs and values come in?

More rules: *Maechi* cannot go into each other's *guti*, so the few occasions we're allowed to talk, we have to do so in the open.

It's so cold when I go to take my shower, the bathroom dim gray. Eventually I work up the courage to throw the first bucketful of icy stream water over myself. Yikes! Then I notice that my right shoulder is covered with perfect beads of water. A faint, cool light gleams through the slatted roof down onto the droplets. The shoulder is round, smooth, the skin soft, the drops so evenly spaced, exquisite. The light so gentle, perfectly placed.

All this beauty and no opportunity to appreciate it! When I'm outside, I feel I should be walking in meditation, eyes on the ground, or sitting in meditation, eyes closed, or doing laundry, eyes on the cloth, the soap, the basin of water.

Why, then, are the plants so carefully tended, the grounds meticulously swept? Do we do it to keep ourselves busy? For the tourists? Or just so we *know* beauty is present?

At famed Wat Mahadhatu in the south, residents are allowed to sculpt with clay. I think that I would like to paint watercolors. Sculpt and paint, write and meditate, sweep leaves and wash clothes on the edge of the jungle. Although I have spent too many hours with prostitutes, child laborers, opium army conscripts, HIV-positive transvestites to be naïve, at times like this, Thailand feels like one big spiritual arena, the natural environment and

this is the last place I would expect to end up, and yet I've done stranger things.

My freshman year I found myself in a small dormitory at the edge of campus filled with other only children and assorted oddballs. (A friend later calculated that by sophomore year ninety-percent of our original dorm members were either popping Lithium or Prozac or had been institutionalized for some period of time.) Chris, a mile away at the upperclassmen's dorms, quickly disappeared into her serious boyfriend and law school applications and the semiprofessional extracurricular activities for which Harvard students are known. And so, isolated from the freshman activities of Harvard Yard, my dorm mates and I stumbled through the college's social maze.

During mealtime, our little band of castaways trudged over to the cavernous Freshman Union and gripped our orange pentagonal trays with quiet hysteria. A few days into the semester, I noticed several long tables at one side of the union populated with black students, many of whom stopped their loud teasing and laughter to eye me as I crept by with my dorm mates. Never having spent any significant time with anyone black, I'd nervously averted my gaze and scampered to my seat, trying not to worry about the nudges, the pointing, the bald over-the-shoulder glances.

There were only six black students in my dorm, including Jim, a giant slab of a boy who cornered me in the laundry room the first week and fastened his meat-hook paws onto my breasts until I, more enraged than frightened, threatened to smash his balls with my jar of quarters. After I reported the incident, full of righteous naïveté, to the administration, Jim was instructed not to come up to the second floor or speak directly to me, a directive which he interpreted to mean he was allowed to stand in the doorway when I came home, eyes slitted with challenge. The lesson learned—that the male (athlete) body is worth more than the female—was colored by race, suggesting a painful lesson—that gender and racial allegiance will be opposed.

✆

AS I SCAN the sea of white cloth and black stubble around me, I recall the first time I found myself in a room filled with blacks. I sat cross-legged on the floor of the Freshman Union trembling at the thrilling, disconcerting beauty. Whenever one of the confident women with her straightened hair molded like shrubbery or one of the muscled, shutter-eyed upperclassmen glanced my way, I quivered, fearful that they would stop speaking their glorious, unintelligible language and point to me. "Hey, you there!" they would accuse. "What're *you* doing here?"

The room spun with directives about where in Roxbury to get something called a Press and Curl (though Chris had told me that for her, Roxbury was where kids pelted her with rocks and told her to go back to Harvard), how not to get off the T anywhere past Savin Hill (or the Irish would do more than throw rocks), how Bob the Chef's was the only place to get good "greens," what sections of Boston were worst for DWB (a condition eliciting many knowing looks and weary head shakes), where in Central Square to buy hair care products, find the AME Church, listen to jazz—all things we obviously wanted to do.

Students on all sides of me laughed freely and loudly, nodded and said *mmm-hmm* just like the women in PBS documentaries about black churches. I felt as I had upon my first trip to Thailand, watching the mouths around me contort into strange shapes that held no meaning. Periodically I glanced down at my forearm for reassurance. I looked black. No one was going to point to me. Truly, adapting to life in the Thai forest is easier. Here, no one expects me to understand. The mere fact that I am trying is my passport to acceptance. Never once does any monk or nun suggest (to my face, that is) that I'm not qualified to wear the robes, that I'm not welcome at the table. Other than my host mother, no person has ever asked me to account for my interest or presence. I am here; that is enough.

occasional ceremony intertwining to inspire and reinspire.

I am now supposed to be mindful of *all actions*, noting everything I do so that every task is a minimeditation. Maechi Roongdüan compares this form of meditation to filling a basin with a slowly dripping faucet, whereas other forms are like making a container, walking to the river, and returning with the water.

She says, "Some people bore a hole in their *guti* for the light to shine through and concentrate intensely on that light; after they have developed their powers of concentration, they seek the truth. But our meditation is for those who seek knowledge right now, those who are in pain. No one hits us, no one scolds us, but our thoughts make us unhappy."

..

Being mindful is what I find most difficult. I am used to being completely undisciplined when alone. It is difficult to watch oneself. It is hard to want something so tedious and boring. I lack humility. I lack a twenty-four-hour dedication.

Only if in teaching you experience yourself as still learning do you have what people call authority. Only if that is the case do you touch people's hearts.

—AYYA KHEMA, *I Give You My Life: The Autobiography of a Western Buddhist Nun*

I'm supposed to be mindful while bathing, so I try to remember all the stupid little movements that go into the act of scooping water from the basin and dousing myself *(lifting, reaching, dipping, lifting, pouring, feeling cold)*. I splash around, getting them mixed up and saying them too late.

The newly ordained *maechi* lights three joss sticks and touches them to her forehead. I smell Jim in the room. In my memory, I see him leaning against the windows with a wall of equally tall, beefy athletes. After the meeting, I had introduced myself to the community service coordinator, asking what sort of programs the Black Students Association ran in the black community. His eyes trained on a cluster of freshman girls next to us who were decked out, like nearly every female except me, in full makeup, tights, and short skirts with heels, he waved a clipboard with a sign-up sheet in my direction and mumbled something about bringing local kids to campus twice a year for a carnival.

"That's it?" I blurted. "Two parties?" I turned to find Jim standing next to me, grinning broadly.

"Hey, chief," he greeted the community service coordinator easily, pretending not to see me. "What it is?"

"My bro-tha," the upperclassman responded, extending his arm and slapping his palm into Jim's. "'Sup?"

They clasped hands, then enacted an elaborate series of grips and shakes and snaps, ending in a half embrace.

"I hear that ball practice is some serious shit," Jim said, shaking his head ponderously from side to side, "but, like, I'm down for the community, you know I'm saying? Where I sign up?"

"A'ight, man." The coordinator thumped his heart twice and then flashed the right fist, thumb facing forward. He nodded slowly, as if weighted down by the enormity of Jim's sacrifice. God in His heaven surely dabbed away a tear. "We sure can use some involved brothers as role models."

Gently (not that I could have interrupted them anyway), I set the clipboard on the table and crept away.

ᴐᴄ

AS THE NEW *maechi* takes refuge in the *Sangha*, the ordained community, it hits me that I've misunderstood Buddhism, thinking that it focused on the development of the individual and discouraged emotional connection to others. But in fact the goal is to love both— oneself and others—without being wounded by that love. Do I even know what that kind of love looks like?

Compounding the pain of imagining myself rejected by the black community in favor of Jim was the irony of having to assume the baggage New England yoked round our necks. Every interaction reeked of racial overtones, from navigating a segregated city with strict territorial markers and the only predominantly (and proudly) white NBA team, to conversations with nonblack students and faculty members who studied us closely for proof of either freak genius or affirmative-action-sanctioned idiocy. Raised by an idealistic white mother, I was as defenseless (and undiplomatic) as a wide-eyed child.

Just as my racial upbringing hadn't prepared me for the tough game of college identity politics, so too had my parents' sixties idealism given me the wrong impression of the student citizen. Where were the new alliances my parents had predicted? Where was that youthful desire both to learn about and to remake the world? Most of my fellow students, well read as they were, focused their efforts on becoming Manhattan investment bankers or joining prestigious "white-shoe" law firms. It was the eighties, social involvement sold to us as a résumé-builder.

I ricocheted between feelings of inferiority and superiority. At nineteen, I was a year older than the average freshman, though my minimal knowledge of the Holy Trinity (the *New Yorker*, the *New York Times*, the City itself) rendered me a child.

After the *maechi* ordination, we sit together, feeling the energy that comes of meditating silently in a group. How odd to live silently with oneself for nineteen hours a day, and yet I sink easily, gratefully, into the silence of temple life, so unlike existence in the West. Even more odd, here I can bring myself to open my eyes and stare failure in the face.

I'm wishing I were anywhere else.

In the middle of soaping my shivering body, I'm suddenly struck by the way the soap lather gleams, faint, cool, on my body in the dim bathroom interior. It's four o'clock in the afternoon, the daylight pure—clear and transparent. It creeps unevenly into the stone room, through the slatted roof, giving my wet skin a dull finish like fine wood. The lather thick and rich as cream.

I regard my palms: soap bubbles up in thousands of swirls against a porcelain background. Perfect droplets of evenly spaced water cover my right shoulder. The scene has the quiet perfection of a still life—one moment captured from thousands that somehow manages to say it all.

Life is no more than this—a series of brief recurring moments—but therein lies the beauty. In impermanence *(anicca)*. In moments of simplicity that cut through the confusion and complexity. One stumbles onto something—a painting of apples, the clarity of breath—and brings order to it all.

As ridiculous as it sounds, everything changes! My depression out the window, I'm delighted and intrigued. Suddenly it makes sense to be mindful; it is a wonder to be able to go slow and appreciate all the marvels of the shower.

I want to see everything! As soon as I slow down and think about it, notation is easy and smooth. There is joy in identifying every little action (some for which I don't even know the words in English) and satisfaction in performing them in tandem with notation.

The Ivy League, I quickly deduced, was not a place to try new things. College encouraged my crazed childhood perfectionism, so deeply bred in most of us that at the merest whiff of failure, we fell apart. In the meantime, being interested in or simply good at something was not enough; one had to excel.

How different it all seems from this world, where all I have to do in order to join the community and receive access to all its privileges is to declare my belief in the Three Refuges and my intention to undertake the rules of training. Perhaps Buddhists understand that we are better prepared to remake ourselves if we are not already convinced of our own inability for redemption.

Both worlds refuse to let me sleep, demanding nineteen hours of commitment. In addition to negotiating course syllabi that assigned several hundred pages of reading per class each week—an expectation I hadn't the foggiest idea how to meet—we perfectionists were expected to Commit (capital *C*) ourselves to a professional level of extracurricular involvement (and then, if necessary, to a swank rest home in which to recover from this Commitment). We lived the ultimate American urban existence, carrying day planners crammed with constant rotations of course lectures and section meetings, athletic workouts and aerobics classes, independent study or lab research projects, tryout duties, lunches with academic advisers, funding meetings to start new organizations we could then claim ownership of, summer internship prep sessions, grant application info sessions, therapy, teas with resident tutors, dorm social commitments, volunteer work, cocktail parties, faculty dinners, club meetings, evening lectures and readings and concerts and performances, late-night study dates. In addition, I spent ten hours a week at my work-study job, eight hours at a new homeless shelter, ten hours codirecting a volunteer program for newly arrived immigrants and refugees, and weekends volunteering with my own refugee family. We were CEOs and soccer moms in training.

§§

AND YET, learning has never been more profound for me than here, in the temple. I have always been an experiential learner, so who better to show up to teach me than the Buddha Himself, willing to be tested by me, a mere novice? *Try this for yourself and see if it fits,* He urges. College, on the other hand, resisted experiential learning, valuing instead abstract intellectualism (a.k.a. Dead White Males and the Women Who Love Them). No one who looked or thought like me was deemed worthy of study.

My anger served me well as I discovered my true calling: social service. It was perfect with its community of students of different races and socioeconomic classes, many on financial aid. Its dewy interest in the world that privileged experience over classroom theory. Its belief that we were the torchbearers of sixties radicalism and social commitment. All manifesting itself in an earnest political agenda that channeled our disappointment in Harvard into empowering (the word of the moment) the poorer communities outside its wrought-iron gates.

By the spring semester of my freshman year, I was fully enmeshed. By sophomore year, I had abandoned my courses for community commitments. My heart thudded with anxiety and relief each time I found myself veering toward the subway, away from yet another discussion section on the ethics of lying (or was it not lying?), another seminar on Southeast Asian refugees, the professor waiting in the courtyard for me to throw off the raincoat I was hiding beneath and appear (like Christ resurrected!) to analyze my current volunteer work. As soon as I missed one section of a course, it was all over. Once I lived through the first skipped class, there was nothing and no one to tell me that my luck couldn't, wouldn't, last. I didn't know the unspoken rules of success.

Imagining that I was conducting the real-life research component

I note everything: brushing my teeth, drying off, wrapping my odd undergarments around me, dressing, putting tiger balm on my mosquito bites, drinking water. I go inside. It is five o'clock, the air perfectly still, cool, new.

When it's time to "check my mood," Maechi Roongdüan calls me outside. She says she will be visiting her sick aunt tomorrow and that my new task is to note and record all the time spent mindfully or in meditation during the day. This is much worse than a simple locker check— it's the Thought Police!

"Were you able to shower mindfully?" she inquires, and I perk up, remembering the afternoon's hard-won success and feeling proud.

Her face smooth as always, she informs me that she stood outside my bathroom and listened. "Hmm," she says, "very fast."

It's like she slapped me twice. Once for each word: Very. Fast. I double over. Shuddering, I throw one leg over the other, my arms around my torso, hugging, holding on.

"You can't sit like that," she reminds me immediately. I careen dangerously close to tears. I can feel them rushing down the ducts. She asks if I need anything, and in the dark, I feel a great wave of loneliness sweep over me.

"I'm so lonely," I want to tell her. "It's so hard!" I'm supposed to give up my friends, family, freedom, conversation, my entire way of life, and become not only a yogi but also a proper Asian woman! I never said I wanted to reach *Nibbana*. Remember, I'm the one here for the sociology?

Seconds later I notice to my chagrin that I am internally noting the feeling (*lonely, lonely, lonely*).

of my coursework (though somehow I neglected to notice that by skipping classes and blowing off homework, I was missing half the equation), I fantasized about bringing it all together during reading period. My final paper/exam/project would be the perfect blend of theory and practice, my learning and actions!

As we roll up the mats and tidy the room, I watch Maechi Roongdüan direct the others. She is mother to us all and yet apart, the one who could give up this earthly life tomorrow without a second thought. She is strong and clear, which is sometimes hard to take but always easy to understand. There is comfort in that. Am I seeking the source of my lost *khwan* or simply another mother, one to replace the one I've outgrown?

Throughout my fall from grace, I knew better than to try to seek help, other than lining up for the freely dispensed antidepressants that every female student of my acquaintance was mainlining. I shuddered at the fragile girls in bicycle shorts who paused in the dining room to do shots of packets of Sweet 'n Low and took my sugar straight. We were all sick. For all the sherry being poured and finger sandwiches consumed in dark-paneled senior common rooms across campus, our interactions with the slightly tipsy Harvard administration were superficial at best. They had admitted us, after all (and given us an obscene amount of money); as for the rest—the incident with Jim had made this clear—we were on our own.

And as for family support, how could I tell my mother, on the rare occasions I could afford to go home, that what we had worked and saved toward was not worth it, it turns out, that this was not the Promised Land?

And so I staggered along, bleeding, until the spring of my sophomore year, when it became clear that I most certainly was going to fail for the first time—both my classes, which I no longer even pretended to attend, and the taut web of social service responsibilities slipping through my fingers.

Until I walked into the lodge we'd rented for the community

service weekend retreat and saw Jim slide his sleeping bag in between two girls. I whirled around to stare at the black girl in charge, who held up her hand and said, "Now, I know what you said about not stepping foot in this place if he came, but he's director of one of our programs, and frankly we need him."

Until morning came and I couldn't propel myself out of bed. On the dark path in northern Thailand headed for my *guti,* I see the moment I've been seeking: me sinking into a peaceful, wordless space, dark as the comforting embrace of a raincoat over one's head. My *khwan* gone.

Instead I say, "I'm very tired after I meditate. Is that natural?" I wonder how in the world I can come up with the six to ten hours of daily meditation she expects.

"Yes," she assures me. "Don't be too serious about it; you're just the beginner. Are your bowels okay?"

She leaves and I creep inside. After flicking on the light, I kneel, arms wrapped around myself, and quietly, mindfully, cry a clear puddle on the reed mat before me.

When I glance up, I notice something on my left cuff: a moth, less than an inch long, absolutely flat, its elongated wings pale and intricate as vintage lace.

As soon as I see it, the moth lifts straight up with long, flat strokes, as if made of paper, and disappears.

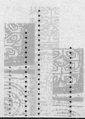

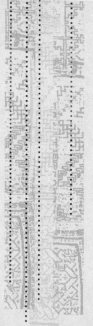

Inside the bod, the ordination hall; Ajarn Boon
to the left, the abbot to the right, before the altar
with the famous Phra Singh statue.

CHAPTER NINE

⳥⳥ The Anthropology of Myself

SATIPATTHANA VIPASSANA IS FIRMLY ROOTED IN PERSONAL EXPERI-
ENCE, PARTICULARLY SINCE THE FIRST STAGE OF THE PRACTICE IS
THE DETECTION OF THE MATERIAL AND MENTAL PROCESSES THAT
COMPRISE AN INDIVIDUAL'S CONDITIONED PERSONALITY.

—*Nyanaponika Thera,*
THE HEART OF BUDDHIST MEDITATION

SOMEHOW, WITHOUT FULLY considering how different my life has become, focusing instead on surviving each hour in the *wat*, each green minute, I make it through the first weeks. When I pause to note this in my journal, the site of so many conversations that have simply moved inward, I realize I have become something of my own subject. *I've become obsessed with documenting everything!* I marvel, the soft, pulpy pages filling with sketches of the *wat* layout and gardens, diagrams of my *guti* floor plan and proper monastic dress. When Maechi Roongdüan brings me two robes from the storehouse, explaining that the tunics my host mother had made with the sleeve seams on the shoulders don't meet Thamtong regulations, I make painstaking drawings of the correct tunic, the sleeve seams midway down the arm.

Part of my journal writing must certainly come from the traveler's desire to capture the exotic details of place, but is it the traveler, immersed, or the anthropologist, detached, who so carefully records these dimensions, smells, and sounds? Or is it someone else entirely—a new role—perhaps the novice seeker?

..
Imagine, I'm still on toilet paper roll number one! For some reason, there are always black lines in the little squat toilet. Hope they're not dead gnats!

Anytime we're outside our *guti*, we're required to wear a long over-robe that wraps around the fitted white jacket and sarong twice, under the right shoulder and over the left. For those of us who are left-handed (i.e., me!), it's a bit of a problem, as the over-robe doesn't allow the left arm to rise above waist level. This makes tasks just a wee bit difficult.

Add to this, the robe is hot and cumbersome. At times, however, I find it soothing to be swathed in so much rough cotton. It makes me feel more like a monk.

Every day I tie my over-robe differently and every day it's wrong. The others must think I'm seriously slow. I start tying it at 8:15. By 8:30 I'm sure it has to be right, but five minutes out of my *guti*, I realize I'm having serious BT (breast trouble), as Scott would call it. Feeling great empathy for hapless nun Maria in

The week before my ordination, Chong and I had spent a Girls' Day Out exploring Chiang Mai City's shiny, pre-tourist affluence. She showed me the latest club kids' hangout—an old-fashioned soda fountain with a stationer/bookstore in back. Over chilled bowls of chocolate ice cream (her favorite) served with tiny silver scoops, she declared, "This place is my *nouveau* favorite." We'd designed a fast, pun-filled blend of Thai, English, and French for ourselves. Her dark eyes sparkled. "*Parfait* after ice cream!"

And truly, the airy room, its pastel wares arranged with as much loving care as a display of intricately carved melon and pineapple at a Thai banquet, shimmered with sugary, Japanese-girl cuteness. Schoolbags of pink and powder blue sported popular Animé characters with spiky blonde hair and huge round eyes. Cartoon book series of Doramon, the magical robot cat (my favorite), fanned out in a kaleidoscope of red and blue. Plastic folders displayed packs of delicate stationery with Asia's ubiquitous "Engrish" phrases—star-crowned angels entreating would-be correspondents, *Please to love my bear hugs party!* bunnies in blue jeans wishing (promising? threatening?), *Good happy everything for my belove* [sic] *kitty; BYOB!*

By then fully in touch with my Japanese inner child, I abandoned the puzzling prospect of inviting my cat to a keg party and headed instead for the latest installment of *Doramon*, bubble-headed cat robot. Doramon had just thrust a round white fist into a magical pouch (in his stomach!) to retrieve something to cheer up his schoolboy pal who was moping at the realization that dinosaurs had never roamed Japan (did that explain the country's Godzilla obsession?) when Chong tugged on my arm.

"Fate, don't you need *un journal* for the *wat?*" she asked, her quick-to-laugh mouth forming a half-open flower of inquiry. "To record your experience?"

"Mmm, good point," I murmured, willing to bet this new development meant time travel for Doramon and Boy Sidekick! As Chong presented an array of sparkly notebooks for my approval, I flipped through the comic, scanning as quickly as my Thai reading ability would allow. I could just see Doramon bobbling along with his oversized head, shielded by cycads and a giant horsetail from tyrannosaurus, the *tyrant lizard*. What Mesozoic mishaps were they bound to encounter?

Chong whacked me playfully on the arm with a notebook. *"Maechi patipat mai dai,"* she teased, *"chop aan* cartoon!" *The nun can't practice; she's busy reading cartoons!*

I grinned and grabbed her weapon. "Oh ho, *c'est* the one!" Unlike the fancy notebooks she'd chosen for me, this one was a standard student notebook with the traditional cloth and cardboard binding. The intricate cover design looked ready to support Buddhist endeavors, pale pink lotus on a green background crisscrossed by darker pink flames like those found on religious scrolls. A wheel of truth glowed inside a sunburst atop the cover. *Parfait!*

"Khop khun maak kha," I'd said, giving flowery thanks in a honeyed feminine voice and making an exaggerated curtsy that threw Chong and the pimply store clerk into paroxysms of giggles they—being proper Thai girls—quickly held up delicate hands to cover.

&c:

MY FIRST FEW DAYS here in the *wat,* I copy out translations of prayers in three languages—Pali transcription, English, Thai. Now, both the sacred and the profane grace the pages. I even call upon my meager math skills to construct graphs and charts of the time spent mindfully or in meditation.

And finally it registers. Not only am I collecting data for an anthropological thesis to be delivered in some future dream sequence (hazy save for the applause echoing through Harvard's marble halls), but I approach life the same way, through detachment and observation, experience reduced to bite-sized intellectual morsels to aid their digestion. Denied an external anthropological subject by Maechi Roongdüan, I've created one for myself *out of*

The Sound of Music, I try to struggle unobtrusively (yet mindfully!) with my breast-wrap as we walk. I feel like the anti-*maechi.*

Week 2
..

Levels 1, 2, 3 Walking for twenty-minute stints each
Level 3 Sitting for fifty-to-sixty-minute stints
Level 3 Eating

Walking Meditation 3
Standing
Wanting to walk
Lifting right/left root
Swinging right/left
Stepping left/right
Wanting to stop

Sitting Meditation 3
In
Out
Sitting
Points (on body)

Eating 3
Seeing food
Taking spoonful
Lifting spoon
Opening mouth
Putting in spoon
Closing mouth
Pulling out spoon
Chewing
Registering taste
Registering response
Smelling
Putting down spoon

Points of Body
(contemplated as second-
ary object in meditation)

1–2 Buttocks:
     right, left
3–4 Inner knees:
     right, left
5–6 Outer ankles:
     right, left
7–8 Tops of feet:
     right, left
9–10 Outer knees:
     right, left
11–12 Thighs: right,
     left
13–14 Hips: right,
     left
15–17 Right waist—
     Heart—Left
     shoulder
18–20 Left waist—
     Heart—Right
     shoulder

··

Today I manage to
spend eight and a half
hours mindfully and
to sit in one medita-
tion session for sev-
enty minutes straight.

I sit in the cave for
twenty-five minutes.
Hot, incredible wind.
I finally see the "eye"
they speak of in medi-
tation texts. At least, I
suppose it's the same
eye. It is certainly
odd-looking.

myself! And hasn't she pointed the way, with her declaration that I am here to prove the truth of the Dhamma for myself? With the story of her own ordination being an experiment against Buddhism?

Somehow I've managed to compartmentalize my mind into both participant and observer, turning one unblinking eye on this bumbling, determined foreign *maechi*. Anthropologist and detective, I search daily for "the material and mental processes" the Buddhists claim make up the individual. In the absence of a science of the Other, I've become enamored of the anthropology of myself.

And so, in preparation for the inevitable encounter, I burn through Buddhist texts in Thai and English at a rate of a hundred pages a night. Every evening I crawl beneath my gauzy mosquito netting, wedge the lavender blanket under my aching legs, and hunch over my kerosene lantern. Some books Maechi Roongdüan finds for me, ending our nightly teaching with a flourish as she produces yet another book with the pale orange paper cover of Buddhist publications from the folds of her robes, a magician unleashing a string of monochromatic scarves. Others I brought with me, figuring boredom would force me finally to study them.

My research until now has focused on the sociological relationship between Theravada Buddhism and gender. Strange as it may sound, I've read very little about the Buddhist tenets themselves and even less on meditation.

I'm thinking about language, I muse in my pink-and-green journal, one in a series of statements that will later read as economical and cryptic as one of Maechi Roongdüan's lessons. In the absence of sanctioned speech, I'm developing an intense, internal multilingualism, a vocabulary of spirituality for which each component of the practice requires its own dialect.

I chant and pray in Pali. For days I listen hard to the chants during mealtime, memorizing the syllables to scribble later in my notebook. Maechi Roongdüan brings me a slim volume of Pali verses translated into English, and by comparing my notes to phonetic renderings of Pali, I'm able to figure out the meanings of the chants. The Pali syllables copied onto the sliver of paper folded into my palm (my chant cheat sheet!) are, however, written in Thai. I transcribe the English transliterations of Pali chants into Thai sounds, as its tonal structure helps to approximate correct chanting tones.

Bowing, I address my fellow *wat* dwellers (the few times allowed) in *pasat phra* (Buddha's or monk's language), a formal version of Thai with fancy verbs such as *rapathan ahaan,* to partake of food (also used when speaking to royalty), and pronouns and classifiers that support the theory that monks embody the Buddha.*

I take my daily instruction next to the stream in English, the language I also use for journal writing and daydreaming.

Finally I meditate and note in standard Thai. One reason is that Maechi Roongdüan teaches me the prompts, such as *breathe in, breathe out, mind wandering,* in Thai. Two, the monosyllabism of Thai verbs makes it easier to note in time to the breath. Three, Thai's lack of pronouns helps to focus on the action rather than the agent, which feels more in keeping with the goals of Buddhist practice. "Mind wandering" (uh-oh—man down!) during meditation seems a much more forgivable transgression than "my (pathetically undisciplined and constantly self-aware) mind is (can you believe it?) wandering."

And yet, for all my quadralingualism, my vocabulary hungers. It's difficult enough to articulate familiar spiritual concepts in English, never mind trying to discuss (even with oneself) an unfamiliar religion in a series of new tongues! Another problem is the particularity of notation. Every action must be broken into its smallest components and noted, requiring a specialized vocabulary. Every evening I pore through the Thai-English dictionary, the Thai-Pali dictionary, and the Pali-English dictionary. My journal swells with

I sketch it in my journal: a round navy-colored pupil and a green iris that keeps changing shape. First the iris is completely round, then pinched at the sides, then flattened, then droopy with an eyebrow, then rectangular.

I write the words "No escape" next to the last sketch. Later I don't know why. Finally it is just an outline of white lines that draw closer and closer until they swallow me.

I have seventy-minute episodes each of seated and walking meditation.

Sitting 4 points for forty-to-sixty-minute stints Increase mindful hours and number of seated meditation stints

---

* For example, when referring to monks, the classifier used is *ong,* the same one used for Buddha statues, instead of *khon,* the classifier used for people.

lists of vocabulary words, ranging from the sacred—*piti* (rapture), *nimitta* (images seen in meditation)—to the mundane—itch, shake, rinse, turn over.

ᛞᚲ

AND AS MY vocabulary and fieldwork notes grow, so does my determination to become a subject worthy of my own study. How to identify the catalyst for my growing obsession with practice? Part is certainly a Western drive to succeed, a subconscious plan to achieve through practice—the only avenue of achievement open to me. Part grows undeniably from the power of what I'm experiencing during meditation: odd visions and sensations I keep to myself, recording them somewhat guiltily in my journal as if evidence of an unbalanced mind. And part is no doubt the ever dutiful student in me responding to any teacher's instruction.

During the second week, Maechi Roongdüan tells me to increase the number of times I sit in meditation each day. We're sitting on the circular stone bench beneath my shade tree, the giant finger of dusk pressing itself into the narrow gully behind us as if into a seam. The sunset air stains everything rosy, including the two of us, and for the first time all day, bugs stop gnawing at me.

"Pardon?"

Maechi Roongdüan smiles at my weak protest, her silent eyes saying, *You think yesterday's task was impossible? Try this one!* She is careful to parcel out challenges in manageable swallows. Even if she weren't my sole source of social interaction, I might follow. She is a natural leader, a no-nonsense preacher with a glittering, critical mind and a poet's furled tongue. What I hope to become. In the meantime, she has decided to ratchet up the experiment.

She nods, fluttering her eyelashes in imitation of me. "Yes, you heard me—increase the number of sittings."

I laugh. "It's like the Elvis song—*all I want is all you've got.*"

Now it's her turn. "Pardon?"

The person who meditates becomes physiologically different from the person who does not. Brain rhythms, heart-beat, blood-pressure, skin resistance—all are changed by meditation. . . . [T]hat is why people who meditate have instinctively taken on a different diet, different clothes, different sleeping habits and a different life-style. They have discovered that certain occupations are incompatible with the meditational thrust that fills their life [*sic*].

—WILLIAM JOHNSTON, *Silent Music: The Science of Meditation*

I've drastically changed my life! I now spend fifteen hours a day in mindfulness. No more than four and a half hours of sleep at night. Two to three naps, which violates *wat* rules, but not more than six hours total prostrate in a twenty-four-hour cycle.

Today we attack *dukkha,* the first of the Four Noble Truths. The inherent dissatisfactory nature of life is the basic premise of Buddhist belief. "Meditation sets up situations where we can see—through our bodies—that life is *dukkha,*" she explains, placing the splayed fingers of her right hand on her breastbone. "This is why you should be meditating more frequently in each twenty-four-hour cycle." More tests for the lab!

And though I'm not convinced I have what it takes to comply with her request, I agree. I'm beginning to see that meditation's focus on the self, which may appear narcissistic or egocentric at first glance, is in fact the exact opposite. It is through the medium of ourselves that we realize the truth about everyone and everything else, all human reactions and worldly occurrences.

During meditation, I witness my body functioning like a miniature cosmos. The *dukkha* arises as pain in my back; the *anicca,* or impermanence of all things, presents itself as the pain fades. So too the cycle of life. Whatever knowledge and experience I acquire relates itself to the crises of humankind, the very flux of the universe.

Before, like many Westerners, I thought that Buddhism encouraged us to ignore worldly problems. I imagined the goal of meditation was to blank our emotions or refuse to acknowledge them, perhaps depositing them in the subconscious to fester. Now I see I was wrong. Buddhism tells us we must deal with the pains of the world in order to conquer them, a lesson I long embraced in political work. I've known since childhood that ignoring the bad only prolongs its reign. And now spirituality, my would-be escape from both society's and my own ills, teaches the same lesson. (Oh, how I should have known!)

As our rosy faces darken and still with the coming of tropical night, Maechi Roongdüan extracts an orange pamphlet from her sleeve entitled *The Foundations of Mindfulness* and talks about the importance of notation. "Awareness serves as a dam to desire," she

In seated meditation I see points of light, another phenomenon mentioned in the ancient texts. It's a relief to find out these are normal occurrences and not evidence of a flipped-out mind.

I've decided to change the shape of my face through massage. I want a smooth, peaceful brow, deeper cheekbones, a sharper chin. I have five mosquito bites on my right eyelid, two on the left.

Today I spend fifteen and a half hours mindfully.

The moment the word "meditation" is mentioned, one thinks of an escape from the daily activities of life; assuming a particular posture, like a statue in some cave or cell in a monastery, in a remote place cut off from society; and musing on, or being absorbed in, some kind of mystic or mysterious thought or trance. True Buddhist "meditation" does not mean this kind of escape at all.

—WALPOLA RAHULA, *What the Buddha Taught*

explains. "By acknowledging our desires, we allow them to build and then fade. Saying, 'I don't want to think about that—it's not good,' allows it to fester. We then act explosively, without awareness—or control."

She begins to gather her robes, one hand twisting from inside, and elaborates. "For example, if a *maechi* develops the desire to go to the movies, she must note, *wanting to go to the movies*. Then she will know herself, her desire and the futility of it. The desire will increase, then eventually pass away." Her eyes twinkle, as if reading my entire history. "Notation gives us the time to establish volitional intention *before* action."

As she stands to leave, the sun drops behind her shoulder. Perhaps sensing my nightly panic as each time I'm left alone, my only human interaction concluded for yet another twenty-four-hour cycle, she smiles gently and tells me that I should be bored or I'm not doing it right (in that case, I must be doing one hell of a job). She departs, moving in that deliberate yet vigorous way of hers, leaving me alone beneath the tree.

In the dark I place my hand on the cement bench, feeling for her warm imprint.

Increase number of sitting sessions to 4-plus
Level 2 Sleeping

Sleeping 2
In
Out
Lying
5 points touching the mat:

    Head
    Shoulder
    Buttocks
    Knee
    Heel

The smell on the way to the meal this morning: jasmine blossoms and earth. Strong, like after a pelting, soaking rain.

*P*ossibly my great faith contributed to slackness in my practice. I was fascinated with everything. My notebook was stuffed with observations that I knew the monks would disapprove of. "Toothpaste tube still hot at nine P.M." "Burmese girls grow their toenails long and paint them."

—KATE WHEELER,
"Ringworm"

For the first time I'm not pretending to work slowly, pretending to be proper, but actually enjoying it, being it.

For all this, I'm still a Western individual. I want to nap and eat pizza. I tell myself, if I'm going to do this for a long time, I want to be the Most Impressive Yogi Ever! Ah, my motives.

Being registered at Wat Thamtong, the temple of residence.
Maechi Roongdüan (in full over≈tunic) on left, flanked by
Maechi Oey; Ajarn Boon and Faith on right.

CHAPTER TEN

∞ *Fieldwork*

MEDITATION IS NOT SOMETHING TO BE TOYED WITH.... IT SHOULD
ALWAYS BE APPROACHED ... WITH THE GUIDANCE OF AN EXPERIENCED
AND QUALIFIED TEACHER.

—*John Snelling,*
THE BUDDHIST HANDBOOK

"IN THE FOREST," SAID THE AJAHN, "YOU DO NOT LEARN FROM BOOKS
AND SCRIPTURES. YOU LEARN FROM NATURE AND FROM THE
NECESSITIES OF LIFE. THE FOREST IS NOT ONLY THE TEMPLE, IT IS
ALSO THE TEACHER."

—*Charles Nicholl,*
BORDERLINES: A JOURNEY IN THAILAND AND BURMA

WE GATHER IN the caves, a flock of white doves with black-stubbled heads, arranging our robes around us like wings, settling in for the monthly *wat* meeting. The other *maechi* and I work studiously not to stare at each other. I can feel their nearness in the stale cave air, smell their breathing fresh and energetic as a breeze. Maechi Roongdüan, flanked by the kindly-faced, wizened Mae Oey, she of the betel teeth, and Maechi Vilawam, grinning as always, cheeks scrubbed within an inch of her life, reviews *maechi* rules and regulations. There are many, ranging from the directive that conversations with men beyond six words must be conducted with mental awareness, before seven o'clock in the evening (the witching hour?), and in the presence of at

Personal goal: Be mindful nineteen hours a day

*M*editation . . . produces changes in the electrical activity of the brain, bringing the conscious and unconscious mind into closer proximity. The conscious mind . . . is thus opened to receive messages and enlightenment from the . . . subliminal depths of one's being in a process that is analogous to . . . dreaming.

—WILLIAM JOHNSTON,
Silent Music: The Science of Meditation

..

I'm sitting with my legs folded in full lotus, so I decide to try meditating that way. In no time at all, my breathing falls away and I'm floating in the darkness, somewhat at a loss. Fifteen minutes later (or so it seems), I have to unfold my legs, though I don't experience any pain at all. I feel completely calm and refreshed. Thin lines of light like television static appear, then the eye develops, becomes the point of light, and disappears.

least one other *maechi,* to the prohibition against standing with one's hip protruding (too kittenish, I imagine).

With her myriad administrative duties, vigorous walk, and voracious appetite for meditation, Maechi Roongdüan, who governs all *maechi* and reports to the abbot, bridges the distance between the two *maechi* groups, workers and meditators. *"Khob khun kha,"* she thanks the kitchen-duty *maechi,* who bow their heads modestly, nesting. For three months at a time, they live in dorms near the entrance, handling reception and cooking for the entire *wat* with food they grow, receive from laypeople, or purchase with donations. As Thamtong is a "supporting *wat,*" providing food and other necessities for all, the other *maechi* can take the tenth vow and spend their time meditating in the interior.

Ask about the mechanics of Thamtong, I remind myself. The *wat* seems to be uniquely free from financial and other concerns. I'm not responsible for anything save my own slow crawl out of ignorance.

As I kneel on my straining knees for what feels like the bulk of my childbearing years, I think that I will surely die. No one else seems discomfited. I try to relax into the sea around me—the blur of gold and ivory faces, bronze and almond hands, teak and sandalwood brows and scalps. Then we chant for forty-five minutes (now I must already be dead and consigned to hell—my born-again childhood friends proved right, after all!). Finally Maechi Roongdüan gives what sounds to my spiritually deficient Thai to be a meditation pep talk. My mind gets up and strides out the cave mouth, joining a huddle of *maechi,* arms around each other's shoulders, robes looped up through their legs.

One rule stipulates that the "elderly" can't ordain. My mind walks back in and joins me on the straw mat. *Is that a transparent, reactionary attempt to destroy the stereotype of* wat *as functioning as retirement homes for childless old women?* it inquires politely, as if butter wouldn't melt in its mouth. *Hush,* I reply. *I'm trying to learn something here!*

At the front of the cave, Maechi Roongdüan declares, "I will not let women over the age of fifty ordain." My mind flashes me a triumphant look. Frowning, I ignore it. Surely she can't be serious! Respect for elders runs deep in Thai society; besides, if one is to champion the cause of women, who more deserving than the middle-aged and elderly? Furthermore, though some of the youngest *maechi* I've ever seen are here at Thamtong, there are plenty clearly over fifty.

"They are visitors," Maechi Roongdüan clarifies when my mind wins out, forcing me to question her during the assembly line for monthly head and eyebrow shaving. The blade flashes in her soft hand as she grasps Pranee's scalp with her thumb and middle finger. "Elderly *maechi* already ordained elsewhere are as welcome as anyone else to come practice." She sees my face and rests the blade against the young girl's ear. "*Maechi* must work hard."

"And they do," I protest. "The elderly ones are in much better shape than I, so why is age a factor?"

Seemingly distracted from the issue, or perhaps seeing the opportunity for a good lesson, she says, "At first this seems like a harder life than lay life, but later it seems easier. When you work here in the *wat*, you reap only benefits, not sorrow."

And having learned, like any good anthropologist, to keep one's mouth shut and one's pen ready, my mind relinquishes the elderly. As for me, I'm in Good Traveler Mode, so caught up in thinking I want to live like a permanent resident that I'm able to swallow strange local customs in a single gulp! The thought simultaneously intrigues and scares me—to work harder than ordinary people, reaping only benefit. It's the very strategy that propelled me out of my hometown and into Harvard, and again out of America and into native society. Now it thrusts me into the study of myself as I accept Maechi Roongdüan's challenge to accelerate my daily practice.

We hold a meeting that evening, my mind and I. First I resolve to live by the letter of the law, as do the permanent residents. I kneel on

Some researchers have claimed that the beneficial effects stem from the lotus posture. They refer to the straight back, the balanced position, the slightly touching fingers and slow breathing as conducive to the deepest human relaxation. Furthermore they claim that next to the lying down position, the lotus is the posture in which the least energy is expended.

—WILLIAM JOHNSTON,
Silent Music: The Science of Meditation

As a result of insight, a brilliant light will appear to the meditator. There arises also in him rapture, causing "goose flesh," falling of tears, tremor in the limbs. It produces in him a subtle thrill and exhilaration. He feels as if on a swing. He even wonders whether he is just giddy. Then, there arises tranquility of mind and along with it appears mental agility. . . . Both body and mind are agile in functioning swiftly, they are pliant in being able to attend to any object desired. . . . One is free from stiffness, heat or pain.

—MAHASI SAYADAW,
*The Satipatthana
Vipassana Meditation*

I finally sit right, feel lighter. A wild meditation. I'm breathing deep, ragged breaths, my chest light, and rather than picturing my abdomen in my mind, I try to move my consciousness *inside* the abdomen. At last I do. I think

the wooden floor and pack up my jars of instant coffee and sugar to donate to the *wat*. Though such intoxicants are technically allowed to help us stay awake in the post-meal hours, I will instead increase my water intake and avoid sleeping more than six hours per night.

Together my mind and I discover that mindfulness increases when I alternate active chores with seated meditation. It also helps to shower and drink water before sitting. By the second week I manage to sit in meditation five or six times a day and sleep less than five hours a night. *The change continues!* I declare in my journal. *Today I feel like a real* maechi.

Finally I understand why the others appear to move so slowly, as if the green air were molasses dragging against their white-clad limbs. It is the constant mindfulness, and only by inhabiting the same awareness can one replicate their movements. We discover that I have to be mindful at all times; this life requires constant vigilance. When I sit and lose myself in a book, I am a mass of itches and unconscious acts—crossing and uncrossing legs, flipping pages, rubbing spots before I even realize I itch. My entire behavior counteracts what we're trying to achieve. But when I walk in meditation or engage in any other mindful activity, pain isn't important; I want to go slow; I want to be mindful always.

Prior to my ordination, life teemed with reasons not to pursue anything difficult: I was tired, my stomach hurt, work was a chore. Now I see what people mean about Buddhism being in the practice, in the doing. It's a bit like being a writer, though one can make an argument for writing while not writing (a Zen-like statement if ever there was one!). Figuratively, to be Buddhist, one has to be moving as a Buddhist. If one lies down on the job, one is not being Buddhist, regardless of faith.

தை

BUT IT IS my four-year-old goddaughter Annie who will teach me my name.

"Auntie Faith!" she shouts, closing her eyes, throwing open her arms, and lobbing herself off tabletops, chairs, the back of the living room sofa.

I scream and lunge forward to catch her before she hits the floor. Her body tumbles into my arms, warm and sweet, purring with laughter. She scrambles out of my arms, eager to begin anew.

Though I've only been in town a day and it's been a year since she last saw me, she does this over and over, anytime I'm in the room. The second I step foot through the doorway, I hear the call—*Faith!*—and feel the rush of wind as she leaps.

"Annie, sweetie," I beg, "please don't do that. What if I can't reach you in time? You'll hurt yourself."

But she is giddy with laughter and doesn't hear. Besides, she can look in my wet eyes and see that I don't really want her to stop this odd enactment of the pact between us. It began four years ago, with her arrival—a full month early—in a shower of blood, endangering both her mother and herself. "Because you were in town waiting to see her," her mother, my best friend from high school, swore, weak but amused. Given her determination to meet me, catching her is the least I can do.

I watch her perched atop the arcing back of the sofa, the quintessential blonde angel, her mother's Mexican blood hidden deep within. Her sapphire eyes are confidently shut, translucent lids blued with delicate veins, arms outstretched. This is what love looks like.

And I think for a moment that no one has ever loved me like this before. With such fierce trust, complete faith!

�

DURING SEATED meditation my mind finally sees the truth of something Maechi Roongdüan had told me: Buddhism (or any religion, I would hope) cannot tell us what to do. As she put it, notation, however, gives us the time to let our acquired personal wisdom

"down," and my consciousness goes dark. There is no picture of my body in my mind.

All of a sudden, my body jumps, jerks, like my heart will burst, and I almost choke on my breath. Then I can't feel my breathing at all. I have the sensation that I'm floating and not breathing at all, which scares me. Will I forget to breathe and suffocate?

A fuzzy pinkish redness appears, blossoming out, peaceful and soft. The pinpoint of light I saw in meditation all yesterday flashes for a second. My body starts to shake as if it would fall over. I note this, and the arrival of a blue haze. My legs, which have fallen asleep, start jerking, and I come out.

Today I sit in meditation on six different occasions, though I'm a little depressed about a new development. After five minutes, the breaths disappear, and I have ten minutes of peaceful, floating nothingness, which inevitably gives way, leaving me sitting on earth. I blink, wondering, *Now what?*

Sitting 8 points
··
Levels 2 and 3 Walking for forty-five-to-sixty-minute stints each

The Middle Path
(Noble Eightfold Path)

A. FIRST VIRTUE:
Wisdom
1. Right Understanding—Understand the Four Noble Truths
2. Right Thought—Thoughts of selfless renunciation, love, nonviolence to all

B. SECOND VIRTUE:
Morality/Ethical Conduct
3. Right Speech—Abstain from lies, slander, verbal abuse, gossip

show us. As our emotions register on our consciousness, we are able to make choices about our reactions; Buddhist practice thereby leads gently, gently, to better conduct.

I feel myself smiling, my heart light. It is this primacy accorded my own knowledge that allows me to venture into this foreign territory without fear.

The Middle Path, I scrawl in my journal after a meditation session, this shorthand reference sending me to my texts to study the Noble Eightfold Path. According to the Dhamma, the path to salvation is made up of eight actions, loosely divided into three virtues, which should be developed simultaneously through physical and mental discipline. Because this path avoids the extremes—the search for happiness through sensual pleasures and the search for happiness through self-mortification—it is known as the Middle Path.

I study the virtues. The first is wisdom. By developing it, the other two (moral conduct and mental discipline) will follow. The more I read, the more I realize that I have no personal knowledge after all. My mind chuckles. What I imagined to be my own interpretation of Maechi Roongdüan's teaching—that notation accords space for wisdom—is in fact a basic Buddhist strategy. *Improved concentration allows the individual to analyze mental and physical phenomena in terms of the three characteristics of existence,* one teacher puts it. Buddhism has already anticipated my conclusion, years before I make it.

Practice is so different from reading theory! I marvel to my journal. My mind snorts. *Hey,* I protest, *I'm young, after all, still new to academic discourse and theoretical analysis.* As I begin to study the basic beliefs of the religion of my ordination, I see that reading or discussing even the most basic concepts, like *dukkha,* in spoken language is like trying to understand poetry poorly translated from a non-Romance language. Words can't begin to capture the true essence. Meaning only becomes clear in meditation.

And yet, for all the limitations of written translation, the meditation manuals Maechi Roongdüan pulls from her sleeves, a mother hen producing an egg still warm to the touch, are incredibly savvy, predicting the personal experience of the meditator with terrifying accuracy. I learn that the accepted technique for teaching *Satipatthana Vipassana* (Insight Meditation) for the past hundred years or so is immersion. No preparation or theory beforehand, just the guidance of a teacher with a light touch. (So my rash, seemingly foolish decision to ordain without prior preparation was actually the best preparation of all.) My mind smirks.

I see that I am on a carefully determined, time-honored path. More amazing, I encounter my thoughts in the pages of foreign texts, recognize myself in the examples of novice meditators from ancient India. *The moment the word "meditation" is mentioned, one thinks of an escape. . . . Distractions should simply be noted until they diminish, which will occur if awareness is conducted without "nursing" these feelings. . . . There arises in [the meditator] rapture, causing "goose flesh," falling of tears, tremor in the limbs. . . . People who meditate have instinctively taken on a different diet, different clothes, different sleeping habits. . . .* All are me—a twentieth-century Western biracial individual. I am the subject, and my experiences and responses, far from being unique, are standard, in fact centuries old.

The light-handed teacher in this instance, Maechi Roongdüan, confirms the experiment. One evening she tells me that following Buddha is like stalking the legendary giant elephant with only partial information. She points to the swept dirt beneath our dusty toes: "Those who study its footprints are the learned who have faith." Her finger points to the pristine cement walkway: "Those who study the width of its path are like those who follow precepts." Now we are looking up at the glossy trees shading us: "Those who study the height of the broken branches in its wake are like those who meditate."

We stand up and stroll past the water cistern and back dormitory to the dark forest entrance. The cement walk gives way to a

4. Right Action—Abstain from destroying life, stealing, sexual misconduct
5. Right Livelihood—Abstain from selling arms, alcohol, poison; cheating; killing animals

C. THIRD VIRTUE: *Mental Discipline*
6. Right Effort—Prevent/stop evil states of mind; cultivate wholesome states
7. Right Mindfulness—Cultivate awareness of body, feelings, mind, things
8. Right Concentration—Develop high levels of concentration

··

Bored. I want to go home.

*I*n the first stages, the teacher provides basic instruction without theoretical explanation, and yogic exercises are performed without goals beyond the training itself. Improved concentration and awareness . . . allow the individual to analyze mental and physical phenomena in terms of the three characteristics of existence, that is, *dukkha*, impermanence (*anicca*), and egolessness (*anatta*).

—NYANAPONIKA
THERA,

The Heart of Buddhist Meditation

*W*e cannot achieve [understanding of the Four Noble Truths] by means of our five senses and our usual way of thinking. For this, another level of consciousness is necessary, which we can attain in the meditative absorptions—in concentration without thought.

—AYYA KHEMA,

I Give You My Life: The Autobiography of a Western Buddhist Nun

bumpy dirt path worn over sharp rocks and exposed tree roots. We peer inside the forest: "Those who study the havoc its sharp tusks have wrought have achieved wisdom," Maechi Roongdüan says. "The beast itself is the Buddha: Those who know the Dhamma will know him."

She leaves me among the twisting vines. I wonder, who is it I have been preparing to meet on the path and will I know him or her? Against a background of chirping lizards and frogs, I study a tiny green placard nailed to a smooth tree trunk. It's calligraphed in white with Buddhist verse I can't for the life of me understand. And then my goal becomes obvious, so clear it's nearly cliché: Faith, in all senses of the word! The anthropologist in me stalks along, observing the marks I leave as I tear through the underbrush. The traveler in me pants and steams, hard at work in the jungle. And the seeker in me closes her eyes, stretches out her arms, and lifts her foot to take the next step on the path she cannot see. She is true faith!

	NEW PERSONAL SCHEDULE
3:30 a.m.	Wake up mindfully—Start active!
	Clean (*guti*, bathroom, dishes)
	Exercise
	Sitting Meditation 1, Walking Meditation 1
	Rest thirty minutes
7:00 a.m.	Sunrise—Sweep grounds
8:30–10:00 a.m.	Mealtime
	Sitting Meditation 2, Walking Meditation 2 and 3
10:30 a.m.	Rest thirty minutes
	Shower; Coffee; Sitting Meditation 3
1:00 p.m.	Meditation (Sitting Meditation 4, Walking Meditation 4)
3:00 p.m.	Chores
	Wash clothes; write in journal; read Buddhist texts
4:00 p.m.	Prime meditation time—Go to cave or be outside!
	Sitting Meditation 5 (longest), Walking Meditation 5 (longest)
6:30 p.m.	Sundown
	Daily instruction with Maechi Roongdüan
7:00 p.m.	Rest thirty minutes
	Shower
	Clean bathroom
	Exercise/massage
	Sitting Meditation 6
11:00 p.m.	Go to sleep mindfully

Walking Meditation 4
Standing
Wanting to walk
Lifting right/left heel
Lifting right/left foot
Swinging right/left
Stepping left/right
Wanting to stop

*B*uddhist meditation does not aim at control but at liberation. It is a process in which the development of awareness and insight are central. Trance states and supernatural powers . . . are incidental to its goal.

—DONALD SWEARER, *Buddhism in Transition*

My face is covered with a soft goose down. It frames my face like guard hairs. The skin seems to be getting tight on the bones, but I'm not sure if that's because of massaging it or if the skin is just getting drier. What am I becoming?

In my study of myself, I cannot fail to notice that the day I slept the most was my worst in terms of practice.

RECORD OF MINDFULNESS

	Day 10	Day 11	Day 12	Day 13	Day 14	Day 15
Number of Episodes Walking	2	2	1	2	3	5
Longest Episode	90 min.	75 min.	25 min.	100 min.	120 min.	120 min.
Quality of Episode	—	—	Poor	Good	Great	Fair
Number of Episodes Sitting	5	5	5	8	6	7
Longest Episode	115 min.	130 min.	115 min.	100 min.	136 min.	170 min.
Quality of Episode	—	Good	Good	Poor	Good	Fair
Total Time Sitting	3 hours 25 min.	3 hours 25 min.	2 hours 20 min.	3 hours 35 min.	4 hours 15 min.	4 hours 50 min.
Total Time Mindful	14 hours 40 min.	14 hours 20 min.	12 hours 20 min.	13 hours 50 min.	10 hours 20 min.	12 hours 35 min.
Quality	Good	Good	Poor	Poor	Okay-Good	Okay
Sleep Schedule	11:00– 3:30	12 :00– 4:40	11:30– 5:00	11:00– 3:00	12:30– 5:00	10:45– 3:30
Total Hours	4 hours 30 min.	4 hours 40 min.	5 hours 30 min.	4 hours	4 hours 30 min.	4 hours 45 min.

Case in point: on Day 12, I slept more than five hours. I only walked once the entire day (poorly), and that was for a meager twenty-five minutes. My total sitting time for the entire day was a mere two hours twenty minutes. Compare that to Day 15, where I slept less than five hours. That day I walked five separate times, the longest episode lasting two full hours, and sat on seven occasions, with the longest stint nearly three hours! Even a math idiot like me can figure it out: my mindfulness plan is working!

I've decided to stop writing every day in my journal. So much is happening that I don't have time to write it all down, even if I had the vocabulary to describe it, even if it could be captured on the page. Besides, one day blurs into the next.

Immediately after ordination, on the steps of the bod of Wat
Phra Singh. Note the näga *sculpture on the steps. In temple
architecture,* nägas run down the edge of the roof, or flank
the staircase that ascends to the vihara (sermon hall) or bod
(ordination hall).

CHAPTER ELEVEN

⟐⟐ *Pilgrims*

I AM ATTACHED TO ESCAPE, TO THE ILLUSIONS OF "THE ROAD" AS
WELL AS TO THE BAREST "NO EXIT" CUL⟨DE⟩SAC. I AM ATTACHED TO
STUDYING DHARMA AND FORGETTING DHARMA. AND ABOVE ALL
I AM ATTACHED TO MY SUFFERING, WHICH IS SO INEXTRICABLY
WOUND UP WITH PLEASURE AND COMPENSATION.... I AM ONLY A
TOURIST ON THAT BROAD AVENUE LORD BUDDHA REFERRED TO AS
THE "MIDDLE WAY."

— *Rudolph Wurlitzer,*
HARD TRAVEL TO SACRED PLACES

LIFE IN THE TEMPLE is organized in threes. Every morning I put on
one of the three robes that mendicants are allowed to own and walk
to the *sala* with its triple-tiered roof. Before meditating I bow three
times; afterwards I chant three verses apportioning the merit of my
act to all creatures in the world. At night in my *guti*, I study the *Tip-
itaka*, "the three baskets of the Buddhist canon." Every afternoon I
take refuge in the Triple Gem, declaring my belief in the Buddha,
his teachings, and the ordained community. All this is surprising and
not surprising. I know from my first experience in Thailand that life
in a Buddhist country is shaped around the broad avenue, the "middle way"—two extremes and a middle, the third option completing
an equation of perpetual possibility. It's a comforting rhythm, as satisfying as a beginning, middle, and end. And yet, the idea of a trinity is foreign, the antithesis of my basic religious upbringing.

I was raised Unitarian, that is, raised not to need religion or to believe in magic, but rather to intellectualize spirituality, in a dry valley of emotional Trinitarians. This religious upbringing occurred in Sunnyside, a town in rural Washington State, constructed on land purchased by the Progressive Brethren Church in order to build a Christian cooperative community. After the forced removal of members of the Yakama Indian Nation in 1855 (an act of dubious Christianity, cooperation, and community), the territory was quickly settled by immigrant farmers of European Protestant origin. A hundred years later, at the close of the sixties, when my mother returned to her hometown with me in tow, the farms and ranches and orchards were drawing a different breed of cooperative Christian—this time, Catholic field hands who arrived from Mexico in a big, harvest-driven loop via California and Texas. My family was outnumbered, our wagons in a circle, our backs against the hills.

As I pace in meditation deep within the gully of northern Thai rock, tracked by butterflies, I marvel at how temple life is so inextricably connected to landscape. The very air—soft, rosy—seems to lend itself to transcendence, clear streams bursting out of dark forests to announce inspired realization. The landscape of my childhood was more conflicted, generating an equally conflicted response. Like much of small-town America, Sunnyside was stratified into lowland and highland. Everyone who resided up on the Hill (or out on sprawling ranches that accorded their owners honorary Hill standing) was Episcopalian or Methodist or Baptist or Presbyterian. Emboldened by their velvety lawns and perhaps the view, they claimed status as *the* Christians. The rest of us, consigned to the lowlands, were by extension not. This included the majority of the town, particularly those who were Catholic or Mormon or born-again into any one of the tiny new evangelical churches that were continually forming and separating at any time of day (so many that our town, population 6,000, was reportedly listed in the *Guinness Book of World Records* for having the most churches per capita, small-town division).

Despite having leapt at the chance to purchase stolen land sanctified by cooperative Christians, my grandparents demonstrated little interest in church. Mummi, raised in the dour Lutheran Finnish tradition, preferred to discuss spirituality with the family and spend Sunday mornings quietly in the garden. Old Pappa, my political gadfly grandfather, took pride in being Sunnyside's only "out" atheist. My mother was a blend of the two. Her long-standing interest in the world encompassing religion as well as politics, she read everything she could lay her hands on. By the time she joined the Unitarian church, taking Mummi along, she had constructed an entire religious curriculum (with weekly homework!) in anticipation of my eventual birth and upbringing.

Every Sunday I had a lesson plan cobbled together from anthropology textbooks and another *Time-Life* series. After memorizing the names of the major prophets and the basic tenets of belief, I would peck out an appropriate hymn/chant/gospel on the piano, accompanied by my mother on black plastic recorder.

"The important thing to remember," she would stress between puffs on the bizarre, foul-tasting instrument, "is that all religions teach us to recognize our human connections to each other."

I nodded and plucked away at the keys, systematically destroying "Amazing Grace."

The unspoken subtext: Just don't get caught up in their mystical mumbo-jumbo!

Each month we honored some religious (pagans welcome!) holiday, my mother daubing our foreheads with turmeric paste for the Jain New Year, setting out bowls of water and candles for Samhain, substituting saltine crackers for matzo at our makeshift seder. Whenever you're ready, she reminded me over our mispronounced mutterings while lighting the *kinara* ("*Umoja* means unity . . ."), reading the Haggadah ("We were slaves of Pharaoh . . ."), reciting the *shahada* ("There is no god but God . . ."), you can choose the religion you want. The offer left me open to the possibility of non-

Western religion while at the same time closing the door on actual religious belief.

⊗⊛

ONE SUNNY AFTERNOON before my ordination I sat studying on the terrace of the Riverside Tea House, a restaurant-bar on the Mekong River. A young white woman with a bright smile approached and asked to join me.

"Do you mind? I don't want to bother you, but it's great to see another American. We've been here three years."

"Please." I moved aside my stack of books. "Three years? How great!"

"It's okay." She sat down, picking up the top book. "You read Thai? That's amazing."

Thailand had taught me modesty. "Well, I'm sure I'm nowhere near as good as you, living here three years."

"Oh well." She avoided my eyes, gazing instead out at the muddy river. "I haven't really got the hang of Thai yet."

Now it was my turn to avoid eye contact, casting my puzzled glance over the railing.

Though obviously in her late teens or early twenties, with a head of golden ringlets, she had the calm demeanor of a much older woman. There was also a vague aura of sadness, a seriousness, clinging to her like perfumed oil. A thought flickered through my mind: we might be friends, in spite of my general no-expat policy.

Every since my year as savior of Thai-American exchange programs, I had worked hard to distinguish myself as the Ultimate Traveler. Scott and Angel joined me in this. We prided ourselves on sensing the subtle nuances of Southeast Asian body language, the violation of which we knew could destroy an entire universe of possibility. We never showed our feet or touched another's head. We worked on beautifying our *wai* and scaling down our oversized American movements. We entered *wat* on our knees and used respectful pronouns when addressing elders and monks. We avoided tourist hangouts, instead cultivating Thai friends and practicing our tones and idiomatic expressions. We ate spicy food and sticky rice with our hands, ladled cold water over ourselves before meals and bed, tied sarongs when at home, bargained like mad at the market. We were Authentic!

Only rarely did we allow ourselves to respond to that hunger for the kind of conversation compatriots far from home share. There was, however, something about this girl. I imagined that this could be a real friendship, not just an excuse to speak English, use arm gestures freely, and reminisce about chocolate-based foods.

We chatted easily about the States, exchanging the small facts that anchor our overseas identities to a common plane. She beamed that generous grin. "I'm so glad I saw you today,"

Such openness is rare. I grinned back. "Me too."

"So," she said, fingering the spine of one of my Buddhist textbooks. "I see that you're seeking. I know that Christ would love to have you. Have you considered Him?"

My stomach lurched, nearly tipping into the river below. Inwardly I cursed. I was wide open. I should have guessed! I stood up, swaying a bit. "I'm sorry, I have to go." I tossed a few red bills onto the table and scooped up my books. "Bye."

"Wait—" She held up her hand. "What's your name?"

I shook my head and headed for the stairs. I too was on a mission, plump with self-righteousness. As far as I was concerned, Christian missionaries were nearly as deluded as the sex tourists, both groups living out their fantasies on a foreign landscape. (The Mennonites, their cat's-eye glasses, long dresses, and bonnets blocking the tropical sun, seemed particular confirmation of this.)

The girl trailed me down the stairs and stood beside my red motor scooter as I dumped my books into the basket and strapped on my helmet. "Please." She put a nail-bitten hand on my sleeve. "Just tell me your name."

"It can't really matter." I tried to speak as gently as possible. "I'm leaving."

"Please." Suddenly she looked as young as she was. "Why can't I know?"

I muttered "Faith" under my breath, knowing full well that upon hearing it, any proselytizer worth her conversionary salt would conclude that the salvation of my eternal soul was a personal test from God, the one deserving all the extra credit.

She flinched, as if I were mocking her. Her eyes widened and pooled. "You were sent to me," she breathed, her sadness so thick around us I nearly choked. "Don't you see? There must be a reason your name is Faith."

I backed the scooter away. "Yes, there is indeed."

The rest I kept to myself. The reason had to do with being born in a home for unwed girls run by the Salvation Army, whose officers tried to terrify my mother into believing that her unborn child was evidence of purity lost and that moral rehabilitation was only possible through giving me up to a childless, God-fearing couple. It had to do with a nineteen-year-old girl, disowned by her family yet refusing to relinquish me. It had to do with her ability to defy the Soldiers in God's Army—her own small resistance against the Crusades—and her staunch, blind belief that what she was doing was right, despite what they and her family and even God and country said.

I revved the engine and disappeared in a cloud of red dust. Hell yeah, Faith!

ෝ

LIKE MOST WESTERNERS who turn to Eastern philosophy, I had a fraught relationship with Christianity, though as someone raised outside the tradition, I found its potential toxicity more like second-hand smoke. Unlike many of the recovering Catholics and Protestants and Jews around me, I didn't worry about burning in Hell's sulfuric pits; I was, however, shy of organized religion, my throat still raw from the smoking fire of zealotry. My childhood girlfriends, who lived up on the Hill, were convinced that I was going to everlasting hell. There were any number of reasons. First was my refusal to accept Jesus Christ ("J.C." to those in the know) as my Personal Savior. Second was my lack of membership in any one of Sunnyside's fluctuating number of churches. Third was my insistence that Catholics and Mormons (even Holy Rollers) were Christian too. Periodically they felt compelled to warn me of the ignominious fate awaiting me, particularly after stints at summer Bible camp, from which they returned rearranged into new social constellations and vowing to stop sneaking Southern Comfort from their parents' liquor cabinets and letting their boyfriends feel them up.

This time they meant it! they assured me, speaking with all the formality our new relationship required. J.C. loved *them,* after all, as He always made abundantly clear (usually on the final night of camp). The final night jamboree (always spoken of in whispers and accompanied by a meaningful glance to someone who had witnessed its mysterious wonders) was an event I could never, ever hope to understand. From what I gathered, it seemed to consist mainly of long sessions of lip-synching to Christian rock music and tearful testimonials from overwrought teens, interspersed with prolonged bouts of hugging.

My friends sighed in unison, dreamy-eyed, remembering the jamboree. After a moment, one would ask me to explain what it was I believed again?

At these moments Unitarianism felt maddeningly inadequate. Why couldn't we have even the basic trappings of respectability? The nearest church was forty miles away, and without a car, my mother and I rarely attended. Worse still, its name—the embodiment of its sole doctrine, a belief in the oneness of God—was dangerously close to the Reverend Sun Myung Moon's Unification Church.

"Uni-*what?*" Cheryl's head spinning rivaled that of Linda Blair's, aided by an eerie round-nosed, pouty-lipped resemblance to her idol (*The Exorcist* was all the rage among the God-fearing set). "You mean that cult? You and your mom are *Moonies?*"

Were we? I didn't think so. Hell, our members were so liberal they rarely married, let alone signed up for mass group weddings. "No, no," I tried to explain. "We're a legit church. Been around for ages." I decided to skip our illustrious beginnings in sixteenth-century Transylvania and focus instead on early connections to Presbyterians and Pilgrims (everybody likes Pilgrims!).

But the years of drawing colorful Pilgrims and Indians, tracing our hands to make turkeys, were over, and I was never quite believed.

My mother didn't have a liquor cabinet, and I didn't have a boyfriend to tempt me off the path of righteousness, which perhaps accounted for my laissez-faire attitude toward the disposition of my Mortal Soul. And though I carried a card in my wallet printed with the *ABC's of Unitarianism* (apparently as difficult a subject to master for adherents as for skeptics), it was easier for me to tally what we *didn't* believe in.

I got as far as No Trinity.

Cheryl, my on-again, off-again best friend since first grade, shrieked and promptly declared her intention to ask her church youth group to take a break from playing rock records backwards in the church basement (a tireless attempt to intercept messages from Satan before they got to less vigilant souls) so that they could devote an entire afternoon to praying for my embattled soul.

The others solemnly nodded their agreement.

☙❧

AFTER A WHILE I accepted Cheryl's invitations to accompany her family to First Baptist; I was keenly aware of the social jockeying that transpired during church and the long, gossipy phone calls afterwards. If I wasn't there in her family pew, shuddering my way through the minister's incomprehensible grammar, Anita, whose father owned the sole Chinese restaurant, was only too ready to take my place. Already she was nipping at my heels in school, determined to oust me from my position as number one Minority Smarty-pants. I knew she had designs on Cheryl, the arbiter of middle school and junior high taste.

ॐ

ON MY EIGHTEENTH BIRTHDAY, the Unitarian Universalist Association welcomed me into the church, sending along an autographed copy of Albert Schweitzer's autobiography. Thrilled to be welcomed into anything, I frequently reviewed the inscription on the frontispiece, though I never got any further in the book. I knew that Schweitzer was considered good because of his work in Africa, and somehow imagined that he amounted to the equivalent of the Unitarian pope. What I particularly appreciated, however, was how Unitarianism seemed to be free of the rituals and secret trip-ups found in the exacting world of Christianity.

One of my first times at First Baptist with Cheryl's family, I had crushed the Host. It was Communion Sunday, my first, and not understanding why I had been handed a tiny dry cube of bread along with a glass thimble of grape juice, I turned to Cheryl. "What's this?"

As the words left my mouth, my thumb and forefinger inadvertently snapped together, crushing the body of Christ into a fine white powder.

"You smashed it!" Dink marveled, looking both scared and delighted.

"Is that bad?" I glanced down, not quite sure what to do with the holy crumbs. "It's only a crouton."

Cheryl doubled over, clutching her stomach through her lacy Gunne Sax dress. "You killed Christ!" she whispered. "That's the funniest thing I ever saw!"

Dink fell atop her, bone-straight hair forming a curtain, "She called Christ a crouton!" Giggles waved up and down the pew.

Immediately I started formulating excuses to placate the deacons who would certainly rush over in a pack to stone (did Baptists stone?) me. ("Satan's minions moved my fingers!" I would plead.) But no one came. And so I knocked back the shot of sweet grape juice when instructed and felt the space in my mouth where the wafer (as they called it, despite its cube shape) should be and awaited some explanation as to why today was Baptist Snack Day. When this didn't come either, I committed everything I had seen to memory so that later I could ask my mother to explain.

When Albert Schweitzer showed up to lead me down the path of adult Congregationalism, I had already accepted the Unitarian philosophy that all humans are interconnected and no individual can call herself free if another is fettered. This wasn't a religious belief, however; it was my social commitment, my job, my vocation. I was interested in religion in the way I was interested in all academic subjects. I had skipped away from my first year in Thailand with no more than a seventeen-year-old's respect for cross-cultural experience. Where we ate bread and potatoes, the Thais consumed rice; where we used machines, they employed people; where we privileged Christianity, they offered Buddhism.

Both the church and my mother supported this intellectualization of religious experience. Basing their beliefs on Enlightenment ideals, the Universalists had long rejected the miraculous elements of traditional Christianity, while Unitarians had replaced the Christianity and Bible of their Calvinist Puritan roots with reason and morals. Both doctrines were congregational, emphasizing the duty of each congregation to make its own decisions, and stressed a scientific view of the universe.

When the two churches merged in the early sixties, forming Unitarian Universalism, the ideal religion for my mother was born. Rationalism and morality were her twin gods. For all her interest in organized religion, she taught it as a social science, a necessary opiate when political morality faltered, as far from transmogrifying croutons and records played backwards in church basements as she could drag it, oh, please Lord!

Interpreting the Unitarian belief in universal religious experience and the Universalist belief in the salvation of all souls to mean that all religions were the same, I maintained a benign, democratic disinterest in them all (Great! No thanks). Christianity was the only one that got an emotional reaction, a spurt of nausea and a tingling at the base of my neck, the same feeling I got the day I left First Baptist.

I had come across Anita's mother, freshly discharged from the sanitarium, standing in the vestry with two women who were telling her in loud, bright voices to sing for the minister. Anita's mother beamed and belted out, *"Zhe-sus rove me dis I know,"* in a thick Mandarin accent, glancing from one face to another for approval as the minister and the two women chuckled and actually (or did I just imagine it?) patted her on the head. As I marched out the front door, permanently vacating Cheryl's family pew for Anita, I thought little about religion and not at all about spirituality.

෨෧

THE YEAR AFTER my acceptance into the Unitarian church, I ran away to college. Upon my escape from 360 days of sunny cooperative community, my resentment of Christianity blossomed like a bloody flower in my chest. When first I encountered the occasional zealot in Harvard Square, I cringed at the Question—"Do you know Christ?" (a query so strangely phrased I had to suck in my lips to stop from quipping, "What, in the biblical sense?"). Something about the tone reminded me of the voice Cheryl used to announce that once again during the two short weeks of Bible camp her new best friend was now Kelly, with her eager horse face, or Deanna, who was just boring enough (or was it smart enough?) to agree with everything Cheryl said, or René, who would later be deemed too sluttish to retain that special status.

After a while, newly free in Boston, the world headquarters of Unitarian Universalism, I could grin. "No, I don't know Christ, and I don't particularly want to."

I was grateful for the strong Jewish presence on campus and the powerful way it curtailed Christian entitlement. We were all expected to know when the High Holy Days were and the proper pronunciations of words like Shabbat. Finally my mother's version of the world applied: other, equally legitimate religions existed!

⚫⚫

AND SO BUDDHISM fooled me. More philosophy than tenet, a contract with the self, a balm on the soul of someone who would rather put a raincoat over her head and stumble around blind than ask for help. I did not recognize it as religion, or my interest in it as spiritual quest.

The study of Buddhist nuns was simply the perfect blend of my social and academic interests. Check it out! I would investigate a dispossessed segment of society. I would contrast the Thais' dismissal of *maechi* to their reverence of monks. I would bring to light an image of Thai women that challenged the bar girls and masseuses and whores. I would rest from the sun in beautiful temples. When Ajarn Boon suggested that I ordain, the anthropological value was immediately apparent.

During meals I find myself staring openmouthed, feverish, at a photograph hanging in the *sala*. It is rumored to be an image of the Buddha that appeared mysteriously on the walls of a cave, a Buddhist Shroud of Turin. Day after day, as I study the blurry image of a handsome Indian man in dark robes and twisted hair, I listen to the soaring highs and guttural lows of the chanting, letting it swirl through my blood. I collect stories of monks levitating in remote mountain monasteries and learn to slow my own heartbeat in med-

itation. I see visions of people I know and eavesdrop on the conversations of those I don't, all the while sitting in my *guti* in the forest,
feeling consciousness leave my body and go careening over the
green-and-gold rooftops and into town. Everywhere around me is
magic!

And so, after twenty-two years of Unitarianism, I step easily,
unwittingly, into a trinity. Tricked! Each time my forehead touches
the straw mat, I ask myself if I do in fact believe what my lips are
saying, that I can take refuge in the three pillars of Buddhism, while
another mouth, a tiny one in my heart, opens and fills, sating a
hunger I didn't even know I possessed.

*Immediately after ordination, on the steps
of Wat Phra Singh, holding flower offerings
on a footed tray.*

CHAPTER TWELVE

❧ The Body of Woman

FAITH IS AN ACT OF THE WHOLE PERSON, OF MIND, WILL, AND HEART.

—*Abraham Joshua Heschel,*

MAN IS NOT ALONE

WHEN MAECHI ROONGDÜAN returns in the evening from visiting her sick aunt, she stands outside my *guti* and calls softly: *"Maechi!"* I emerge to find her standing beneath the tree, hands folded together before her, face gleaming rosy and tight. She grins as if she's missed me.

I grin back, surprised to find that, despite how relaxed the meal and general atmosphere have been in her absence, I have missed her too. An entire conversation takes place in our silent smiles.

"Sit with me," she invites, lowering herself onto the circular stone bench, white robes billowing about her, as if into a pool of milk. Though her posture is erect as ever, I recognize this moment between us as soft. As if to confirm this thought, she announces: "You may interview me."

I try to recall all the questions I've been storing up as I study, obey, resist, admire her. The sociological markers I've developed suddenly pale at the prospect of reducing her to a subject. How to capture the root of spirituality in a case study? Which research question can unlock the secret to religious determination?

I start small, hoping for inspiration. We blow through the basics, establishing that she is thirty, has been ordained five years, and was raised in nearby Hod Township. Like many ethnic Chinese,

..

I want to meditate in the cave, but some tourists are playing inside for what seems like an eternity. I wait thirty minutes on the lower ledge. If I were they, the weary traveler (and hasn't it been so in the past?), I would be irritated with *me,* the would-be obstructionist *maechi* who thinks she needs to meditate in the most beautiful part of the *wat*—though her eyes are closed!

Realizing this should be enough to reduce my annoyance, yet I cling to irritation. The tourists burst out, giggles fading in the open air, at the sight of me.

*E*arly each morning, carrying his alms-bowl, the [monk] makes himself available before the houses of the laity to receive food offerings. We may say he is begging. Actually, he is providing opportunity to the layman to earn merit through giving. The [monk] is indifferent—he should not care whether he eats or what he eats. While he receives and eats this food he is to think, "I eat in order to sustain my body, not in order to enjoy eating."

—ROBERT C. LESTER,
Theravada Buddhism in Southeast Asia

her family is a poster child for Thai middle-class aspirations. Two of her siblings have inherited the successful family business, while the other three work as members of the Middle-Class Trinity: doctor, policeman, and school headmaster! I nearly burst out laughing.

Not surprisingly, for years her family vehemently opposed her ordination. They asked, "Why would a college-educated woman want to adopt a profession that people scorn?"

Maechi Roongdüan admits that she herself wrestled with the idea of ordination for six years. "I didn't believe that the historical Buddha had really existed," she says easily, as if she had just stopped by for tea and to discuss the PTA bake sale. "I thought Buddhism was a story fabricated to restrict people's activities, a philosophy to discuss and dream about."

I glance around at the bare walkways, the empty gardens, terrified of having inadvertently solicited this, the most blasphemous statement I have ever heard any Thai—devout or otherwise—utter.

I lean forward. "You didn't believe he *existed*?"

She shakes her head. "No. I decided to ordain to disprove Buddhism."

Blinking, I fold my hands in my lap and wait. The interview is hers. I have no idea where to go with any of this.

Against the gentle clicking of the geckos scampering in the leaves above us, she explains how she was nonetheless concerned with spiritual questions: "From the time I was fifteen, I asked myself, Why are we born? My parents suffer, working hard to make money to send me to school and begging me to do well. I in turn have to read and read and try to memorize, which is suffering. And for what?"

She shakes with silent laughter. "So I can get a degree and a job. Then I have to fall in love, get married, have children, and begin to do the same for them—all suffering."

Her dark eyes sparkle with amusement, as if aware of the incongruity of someone with her intellect and zest for life suffering through education and relationships. "But I thought my question was 'the teenage problem,' so I went on."

At Chiang Mai University, where she was studying in the science faculty, she read Buddhist doctrine for the first time. After meeting several monks who impressed her, she decided to test the Dhamma for herself.

She moved out of the dorms and into a *guti* at a nearby *wat*. I smile, remembering how I used to stroll from campus to that very temple's gorgeous grounds, how I once sparred with a Sri Lankan monk there. For the next six years she kept Buddhist precepts and read and discussed dhamma.

"Six years." It feels like a sigh escaping my lips.

She holds out her hand, wrist facing up, and tells me that she used to be fat. "I used to have a curved back and be covered with pimples. All that changed."

My heart flutters with hope, a wood thrush against my breast. We change.

Though she had decided that Buddhist living was the true way to relieve life's suffering, still she resisted ordination. "I saw that *maechi* spend all day selling flowers to get the money to buy food to cook for themselves. What if we have no money, no food? What is the use?"

I think about the *maechi* who once tucked a buttery flower into my hand like a devotee affixing gold leaf to a Buddha statue. There is use.

Maechi Roongdüan continues her gentle critique of the church: "Men become monks to follow tradition or seek education; everyone is happy. For women, no one is happy. *Maechi* life is very dry and difficult."

Then she met a forest hermit monk. "I had no interest in the life of *maechi* until I met this one monk. He lived without wearing the shoe or having the money. He was vegetarian. I expected him to be so thin, but he was tall and—what do we call it?"

··

I detest tourists! In the morning a group of laypeople with *Aerobic Dance, Tapae Township* inexplicably printed in English across their bright blue T-shirts and matching visors visit the *wat*. First we hear them chanting over the loudspeaker. Then they ring the bell, which sounds very urgent and medieval, like a plague warning.

We are on our way on the path alongside the stream when Mae Oey, the most senior *maechi*, comes out and tells us to go back. The visitors are still conversing with the abbot, she explains.

Oh Buddha, when you only eat once a day and always at the same time, and your stomach and bowels have been empty for a good twelve hours, the withholding of sustenance is pure torture!

No one among us is amused. As we turn back to our *guti*, I want to curse the merit-hungry laity for messing up our schedule. Though the famed reciprocity of Theravada Buddhism sounds delightful in the abstract, with monks and *maechi* nobly ministering to the psychic and spiritual needs of their communities (hurrah!), which in turn provide physical support, in reality it places the *Sangha* under the laity's thumb.

She snaps her fingers, and a gecko that has descended partway down the tree trunk, whips around and scurries up, rustling the leaves. "Handsome. Yes, very powerful. He would go alone into the forest or to the top of the mountain for three months at a time."

Her dark eyes widen, recalling her amazement. "I thought, how could he live like that? I thought, if he can do that, so can I."

I exhale, *ah,* startled at the poetry of her words, the familiarity of her thought process. Moving immediately from questioning how a thing is even possible to declaring one's own readiness for the same challenge is how I too was raised, isn't it?

She decided to ordain. A few days prior to the ceremony, she meditated for the first time and began to experience an unprecedented happiness, such that "every other happiness seemed coarse by comparison."

This reassured her that practicing asceticism and meditation would make ordination bearable.

She shrugs, a secular gesture. "So I came here to Thamtong and have lived on one meal a day, without shoes, money, meat, for five years. And I see that we can live like this. Before, I believed the doctor; I studied science. But no, this is healthy."

She pinches the milky skin of her left wrist with her right thumb and forefinger. "I haven't been to the doctor in ten years. It is the simple, the very clean life."

☙

LATER, AS WE sweep the cave, Pranee, the youngest *maechi,* whispers that it took years, but Maechi Roongdüan's family has finally accepted her ordination. They are in fact financing a private *guti* for her. Maechi Roongdüan does the actual building work herself—by hand.

Pranee grins as she drags out the large mats and hoists them over the stone railing. The balusters, carved angels with ornate headdresses and enlightened beings from the Buddhist pantheon, watch from their posts, every meter along the handrail. Pranee's smile can make you believe that ordination is a continuous slumber party. "Maechi Roongdüan can do it all!"

I grab the edge of the mat with both hands and help her shake, thinking of Maechi Chaloon. Before my ordination I had gone in search of her, having heard that she'd been ordained at one of Thailand's most famous *wat* since the late 1950s. Ducking the flower-toting crowds milling about the gilded *stupa* and tiered umbrellas, I found a caretaker who directed me to a *guti* perched on the side of the mountain. There, a dark-skinned, vibrant-looking *maechi* knelt amidst rioting flower and vegetable gardens. With an expectant smile, as if she'd known I was coming, she returned my *wai* and handed me a glass of cool water. We sat in the open doorway of her *guti* while Maechi Chaloon explained that when she ordained twenty-seven years ago, at the age of thirty, few temples in the north accepted women.

"Most *maechi* were old women waiting to die. To be allowed to exist at the *wat*, they had to live and work under the thumbs of the *phra*." Nonetheless, she ordained, taking all Ten Precepts. Eventually she concluded that the stricture against money was limiting her freedom. She made a small gesture, hands palms up. "Going on alms rounds was dangerous or fruitless. Often I ended up hungry."

I found it hard to imagine anyone turning her, with her smooth brown face and taut muscles, away. "Why this particular *wat*?" I asked. I could count the number of *maechi* on one hand.

She explained that she'd been impressed by the abbot and the peaceful setting. "When I first came, it was still jungle. There were bears and tigers, no tourists, few *guti*. Another *maechi* and I weeded the side of this hill alone."

Laughing, she pointed out the door, sweeping a graceful hand, fingers bending in the backwards arc of Thai classical dance, toward the jumble of vegetation. "No one forced us—but who would do it and keep the *wat* orderly if we did not? Our hands were *ripped!*"

Devotees give to the robe, not to the wearer. They believe it is a ritual for the making of merit, for a better rebirth. If a monk thanks the giver, then by treating it as a personal favour, merit is not gained.

—TIM WARD,
What the Buddha Never Taught

..

In a way, the order is like a faculty at a university. We have to perform well enough to be famous enough to attract followers; it's much like the pressure on professors to publish and lure a new generation of students. Devout followers offer merit-making necessities. Students who happen to glean an education from this atmosphere will go on to become professors themselves, thus ensuring the continuation of the whole parasitic cycle. Is that what we are?

*D*evout Buddhists
may give food offer-
ings regularly in the
morning, send money
contributions to their
neighborhood monas-
teries, or contribute
to some meritorious
causes such as build-
ing an Uposatha hall.
. . . Thai calendars
usually show a special
day of every week . . .
known as Wan Phra,
or the Buddhist holy
day, when the pious
are often especially
active in their merit
making. They may
take food offerings to
the monasteries or go
hear special sermons
and observe addi-
tional precepts.

—PHRA
   RAJAVARAMUNI,
*Thai Buddhism in the
Buddhist World*

I want nothing to do
with the laity. If I had
but an ounce of *metta*
(loving kindness), I
suppose I would wel-
come their loud inter-
ruptions, their spoiled
children running up
and down the paths in
their Mickey Mouse
T-shirts and baseball
caps, their picnicking
on our meditation

Once again she turned her palms up, this time showing me a cracked riverbed of scars. "I could have asked for help, but I gave up my family and wanted to help myself."

I sucked down my second glass of water as she watched me from beneath nonexistent brows. "*Maechi* life used to be hard, truly hard."

I nodded. I believed her. "Maechi, what was the life you left behind? What was your family profession?"

She smiled, a dark blossom on a stalk of white cotton. "Gardeners."

Her gaze caught the setting sun, hovering fat and orange among the vegetables. "It used to be *anything* would grow here—bamboo, mushrooms. . . . We didn't have to worry about food. We would gather it and preserve the surplus." She watched the sky turning red around her mountaintop gardens. "Sometimes I would go to bed and just think, How is it *possible* to have such happiness and freedom as this? So much happiness and so much freedom!"

Bowing, I thanked her and crept away.

I watch Pranee spread out the clean mats and wonder what life awaits her.

In the bus down the mountain, a jovial middle-aged tourist with a camera around his neck had asked me about the temple. Still glowing from my visit with Maechi Chaloon, I told him what I knew of its religious significance and tossed in some tips about other important *wat* in the area.

"I am from Sviss," he'd declared. "You too make the tourism?"

"No, I was visiting a Buddhist nun."

"Ah, nuns," he said, cocking a brow and winking. "You cannot make the sex, that is so. Yes?"

THE NEXT EVENING as darkness descends to meet us beneath the tree, Maechi Roongdüan tells of her three-month *thudong,* hard practice pilgrimage, the most profound moment of her ordained life. Traditionally such pilgrimages consist of trips to the deep forest, mountain peaks, or cremation sites for solitary intensive meditation, though they can also entail working on a specific weakness.

At her announcement, I lean forward to make sure I heard correctly. I've never heard of a woman going on *thudong*.

"Yes, *thudong*," she repeats, her face glowing in evening light. She, Maechi Vilawam, and three others traveled from one end of Thailand to the other, starting in Chiang Mai's northern mountains, moving down through Bangkok's central lowlands to Songkhra in the deep southern tropics of the Malay Peninsula, then looping back up through Bangkok and over to Issan, the dry, poverty-stricken northeast.

All five were vegetarians and used neither shoes nor money. All each one carried was an umbrella, a mosquito net, an alms bowl, and the robes on her back.

"We would flag down buses and explain that we do not carry money. If the driver allowed us to ride, we would bless him; if not, we would walk."

They rose at three-thirty every morning to meditate and talk; at six-thirty they went on alms rounds; the rest of the day was spent preaching and traveling. The first time they received alms, one of the *maechi* burst into tears.

Like many Thai, Maechi Roongdüan smiles equally at joy and sorrow and a combination of the two. The corners of her mouth curve upward gently as she explains: "She said she didn't believe that she would ever receive alms in the body of a woman."

In the north, Maechi Roongdüan was surprised that the Hmong tribespeople, who don't speak Thai and aren't Buddhists, shared their meager supplies of rice and fruit. One man chased after them with a full stalk of bananas cut straight from the tree. Forbidden from touching or interfering with the offering until the end of alms rounds and subsequent blessings, Maechi Roongdüan tried to use a

benches as if this were a Disney exhibit—*The Ride of Golden Temples*. I would find their interest in the *wat* promising and good, but I am not Ajarn Suchin, so all I want is my meal!

Inside my *guti*, I fume, trying not to think about the roiling acids attacking the lining of my stomach. Attempts to focus on my breathing, *In-Out*, only heighten the attention on my belly.

After thirty minutes, the bell rings again and we gather anew, tension coating every mindful gesture. As we approach the bridge, I see the blue-clad Aerobic Dance Tourists of Tapae Township scattered across the path like so many Smurfs. My heart sinks. Not again!

one-handed form of sign language to explain that he should divide the giant bunch into five smaller ones for each of them.

She laughs, manipulating her fingers in the dusky half-light to show the difficulty of gesturing while holding a large alms bowl. "He didn't understand."

Eventually she staggered away under the immense weight of his generosity, a hundred bananas poking out of her bowl like the giant golden hand of Buddha.

When the *maechi* returned to Thamtong, the abbot forbade them to go on pilgrimage again. Maechi Roongdüan does a pantomime, by now nearly a silhouette in darkness, sheepishly recalling the abbot's presentation of scripture after scripture stipulating that women cannot go on *thudong* or sleep alone in the open.

"But," she says, eyes catching the last light and twinkling, lips curving imperceptibly upward like a Buddha statue, "I have already done it."

The means of achieving Buddhist goals is through meritorious action and the accumulation of merit. There are traditional merit-making acts, such as giving alms to monks, building a temple, "giving" a son for ordination into the Sangha, etc.

—THOMAS KIRSCH, "Buddhism, Sex Roles and the Thai Economy"

Upon seeing us, the Dance Tourists spring to either side of the path and kneel, even the young men, pressing their bare knees into the sharp gravel. Their hands form a phalanx of *wai* we pass through, a gauntlet of humility.

In that moment I understand Maechi Roongdüan's story about the *maechi* who cried the first time she received alms, and I have to fight back the tears threatening to leak out of my own eyes.

Temple Cave: Maechi *doing walking meditation in the caves of* Wat Thamtong *temple of residence.*

CHAPTER THIRTEEN

⊱ Hungry Ghosts

REALIZATION OF THE DESIRES THAT GOVERN ACTION ALLOWS THESE
DESIRES TO CYCLE AND CEASE; EITHER IGNORING OR JUDGING
DESIRES LEADS TO ACTION WITHOUT CONSCIOUSNESS, WHICH IS
SUBJECT TO *KILESA* (DEFILEMENTS, IMPURITIES, PASSIONS).

— *Nyanaponika Thera,*
THE HEART OF BUDDHIST MEDITATION

DURING THE HOT SEASON the mountains are dry and the monks wear bright orange robes. In the middle of the night I awake to the crackle of activity. Bare-shouldered monks in only their under-robes dart past my window, disappearing into the forest on our side of the stream. Their dogs tense, bristling. Circles of light jump along the dark pathways, carrying with them flashes of white, the suggestion of women's voices, high and rapid.

Pranee, the youngest *maechi*, stands high on the mountain face, beating the earth with a broom. Her *guti* is on fire.

During the hot season the dry underbrush surrounding the *wat* frequently bursts into flame, the unfortunate side effect of the slash-and-burn farming techniques the local villagers use in the deep forest.

For some reason no one remembers, the *wat* was built at the forest entrance, a physical reminder of the reciprocal relationship most *wat* and villages seek. To enter, the villagers are always marching along the row of *maechi guti*, barefoot, faces blurred under dustings of black ash and red soil. In the indigo work shirt and straw hat

..

I'm now supposed to be mindful of *everything I touch* and *every desire.*

..

Today I take even less food, barely covering the bottom of the bowl. Once I taste how delicious it is, I regret my restraint, but by the time I've mindfully chewed every bite, even that small amount is too much.

*L*ogic tells us that a decision to give up the ordained life may relate to problems in maintaining celibacy.

It has become something of an "in" joke in ordained circles that no one gives up their [*sic*] vows due to an overwhelming desire to eat after noon.

—KARMA LEKSHE TSOMO,

Sakyadhītā: Daughters of the Buddha

I am a very bad *maechi*. Last night I slept maybe one hour; otherwise I spent the entire night dreaming about every man to whom I was ever attracted. The dreams were quite simple. The men are touring the temple, and just as one walks by my *guti*, out I step ever so demurely. "Faith!" he exclaims. "What are *you* doing here?"

We talk properly, as befits a *maechi*, but there's something about the length of time he looks me over. I only sense this,

of the Thai farmer, red checked scarves ringing their necks and machetes wedged into waist sashes, they are eerily reminiscent of the Khmer Rouge, who still wander free, not so far away. I see them on the path outside my *guti*, the occasional flash of square white teeth, and remind myself that they are farmers, not killers. I hear them in predawn darkness, laughing and chatting in northern dialect, and again upon their return in late evening. This odd commuter trail.

When the water buffalo aren't being used in the rice fields, the villagers husband them back near the waterfall. The *wat* provides free grazing land as well as a deterrent to theft. In a Buddhist country, who would be bold enough to steal a buffalo and walk it through a gauntlet of living merit fields, along gardens of eggplant and holy basil, under the bower dripping with frangipani and jasmine, past the reception area with its bamboo cages of songbirds?

&

THE DAY AJARN BOON and I visited the *wat*, the day I decided to ordain, I remember being struck by the sunlight, the heat, the activity, the feverish colors of the monk's side of the stream. "It is called Wat Thamtong because of the caves," Maechi Roongdüan had explained. "*Tham* means caves, *tong* gold." *The Temple of Golden Caves*. I had no idea that at night it would be the *maechi* side bursting into flame.

That day as I stood panting from the hike beneath a blistering sun, I made a decision to ordain. A decision based on desire. True, it was the desire to live a life free from desire, but it was a hunger burning in me all the same.

&

THE POOREST LOCAL farmers don't have water buffalo or even flat farmland to work. They are the ones who claim the jungle, hacking and burning the thick undergrowth, frequently leaving patches to smolder. So all hot season, *maechi* climb the mountain with brooms and buckets of water to put out the night fires before they reach the *wat*.

The burning is not intentional on the part of the villagers, Maechi Roongdüan explains. "Just as every day the leaves fall and we must sweep them, so too the villagers must farm in order to eat. It is life."

I can smell the burning of Pranee's *guti* now like a scorched pot. I wonder if I, in my poorly managed robes that keep unfastening themselves from this Western body, can be of help. Me, with my poor night vision and dried-up contact lenses. Or will I just distract as usual—the fragile foreign *maechi* giving everyone more to worry about? In my own country, I am surely more useful.

I take one agonized step toward Pranee and her burning home.

Maechi Roongdüan appears on the path with a bucket in each hand, the contents lapping softly against the plastic sides like bathwater in a tub. "We thought of waking you to help," she says, "but this time Ajarn Suchin sent the monks across the stream to help."

As usual, her face is wide, smooth, her smile rippling gently like a stream. *"Mai pen rai,"* she trills the Thai's favorite phrase. *Don't worry.*

I sense rather than hear a sudden intake of breath, a collective unvoiced gasp like the absence of wind on a hot day. Maechi Roongdüan spins around, the water in the buckets scattering in an arc of droplets around our bare feet, staining the earth dark red.

A monk stands stranded high on the rock face, encircled by a ring of fire. Hungry, glowing flames the color of his robes lick at his calves and thighs. It resembles some horrific circus act. Pranee, still keeping the vow of silence, stares. Her face is orange and fluid, reflecting the monk like an unwilling mirror.

An early memory pushes its way into my consciousness: the black-and-white image of an elderly monk steadily pouring petrol on himself in a busy midday street and then setting himself alight.

of course, as I am staring at the ground.

The next thing I know, we're in my college dorm room; there's beer; I have hair! I anger the man, who becomes aggressive, forcing me to my knees. We have frenzied sex in the hall, on the table, up against walls. Then we eat chocolate chip cookies. Not just any chocolate chip cookies, mind you, but bittersweet chocolate with macadamia nuts (at five dollars a pound) from that little shop in Harvard Square. Then comes the next visitor.

Needless to say, I am exhausted when the three-thirty bell rings. So that it looks like I am meditating, I turn on the light and put on my robes—in case of a surprise summons—then go back to sleep. When I get in line at eight-thirty, I notice the other *maechi* smiling. I must seem utterly hopeless and bedraggled.

The food is absolutely delicious, perhaps to make up for the fact that they only had three dishes yesterday and then ran out of those. As the last to eat, the *upasika* and I were given a can of sardines to flesh out our meal. But today there are dried honey bananas, shrimp crackers, vegetarian chili paste, relatively edible leaves and grass, even a potato and fish casserole that tastes like Grandma's Finnish *kalavuoka* (but with flavor).

I spend the entire meal worrying that I haven't taken enough food. In the end, not only am I unable to finish, I feel bloated. Why? As usual, I eat considerably less than everyone else, though I'm much larger. Is it my mind-set? Am I eating more quickly than I realize? Does the Buddha want to teach me a valuable lesson about gluttony?

Processing back to the *guti* after the meal, I hear a noise and, turning, catch a vision of fire across the stream. Three monks, their sashes

Flames roaring up his body as he sits immobile, chanting, palms clasped together. Women and men charge forward, faces and bodies dropping before him, prostrating themselves over and over. The air fills with wailing.

I scream and my mother rushes into the living room, a jar of home-canned peaches in one hand. She swoops down and scoops me under one arm, heading for the hallway. It is too late. This becomes one of my earliest memories.

Am I only a toddler, inexplicably watching Vietnam's Buddhist Crisis of 1966 as it unfolds on American television screens? Or is it years later, perhaps a war documentary with footage of Thich Quang Duc, the seventy-three-year-old monk who performed the first self-immolation the year of my birth?

My mother cradles me in the hallway, preventing me from seeing the rest of the story: the flickering black-and-white monk becomes a charred skeleton. His ebony bones list to the side, slowly, slowly, hands still locked together in a *wai*, brittle limbs collapsing, fluttering like a negative of leaves, like a river of red paper after the Chinese New Year. His prayers linger on the smoky air.

I go to bed early. This is one of my earliest images, this charred monk, and the Napalm Girl running down the road, arms outstretched, skin dripping off her body in sizzling strips, and the plump, golden peach orbs swirling, suspended in clear viscous liquid. I have nightmares about Southeast Asia for years.

Two decades later, I stand rooted to the foot of a fiery mountainside in Thailand. All around me, monks and *maechi* spring to the aid of the young monk, slapping the earth before him with straw brooms, forming a human chain up the mountain, passing bucket after bucket from the stream. The thick air sparks and glows. Water spatters at the monk's feet with great hisses.

Maechi Roongdüan nods briskly at the rescue, and I remember to breathe. The air rushes out of my lungs.

"See? It's just like trying to extinguish our *kilesa*." *Cravings*. She sounds almost triumphant. She hoists the lap-lapping buckets of water and disappears up the side of the mountain, leaving me alone on the dark path.

॰॰

THE NEXT DAY, holding a finger to her lips and whispering so that we don't get caught talking, Pranee shows me her replacement *guti*. Unlike the standard wooden hut built on stilts to discourage cobras and other invaders, it is a small, dim cave in the side of the mountain. Just large enough for a lumpy pallet on a bed of rocks.

I pull back the stiff tarpaulin curtain, dip my head inside again and again. The murky stone walls resemble an underwater grotto, full of dark crevasses. I draw back, terrified, thinking about creepy crawly things and how superstitious most Thais are.

Pranee scoffs. "Ghosts are for idiots!" she declares, her sunny, scrubbed face lighting the rock. "The only place they exist is in the mind!"

She tells me about her old life. Her parents farmed up-country. She was one of seven children. Maechi Roongdüan lets her and Theew, the swan-necked twenty-one-year-old, speak together occasionally because "silence is most difficult for the younger ones."

Later that evening she gets permission to visit me and waits on the walkway outside my *guti*. She tucks a few fading snapshots into my palm: one of her parents in farmer dress, one of herself in her primary school uniform.

"Will you go back?" I ask.

"Maechi Roongdüan is my mother now," she answers. "And the others are my family."

She tells me about the time Maechi Roongdüan took them for a weeklong meditation retreat to an abandoned crematorium. According to my Buddhist texts, graveyards, crematoriums, and corpses are all traditional settings or subjects for meditating on *anicca*, the impermanence of life. Pranee explains that the place was

high and wide, stand at different levels on the brick-red riverbank in the bright sunlight. They wear only under-tunics—arms, shoulders, upper chest, and calves bare—overrobes meticulously pleated and draped over their shoulders.

They are rinsing out their black-and-gold alms bowls with the easy synchronized movements of a work crew. After swirling water in the bowls, they toss it onto the bank below with a great *splat,* staining the earth dark copper. Three dogs, large and golden, run back and forth, barking, frenzied.

*M*en who live dominated by anger, hate, and violence will be punished in the hells. Those dominated by concern for food and sex will undergo punishment in animal forms, and those dominated by greed will suffer as hungry ghosts in the purgatories.

—S. J. TAMBIAH,
World Conqueror, World Renouncer

Good sitting meditation for seventy minutes in the cave. After the customary thing—space getting darker and darker before my eyes—my face feels like it's zooming forward on its own, rushing through a dark tunnel. Then it begins to drip off, the flesh melting down and oozing off the bones. Strangely, it doesn't *hurt*.

Figuring that the veil I wear over my head to protect me from the sun and insects is slipping, I open my eyes. The gauzy material is perfectly in place, draped over my head just as I had left it.

I wonder if there is a ghost in the cave. Each time I close my eyes I hear someone coughing, walking on the floor mats, prickling me, pacing back and forth. Each time I open them, no one's there.

stiflingly hot and *maechi* kept fainting during meditation. After three days, everyone except Maechi Roongdüan wanted to go back.

"She wants us to know about bodies," Pranee says, her eyes glittering with an emotion I can't place. "About death."

ᘓᘔ

RESTLESS AFTER THE enforced seclusion of the rainy season, Maechi Roongdüan takes *maechi* on a *thudong*, a pilgrimage, to a local teaching hospital.

On the drive I gaze at the road, memorizing the colors of the Thai countryside, the emerald, jade, rose, aubergine, celadon. Before I realize it, we are standing in a chilly hospital room crowded with unsteady medical students, *maechi* in solemn white, and a few locals who seem to be here just for the fun of it.

The cadavers arrive on wheeled cots: a man with the skin of his head already folded back like a disassembled android, revealing red and blue veins of circuitry; a yellowing woman with a long pelt of hair clinging to a flap above her severed ear; a child. Though the room reeks of formaldehyde, I worry that I will be able to smell the stench of decay. It's like my certainty at the dentist's that the Novocain will wear off any minute, revealing the white-hot agony of the drill. Of course, it never happens, but the fear is so strong I interpret every sensation as pain.

Fingering stainless steel instruments with dusted latex gloves, the students tell quiet jokes and get to work, peeling the man's face off to get at his skull.

"That's all we are," Maechi Roongdüan says, lining us up and coaxing us forward. "Flesh and bone, some breath."

Breath. Breathe. In and out, in and out. My breath clings to the pale gray walls, to the metal trays, to the wheeled cots, leaving tiny droplets like perspiration. A sheen of my panic coats the room. I learn that a dead body is far worse than a live one.

I remember the body I did not see. Freshman year at college I worked with refugees from Laos newly arrived in the United States. Entrusted with two families, my volunteer partner and I were supposed to befriend the children and help the parents navigate the confusing waters of U.S. immigration and social services. We were supposed to convince them that America wanted them.

The families had been settled next door to each other in a run-down apartment building in Dorchester, Boston's most segregated neighborhood. The nearest T stop was in the white part of town, several long blocks away. The first time we visited, the children scolded us for arriving so late in the afternoon. *Bad people come out in dark,* they warned us. *You leave by four!* My partner, queasy from an encounter with a rat in the bathroom, nodded.

Next time, we came in the morning, tripping across a minefield of hostile glares from white men outside the Irish pubs dotting the street. We arrived to find one of the sons, a teenager who worked the graveyard shift as a busboy, sprawled on the sofa, face swollen and head bandaged. *The bad people catched him as he walk home,* the kids explained in hushed tones. *They thought he Vietnamese.*

"We help America against Vietnam," the father protested, his one good eye searching ours with milky urgency. "That why we must to leave." He spread his fingers, palms up. "We lose everything for USA."

My partner and I squinted in sympathy and left early, sunk in the realization that the family needed more than we had to give, hoping my partner's pale skin would keep the red-eyed, red-faced men at bay.

I began to develop stomach pains on Saturday mornings. Friday nights I dreamed about the long, jolting T ride to Savin Hill; the trudge down gray streets speckled with dog shit; the gauntlet of drunken men; the apartment smelling of urine and *gapi,* fish paste; the hunger of kids convinced that I didn't love them enough, convinced that each visit would be my last.

The ten asubhas (impurities) one may focus concentration on are as follows:

1. a swollen or bloated corpse
2. a corpse brownish black or purplish blue with decay
3. a festering or suppurated corpse
4. a corpse splintered in half or fissured from decay
5. a corpse gnawed by animals such as wild dogs and foxes
6. a corpse scattered in parts, hands, legs, head, and body being dispersed
7. a corpse cut and thrown away in parts after killing
8. a bleeding corpse, i.e., with red blood oozing out
9. a corpse infested with and eaten by worms
10. remains of a corpse in a heap of bones, i.e., skeleton

—MAHASI SAYADAW,
Purpose of Practising Kammatthana Meditation

The sophisticated meditator understands that gods, demons, and ghosts are personifications of desires, anxieties, fears . . . [and] ignorance and does not deprecate the man of less sophistication who objectifies and personifies, who gives gross form to the same realities.

—ROBERT C. LESTER,
Theravada Buddhism in Southeast Asia

..

Maechi Roongdüan explains the concept of rebirth. She says that there are many kinds but two main ones: the abstract concept, rebirth in the mind, and the version for the layperson, known as reincarnation. The latter exists "because the laity cannot understand the finer points of the other, especially if they haven't practiced.

"If we tell them, live by the Five Householder Precepts because society will not worsen if every-

One Saturday morning I called my partner and told him I was sick. It wasn't working out; we weren't helping anyone. I spent the day huddled in bed, as I'd done in response to most things since arriving at college.

That evening the television news reported that a black man had been killed at Savin Hill. The camera showed our T stop and the street we walked along each week. The reporter explained that white men from one of the local bars spotted the man waiting for the train and taunted him with racist epithets. They then got baseball bats and chased him onto the railroad tracks, where he ran headlong into an oncoming train. He was killed instantly.

"Well, he shouldn't have been here," a white-haired grandmother type snapped at the reporter. "This is our neighborhood."

I huddled under the covers, my rage a cancer gnawing at my gut. Through pain came understanding, as I realized that the kids' terrified accusations were true. I didn't love them enough. I didn't love anybody enough to let go of fear.

SUDDENLY I AM face to face with a beautiful, rotting boy. All around me, Thais whisper in a vocabulary of sensationalism I can't quite understand. The boy died in some mysterious, violent way. His body is being preserved until the trial is over.

I am failing the exercise. Instead of focusing on the impermanence of the body, I find myself wondering about his short life. What are they whispering behind their fluttering, birdlike hands, their white masks? I hear the word *pa,* father. Did his father kill him? Is that the reality my vocabulary cannot embrace?

My stomach lurches, and at the edges of my consciousness I recognize my old friend—rage, nearly a stranger now. For Buddhists, there may not be anything sacred in the bodies of the dead, but the presence of tourists in the room, gossiping, brings hot bile to my stomach.

I smell the gases leaking out of my pores, sour. Gold Bond medicated powder ringing the necks of the female medical students. Acrid rubbing alcohol clinging to the tips of instruments cutting through flesh. Focus on that!

The dead boy looks like he's asleep. He has waxy, veined eyelids; his lips and skin are blue. A grotesque decomposition eats its way down the side of his head like fancy embroidery. Focus on that.

Maechi Roongdüan is at the front of the room the whole time, wanting to see what is what, sticking her hands inside someone's open chest. She is not just Pranee's mother—she is mine, staring unflinchingly at the exposed flesh of man.

"Look at her," Pranee whispers. "She's not afraid of anything!"

I focus on Pranee's eyes. They glitter with the intensity of a malaria victim, dark and sure.

one abides by the Five, they will not believe us any more than a farmer believes the idea of an invisible virus. So lay society believes in merit and physical rebirth."

This interpretation comes as a complete surprise! I too have interpreted Buddhist concepts literally, believing that *kamma* and reincarnation encouraged sloth. I wonder how many other concepts are too sophisticated to be understood without meditating.

Maechi Roongdüan continues, "The rebirth which concerns us is that of defilements, *kilesa*. The Buddha said that every time we are angry, are greedy, are deluded, we suffer rebirth. That's true. When we are sitting in meditation or noting, we do not suffer from those emotions."

She shrugs, her hands folded in her lap. "Is that not right? We exist as *anatta*, No Self. When we are angry, it suddenly becomes: *I* am angry. He did that to *me*. It infringed on what is *mine*. It is *my* right to feel upset." She smiles and turns over both hands, the left one unfolding from the right like a flower blossoming. "We are born. The 'I' comes into being. When we are meditating, there is no self, there is only *Nibbana*."

I catch my breath at the beauty of her words, and she points to the stream, icy blue from the deep forest waterfall. "Meditation is a drop, a drop, a drop, forming a stream of water."

Ordinary man conceives the four woeful states . . . as outside him, attained after death, as hell, as the realm of beasts, of the hungry ghosts, and the frightened ghosts. But in dhammic language the woeful states are experiences here and now: The hungry ghosts of Dhamma language are purely mental states. Ambition based on craving, worry based on craving—to be afflicted with these is to be born a hungry ghost.

—BHIKKU BUDDHADASA,
The ABCs of Buddhism

I want to know about *kilesa,* the Three Cravings (anger, greed, delusion) and the Four Virtues: *metta* (loving kindness), *karuna* (compassion), *mudita* (sympathetic joy), and *upekkha* (equanimity). How do we work actively on developing the four and rooting out the three?

When I'm meditating, I'm fine, but as soon as I open my eyes, I return to anger, to want. I remember every slight. I am a mass of scar tissue.

*M*y first impression of Thailand is of a country sliding out of control . . . full of violent attachments; dark, ungovernable fears; prowling hordes of *pretas,* or hungry ghosts; compulsively expanding, omnivorous populations governed by increasingly insatiable hates and addictions.

—RUDOLPH WURLITZER,
Hard Travel to Sacred Places

Today we have a special meal—Royal Cuisine from the central region, exotic fruits, and dessert. It must be a major Buddhist holiday or at least *Wan Phra.* I am ravenous. I think I may have stretched out my belly yesterday. Am I regressing?

I remember the hungry ghosts, one of the worst punishments in Buddhist transmigration. An evil person is reborn as a ghost with an immense stomach and a tiny mouth. What a simple, terrible punishment! Hunger alone already makes one a ghost, but to be born as a hungry ghost, doomed to an entire lifetime centered on hunger!

At times I think I must be one, a pot-bellied soul with an inadequate mouth. This maneuvering of rage and sorrow and desire, this certainty of not enough food in the bowl which prevents me from enjoying the food already there, this need to conquer new lands, be the best, win friends and influence people, succeed, this expectation of food, love, movement, happiness. This bottomless need I manage must be the American—not the African—half of me.

Maechi *on the pathway leading to forest entrance.*

ᴕᴈ The Nāga Princess

NĀGAS WERE BELIEVED TO INHABIT AQUATIC PARADISES, NAMELY,
THE DEPTHS OF RIVERS, LAKES, AND OCEANS.... [T]HESE SERPENTLIKE
BEINGS WERE ALSO THE PROTECTORS OF THE SOURCE OF LIFE,
SYMBOLIZED ... BY THEIR SELF-REJUVENATION, ILLUSTRATED IN THE
SHEDDING AND REPLACEMENT OF [SNAKESKIN]. THEY WERE VIEWED
AMBIVALENTLY AS EQUALLY DESTRUCTIVE AND BENEFICIAL.

— *Diana Y. Paul,*
WOMEN IN BUDDHISM: IMAGES OF THE FEMININE
IN THE MAHAYANA TRADITION

WHILE PREPARING FOR my vows, I came across the script for higher ordination in which the ordaining monk, after determining that an applicant is free from deformity and disease, asks ten questions to establish that he or she is free to ordain. The question that most disturbed me was, *Are you a free person, that is, not a slave?* The one that most surprised me was, *Are you a human being?* A few weeks before my ordination, Ajarn Boon and I debated the issues over lunch at a noodle soup stand. To my complaint that women had to obtain the consent of their parents and husbands before ordaining, and that slaves and eunuchs were barred from the Life, he countered with a pragmatic look at social relations in ancient India.

"The real radicalism of these ten questions is in what is *not* asked," he said, leaning forward to lift lid after lid on the tiny village of condiments covering half the table. "Consider—no woman had

I'm covered with bites and chapped spots from the neck up. Despite this, I can't believe what Maechi Roongdüan says, that the body is merely a "skin sack." I love feeling the sun on my body. I love the way that, even in the hottest, most stifling crowds, you can actually *pluck* a faint breeze out of the air if you close your eyes and slow your breathing. I love showers.

THE FOUR
SUBLIME STATES
OF MIND

Seated meditation
usually begins with a
recitation of the
Triple Gem and ends
with the following
chant designed to cul-
tivate the Four Sub-
lime States of Mind:

1. METTA
*(universal love and
goodwill for all living
beings)*

All beings
May they be free of
  enmity
May they be free from
  ill treatment
May they be free from
  troubles of body
  and mind
May they protect
  their own happiness

2. KARUNA
*(compassion for all liv-
ing beings who are suf-
fering)*

All beings
May they be freed
  from *dukkha*

3. MUDITA
*(sympathetic joy for
others' success, welfare,
and happiness)*

to explain *why* she wanted to ordain, *whether* or not she was educated, and *who* or *what* she had been before. From the moment she took the vows, she was as much a *bhikkhuni* as any other."

He went to work with a flat ceramic spoon and pair of chopsticks, lifting and stirring. *"That's* your social transformation!"

I grinned, squirting garlic-chili paste into my broth. It washed up against the islands of noodles like a strain of red algae come to claim the coastline. "So what's with this 'being human' requirement? What's that?"

Sweeping his chopsticks aloft like a conductor's baton, Ajarn Boon airlifted several fish balls out of his bowl and dropped them into mine. He resembled a Thai mother in this, covering the terrain with a barrage of delicacies.

"Oh, that's simple," he said. *Plop, plop.* "In ancient India there once was a *nāga*, a great serpent, who took human form and ordained as a monk. He was a devout practitioner of Buddhism, but one night, as he slept, his true form revealed itself, his great coils spilling out of the *vihara* and nearly smothering the sleeping monks."

"Holy moly!"

He laughed, eyes crinkled shut, like a child giving himself over completely to surprised delight, before revealing that the Buddha had forced the *nāga* to disrobe, sadly explaining that serpents could not be monks. "The Buddha promised, however, that the snake's image would henceforth be placed in Buddhist *wat* in honor of his devotion."

Ajarn Boon added that this is also why during the intermediary stage, after a male postulant has shaved his head but before he has taken his vows, "he is called *Nāga*." The snake that exists in the realm between human and monk.

The next day, over a breakfast of roasted beetles and chili paste, Khun Mae told a different story. According to her, the snake king Mucalinda protected the Buddha from rain for seven days while he was deep in meditation. She held up both hands, the size of an

American child's, one with the fingers spread, the other forming a peace sign: seven.

This accounts for the familiar image of a meditating Buddha seated atop a coiled snake with a cobra's hood behind him. The snake as human protector.

My Buddhist texts claimed that images of *nägas* (Sanskrit for serpent) date back to pre-Buddhist snake-worshiping cults and were later incorporated into Hindu and Buddhist mythology. *Nägas* were semidivine beings, half human and half snake, that could assume either form. They began to appear in Buddhist temples as door guardians, represented as either a hooded cobra with many heads or a human being with a snake tail and a canopy of hoods. In the Mahayana Buddhism practiced to the north, *nägas* are even more present—protecting the Buddha's sacred teachings, their princesses achieving spiritual perfection or falling in love with human males.

Piloting my motor scooter through the forest, past teak houses on stilts, small black pigs tied beneath, I was haunted by the notion of the serpent that wanted to ordain. Why, since he had proven himself, could he not remain a monk?

After my ordination, while studying charts of Buddhist cosmology, I realize that all beings are relegated to a place in the cosmic hierarchy as determined by their *kamma*. Lowest are the beings patrolling the realms of hell; next come the hungry ghosts; then animals. Humans exist on a higher plane, primarily because we can stop the cycle of rebirth through good acts and ordaining in search of enlightenment. At the top, various enlightened beings and gods flicker and glow.

Based on this, a snake is clearly a snake for a reason. As a human, he must have damaged his *kamma* enough to be reborn in a lower form. Now, only once he accrues enough merit to be reborn as human can he aspire to the next step: monkhood. Humans build a reservoir of merit through good deeds, gifts to the *Sangha*, having

All beings
May they not be
  parted from the
fortune obtained by
  them

4. UPEKKHA
*(facing all vicissitudes
of life with equanimity
and calm of mind)*

All beings
Are the owners of
  their *kamma*,
Heirs to their *kamma*,
Born of their *kamma*,
Related to their
  kamma,
Abide *supported* by
  their *kamma*;
Whatever kamma
  they will do,
For good or for evil,
Of that they will be
  the heirs.

I'm a bit worried about mosquitoes. I had forgotten, until I reread my journal from my year as a high school exchange student, how sick I got from them. At one point I had 150 bites on each leg and shook uncontrollably, dropping glasses and pens. At night my legs felt as if they were on fire. The bites, clustered together and ringed in gray and purple, looked like a skin disease. It was years before the scars faded enough for me to wear shorts or a skirt without scaring people.

*B*uddhists cannot slaughter or witness the slaughter of animals; but they can eat animal flesh as long as they are not responsible for the termination of the animal's life. . . . In Thailand and Burma, to be truly virtuous, one should never crack an egg. Shopkeepers routinely evade this restraint by keeping a supply of eggs that have been "accidentally" cracked. Wealthy Buddhists

a son (note: not a daughter) who ordains. I wonder how a snake accrues his.

&&

ONE FRIDAY afternoon when I was five, my mother came home from the California junior high school where she taught, surrounded by parched fields, and announced that she had brought me a surprise.

"A surprise?" I echoed, looking up from my perch on the kitchen counter to see her in the kitchen doorway, cheeks flushed pink from the heat, long chestnut hair clinging to her back. I jumped to the floor. "Where?"

She laughed. "It's in my bag in the living room—" she started as I shot past her, out the doorway.

My mother was famous throughout the neighborhood for her surprises. When we were still poor, living on dried pinto beans and rubbery government-surplus cheese, she wrote storybooks about African girls—warrior-scholars who rescued indecisive princes—and illustrated them with her own watercolor paintings. She dug through fabric store bins for felt scraps to paste to the backs of the *Ebony* magazine models that populated my homemade felt boards.

Once she got a teaching job, my mother's quest for the perfect toy, something that would combine my obsession with miniatures with her obsession with history and culture, began in earnest. She could talk merchants out of anything marked *Not for Sale, Display Only, Factory Model* and routinely climbed off the bus lugging suede tepees, beaded African masks, boy dolls with tiny molded plastic penises.

When necessary my mother revised a hostile world. She sewed African-inspired outfits out of faux-leopard-fur scraps for a village of black dolls. She took Tawny Taupe fingernail polish and black markers to my picture books and paper dolls, darkening the pink faces and pale hair to make them resemble mine. She replaced guns with plastic animals and tiny nets. I was nearly a teenager before I realized that (my black, of course) G.I. Joe was actually a soldier and not *Dr. Mark Luther, Global Adventurer and Official Government Archaeologist*!

The California afternoon of my mother's surprise, I rushed to our living room, a tiny box shrouded by thick, waxy drapes drawn against the hot sun. My mother's bag, a straw beach tote with two big loops for handles, perched in the battered rocking chair between a tower of student folders and a canvas satchel bulging with books. Perhaps the surprise was not a toy at all. Perhaps one of her students had given her a batch of homemade tamales, still steaming in their corn husks, or perhaps she had stopped at the bakery across the street and picked up one of the maple bars the lady at the counter always saved for me.

Years later I would learn that the sunny neighborhood of my childhood was as carefully constructed as the toys my twenty-five-year-old mother repainted for me. Our close-knit, child-filled apartment complex and playground abutted a low-income housing project with a vacant lot. My long-standing love of mud pies was born of necessity, given the scarcity of grass. My bakery saint was a point person, paid fifty cents a week to reserve a doughnut and, more importantly, check for me on my daily walk home from the baby-sitter's. And rather than preparing time-consuming delicacies, my mother's students were more likely to shadow her home, chanting "nigger lover" and pelting her with rocks.

But at five, I knew nothing of this, my attention focused instead on my mother's surprise. Upon reaching the bag, I yanked the two handles apart and thrust my face inside, my nostrils just skimming the snake coiled asleep at the bottom.

Too shocked to scream, I snapped my neck up out of the bag and stumbled back. Mouth pumping open and shut, I must have resembled the goldfish we tried raising, a doomed experiment of tiny gold-and-black shadows (leave it to my mother to find an equal number of black goldfish!) who mouthed mysterious, pleading

ask their servants to break their eggs; the master escapes blame because he didn't do the killing, and the servant escapes blame because he was ordered to do it.

—MARVIN HARRIS,
The Sacred Cow and the Abominable Pig

From five-thirty to seven Maechi Roongdüan tells me more about her amazing pilgrimage with Maechi Vilawam and three others. In the deep tropics of the Malay Peninsula, the villagers work at night stripping rubber trees and sleep during the day, when alms rounds traditionally happen. Since it is forbidden to eat after the sun reaches its zenith, this meant they had to go for days without food. They learned to meditate to overcome hunger pangs.

Often, sitting alone in an empty field, Maechi Roongdüan would come out of meditation to find cobras curled up on either side of her ("coiled like little stupas") or with their heads in her lap, perhaps attracted by her body heat. Maechi Vilawam felt that they were being watched over and protected by all creatures.

I was especially offended by the Thai tradition of buying little containers containing birds, fish, and turtles, then setting them free during special occasions. Through this beneficent act the buyer gains "merit" for his next life. Yet it is obvious that the sale of such animals, captured for just this purpose, is a thriving business in death and torture which contradicts the most fundamental Buddhist beliefs. Most of these animals soon die or are quickly recaptured after their release. One vendor told me that she addicted her birds to

vowels from behind the thick magnification of their bowl before invariably, persistently, turning their shimmery apricot-and-plum bellies to the ceiling.

Betrayal! After a minute of startled silence, I fell to the floor hollering.

"Good God, Faith!" my mother exclaimed, hurrying out of the kitchen. "You'll scare the poor thing to death!"

She dipped a pale dimpled arm inside the bag and it emerged, the snake molded to it like a jade-and-silver bracelet. An avenging mythological goddess, the snake's flat head wavering in midair below hers, my mother turned to me. "Where did you learn this sort of behavior?" she asked, the snake's black forked tongue flickering at me like an accusing echo.

∞

TRUE, I WAS certainly no stranger to animals. After the suicidal goldfish came a stream of metamorphosing tadpoles: tails grew and dropped off, one leg appeared without the apparent need for a partner, an entire evolutionary cycle happened over the course of a single night, with tiny, fully formed frogs crawling out of the primordial ooze of my Woolworth's Tabletop Tadpolium. Soon miniature turtles came to share the yellow plastic island and rest under the ragged shade of its snap-on palm tree.

As my mother and I moved higher up the food chain, with hamburger and the occasional pork chop appearing on our rickety Formica kitchen table, I graduated to mammals. For years I ran an elaborate futuristic city of white mice. Typical of home improvement projects, my red-and-yellow plastic HabiTrail was always in mid-construction, soaking up my allowance with its endless additions of tunnels leading nowhere and exercise wheels. On weekend mornings I took the mice into Mom's bed, and as she read aloud from *On the Banks of Plum Creek,* I would watch them burrow beneath the blankets, little mounds busily creating furrows around our lazy legs.

When we moved to my grandparents' farm and stopped eating meat—this time by choice, Mom measuring out swirls of beans and mesas of rice according to *Diet for a Small Planet*—I would finally get a puppy (black and white, of course), a Real American Pet. One afternoon a few months after his arrival, I returned home from a sleepover to find the puppy, whose eye had started bulging out milky blue, mysteriously replaced by a gang of pampered cats. From then on, our house was dominated by Chelsea, a chubby Siamese who could open the refrigerator and hang from a shelf, tongue darting wildly as my mother came running; Beowulf, a silvery blue who responded to voice commands like a dog; and Boromir, a seemingly spineless mutt with a habit of slipping off the porch roof onto unsuspecting visitors and dragging home baggies of half-mangled Twinkies.

Then there were the animals we were determined to save: the revolving series of stray cats and kittens found in irrigation ditches, on the side of the highway, or, once word got out about the "Cat Lady," on our doorstep that we took to the vet for repairs, taught to trust again, and gave away. The spiders doing battle across the ceiling and weaving mummified flies into corners whose execution my mother stayed by placing her rocking chair directly beneath them. For hours she would rock, reading calmly, the spider spinning and dropping perilously close to her nest of cowlicks, while my grandmother patrolled the perimeter with a broom and dustrag, eyes glinting.

Finally there were the buckets of rose-bellied trout I loved to catch but refused to kill. Each summer my mother relinquished me to my grandparents for camping trips, deer hunts, fishing parties, with the provision that everything we killed would be consumed, necessary! My grandfather was a champion fisherman, and we stood together at the edge of the Pacific as the sun stained the morning sky different shades of pink, reeling in catch after catch of muscular fish almost effortlessly, despite the fact that summer-run

opium so they'd return to her. Now, she bemoaned, opium was too expensive.

—ALAN RABINOWITZ, *Chasing the Dragon's Tail: The Struggle to Save Thailand's Wild Cats*

All I have to medicate the insect bites that dominate the entire lower part of my face is a tiny flat tin of Chinese tiger balm, which burns and burns. My ears are scabbed, which reminds me of the time my kitten was having difficulty weaning. All night long he would suck my earlobes and sigh; in the morning my mother would massage Bag Balm (Old Pappa's cure-all) onto my lobes.

My neck is beaded with welts. And the best benefit of being bald: I have mosquito bites all over my scalp—agonized bumps breaking through the hard stubble of my curls. I've never seen so many stupid, creepy bugs in my life!

I never imagined that the vow not to kill would be so complicated, that we would have to orchestrate our smallest action so as to avoid inadvertently stepping on ants. I mean, we are living in the jungle, for Buddha's sake! Unlike other precepts (for example, not drinking alcohol), not killing calls for constant awareness and an immense sense of personal responsibility.

I'm not a particularly good *maechi,* but I'm not a bad one, either, I don't think. How to be a bad *maechi,* anyway? We don't have the resources and power of monks; we're not preaching, advising, blessing, or running universities, so there's not much potential for abuse (besides killing bugs on the sly).

steelhead always slammed the bait and tore up the river mouth. Meanwhile, on either side of us, fishermen squirmed, switching from casting to spin rods, checking reel capacity, fingering heavier fly lines with sink tips, their faces stretched in grimaces approximating smiles.

Later, when we staggered back to the trailer, each toting a bucket heavy with trout, Old Pappa roared. "All those grown men without a bite watching this bitty girl reel 'em in and trying to be excited for her!" He tossed his plaid hunting jacket into the kitchen nook.

I laughed too, but when Mummi wiped her hands on her denim pedal pushers and reached for my bucket, talking of breakfast, I shrieked, *"no!"* No one was going to kill my fish.

My grandparents looked at each other. After a few moments of speechlessness, Mummi tried to explain. "But, honey, that's the whole point of fishing."

I draped myself over my bucket and sobbed.

They retreated. "Okay," Old Pappa reasoned, "that's fine, but we should throw them back then, so they can live."

I sobbed all the more loudly. I had caught them. I wanted to keep them!

No amount of explaining or pleading would dissuade me, and so the bucket of trout sat outside our camping trailer, the steelhead dimming to gray and moving in increasingly listless circles like the goldfish, until one morning Mummi, pinching her nose with one hand, handed me the bucket with the other: "Go!"

I was not alone in my ambivalence about killing. One summer after a twenty-minute battle, Old Pappa wrestled a hoary catfish off the bottom of the lake and into our canoe. It landed on the bottom of the hull with a sloppy shudder that rocked the boat and, immense and dark as a troll, regarded us balefully.

The neighbor boy David and I scrambled to the stern and gaped. "What's *that?*"

Old Pappa grinned and arched his bushy eyebrows. "Cat," he panted. "Fish!" He drew his handkerchief across his ruddy neck and forehead. "They're good eatin'."

David and I stared at the upturned mouth, the thick reptilian skin, the sweeping catlike whiskers. Good eating? The thing looked like a mutant caught in an evolutionary dispute!

Old Pappa shook his head, peering at the catfish's black skin layered with pond scum. "This one must be years old. Sitting on the bottom of the lake all this time."

The ancient fish lay in the hull a good hour croaking for breath. When time came to head back to shore, it was still living, eyes steady, mouth working fearlessly. Old Pappa's eyes bulged too. "I think we should throw it back," he whispered, and still huddled together in the stern, David and I nodded.

ଚ୍ଚ

MY MOTHER'S snake surprise undulated across the summer-peach flesh of her arm, shifting its fluid body into space, then freezing in mid-shape. My mother clucked softly, apologizing for my behavior. "Really, pun'kin," she said to me, "you're so much bigger. He's just a harmless little garter snake. How can you be scared of him?"

She held out her other arm, and the snake draped itself through the air, wrapping her in its muscular embrace. "Don't you want to meet him?" she asked. "He's very sweet. One of my students rescued him from a squirrel, and I asked if we could keep him over the weekend."

She beckoned, waving a glittering, scale-covered arm. "He knows how to play hide-and-seek."

"Huh?" I shuffled forward, watching my mother's pearly nails stroke the checkerboard pattern of its back. Three light green stripes ran the length of its body, marking a beaded pattern that resembled a bolt of fine fabric cascading to the floor. "Is it slimy?"

"Of course not." She held out a coil. "He feels really neat."

Some Ways for Maechi to "Faster Pussycat, Kill, Kill"

- Not studying the path while walking
- Wearing shoes
- Breathing with mouth open
- Breathing through nose without a veil covering face
- Leaving a glass of water uncovered
- Quick, brushing movements

*T*o imitate someone speaking English, Thai children chant, "snake-snake-fish-fish" in English. Apparently the battery of hard *k*'s and satisfying whoosh of the *sh*'s is what the English language, spoken quickly, sounds like to a Thai.

No matter how often I scrub the toilet, gnats drown in the shallow bowl, tiny black lines ticking off my sins like the days of a prison sentence. It makes sense to say "Don't kill animals" when you live in urban "civilization" and everyone is half-consciously swatting anything that gets in her or his way, but I have to say I get very bored coaxing nineteen ants out of a glass just to be able to take a sip of water, of feeling bugs crawl between my legs just as I am drifting off to sleep, of concentrating on *pain, pain, pain* while yet another creature is sucking my blood—the *very* moment I am trying to cultivate compassion.

In the evening Maechi Roongdüan talks about the importance of developing compassion toward all creatures, especially dangerous ones. I'm thinking, *Why?* Sure, we may free ourselves from crippling fear, but since when do the things we fear need our compassion?

I grinned, feeling foolish in the face of her enthusiasm, and poked a middle section, far from the head with its darting, fissured tongue. The smooth, interlocking weave felt pleasantly cool, the way a water-worn stone fits snugly into the palm, not like a fish's hard, articulated scales.

"See?" My mother nodded, smiling encouragement. "Not slimy. Look," she said, indicating several places where the scales rose up a good half inch, forming miniature anthills. "We think he must have been bitten by the squirrel, poor thing."

My fingers trembled over the rise and descent of the squirrel bite. The snake seemed to smile, its mouth curved upward.

"My student is keeping him until he recovers enough to return to the wild."

We spent the weekend hiding behind our few pieces of furniture as the snake slithered through the jungle of shag carpeting after us, and reading the snake books my mother had brought from the school library. By the time I presented my weekend homework report on Sunday evening, I knew all about the thirteen species of American garter snake, how the females are longer and thicker than the males, how they like to live in parks and other human habitats, how the tongue acts as the nose, how they have no ears (so my shouting couldn't have scared him!). I understood garter snakes' importance to our ecosystem, eating troublesome frogs and mice and fish, keeping away poisonous snakes, and I empathized with their bad rap.

But on Monday morning as my mother uncoiled the snake from around her neck, sighing, and settled him into the bottom of her bag, a thought flickered through my mind as quickly as the appearance and disappearance of that black splintered tongue: Neither my delight in the snake's arrival nor my sadness at its departure equaled hers. I was capable of feeling such outrage on behalf of mistreated animals that I would make myself ill, stomach roiling as I passed scabby dogs at the ends of chains, yet I suspected that it was not the same as feeling true affection.

Perhaps it didn't matter. Perhaps the important thing was that by age five I had internalized my mother's code of behavior. I had a crippling sense of compassion and a yearning for others' self-determination. I set impossibly high standards for others and myself and sometimes even managed to live up to them. So what if I lacked what the Buddhists call *metta,* true love?

For years to come I would champion the scabby dog. As a child I collected signatures, formed volunteer organizations, dragged home worm-eaten kittens, visited nursing homes, steeling myself against the smell. In college I mastered a rhetoric of empowerment and social justice, abandoning—as we know—my classes in favor of teaching English to refugees, theorizing about overseas grassroots development projects, organizing homeless shelters. After graduation I would have a series of low-paying jobs in human services, legalizing undocumented immigrants, mentoring girls, smuggling student activists over the Burmese border, inserting myself as a bridge to racial dialogue, plying students with Hershey's Kisses and sympathy on my own time.

I was despairing of humanity, outraged at middle-class complacency, inspired by my colleagues' commitment, ashamed of my own. I acted and I behaved, always hoping, as the Jewish adage reassures, that by going through the motions, faith would surely follow.

Ever since her encounters with cobras down south, she doesn't fear them. When she accidentally steps on a snake on the path, she says, *"Khaw thôod!"* Excuse *me!*

This conversation makes me nervous. So far every issue she's brought up in my evening lesson has been perfectly timed for use in my meditation practice. *Oh no!* I think. *Please don't tell me about snakes falling off the doorjamb of your guti onto your head!* But of course she does.

Once, while she was still in college but living at Wat Umong as a laywoman, she woke covered in white-winged ants. They swarmed over her, on every inch of ground, the sleeping mat, the pillow, everywhere. Unable to move an inch, she switched off the light and began to meditate, praying they'd leave so she could return to sleep and make it to her morning class in time to take an exam. After a while, she switched the light back on and found that they had all disappeared.

*T*he king cobra greets me as I walk down his path one morning. He looks at me lazily, not bothering to arch his black hood. I squat less than two metres away, watching him smell me with his tongue. . . . He has more compassion than us all. He could rise and kill but he chooses to let me work out my *kamma* for myself. . . . Slowly the long muscular body surges across the trail, gliding like a flowing stream. I wait until the tail is swallowed up in jungle, then raise my hands right up to my forehead in a respectful *wai.*

—TIM WARD,

What the Buddha Never Taught

Maechi Roongdüan says the reason she discourages talking is that we still think like laywomen and would speak without meaning. To illustrate, she holds her hand before her mouth and giggles, just like a Thai schoolgirl (and many an adult woman, for that matter).

"Ahaan aroi," she trills, mocking one of the Thais' primary obsessions: *The food is delicious.* She flutters her eyelashes. *"Phom suay!"* Your hair is beautiful! Snake-snake-fish-fish. She is not without a sense of humor, this powerhouse *maechi.*

When I report, slightly embarrassed, that I can only sit in meditation for an hour at a time, she says, "Already?" She looks impressed, which both surprises and worries me. What will she come up with next?

She compares training the mind through meditation to the desire to catch a fish: "We wade into the paddy up to our calves in mud and search. At last we grasp what seems to be a fish, but upon withdrawing our hand, we realize instead that it is a snake. What to do with it? Barehanded, we cannot kill the snake; stuck in the water, we cannot fling it away for fear that it will twist back and strike. So we whirl it around and around above our head until it is tired, then fling it away and run in the opposite direction."

Snake. Fish.

"Two Buddhas Ayutthaya, 1993" by Marcia Lippman.

CHAPTER FIFTEEN

⍩ Lessons in Lying and Killing for the Black Buddhist Nun

ONE EVENING IN the *wat* I fall asleep meditating. I wake at nine-thirty, completely disoriented. My *guti* is dark, my contacts are welded to dry eyes, and my bladder groans. Groggy and half blind, I stagger outside to the bathroom.

Climbing onto the cement block and placing my feet on the grooved footpads beside the basin, I notice the scattering of black lines in the toilet bowl. I groan. More dead gnats! Day after day I clap my palms together over the bowl, careful not to disturb the other *maechi;* I scoop water from a bucket and dribble mini-water-falls of warning, begging the gnats to fly away so that I can pee without committing a sin; I hop from leg to leg, mouthing a prayer of increasing intensity: "Hurry up, hurry up, fly away!" These gnats that have chosen my toilet are my responsibility, my constant, inadvertent sin.

Since they're dead already, I suppose it's all right. I wrestle my sarong up over my hips and squat down. Afterwards, I step off the dais and reach for the plastic bowl to ladle water into the basin to flush.

As I bend toward the plastic bucket, I hear a *whoosh!* Spinning around, I see a rat, its torso nearly eight inches long, fly out of the toilet bowl, exactly where I'd been squatting only seconds before. My groin contracts; the bowl clatters to the floor. A strangled cry escapes my throat.

The rat, propelling itself out of the narrow mouth of the toilet,

..

After Maechi Roongdüan's lesson on developing compassion toward dangerous animals, I go inside my *guti*, open the door, flick on the light, and there, lo and behold, as I had expected (though, damn, not quite *this* soon!), is my test:

..

A huge spider, glossy black, some four inches in diameter, hangs on the wall above my sleeping mat. I sink to the floor and try to calm the panic rising within me. Mentally I fumble for my cheat sheet, the Buddhist answers to get me out of this moment. Awareness! I try to think about what exactly a spider is, break it down into its components.

Contemplation. I focus on the shiny black ball of a body and eight hairy, jointed legs. I consider how irrational my fear is. I breathe.

The spider remains. Ugly, mythic. Scotty, beam me the hell up! I want to run screaming into the night. Not possible. I want to cry, sinking with the realization that from now on we might be roommates. Possible (though not recommended).

When I feel a bit calmer, I close my eyes and try to meditate. I manage a few ragged breaths, a reluctant slowing of the heart, but spend most of my energy fighting the urge to pop open my eyes (*boing*!) and keep tabs on my visitor.

Almost immediately I hear a loud thumping and look up to see the planks of the *guti* wall that connects to the bathroom contracting in and out, one after the other, as if a heavy steel ball were being rolled across the inner bathroom

flies in a liquid, glistening arc toward the door it no doubt expects to find open and the great outdoors beyond. Instead the door is shut. With a great *thwap!* it hits the wood full force and goes berserk.

Squealing, the animal flings itself around the tiny bathroom, twisting up, down, and around. Each time it meets resistance and ricochets faster off the walls, the ceiling, the floor. *Zoom, zoom, zoom!* It flails and shrieks, scattering its foul trail, bared teeth slicing within inches of my hair, my face, my throat, my breasts, my belly, my buttocks, my calves, my ankles.

Still crouched over the bucket, I am paralyzed in the midst of the rat's crazed trajectory, a museum thief caught in a high-tech laser web, Roongdüan in the midst of flying ants, the bare-handed fisherman knee-high in mud. Even if I had the presence of mind to move out of the way, I would have no idea where to go. The rabid rat is moving so quickly, it's everywhere. I hear the crunch of rat muscle and bone against the stone walls, tin ceiling, wooden door.

Somewhere in the recesses of my mind, I know that I can't scream, that *maechi* who've taken vows of silence don't go hollering and running about half naked due to small animals. It takes all my concentration to control this novice body in its stiff white sarong that has chosen this of all moments to begin undoing itself. As my skirt slides down my trembling legs, my heart rises so high in my throat it nearly chokes me. I feel a furry whirr against my knees and the bucket flips over, leaking water onto the cement floor. Liquid dribbles warm along my inner thigh.

Finally the rat finds the drainage hole in the corner and squeezes through, scurrying into the black forest. Throwing open the wooden door, I tear down the stone walkway, running off this need to scream, running toward safety and the open bedroom door at the end of the hallway, running away from the sleeping snake in my mother's bag, the tired snake in my bare hand.

My mind whirls with information, namely, that the rat lives in my toilet, in my private little septic tank, that the black lines I've been cleaning every day are not dead gnats at all but in fact rat excrement, that every time I squat down Asian-style over the toilet there is the very real possibility this typhoid torpedo will come flying up—*whoosh!*—with such force. . . .

I'm several yards down the path in the direction of the deep forest when a worse thought bursts, sharp and clear, through the half-formed jumble crowding my brain: *Snakes!* Here I'm running from a solitary rat, headed straight into the night jungle! I imagine a nest of king cobras, coiled in muscular anticipation, just inches from my bare feet. I can practically see them rise up and tremble, their shadowy hoods flared, hear them spit and hiss.

"Gack—!" I pivot and head back toward my *guti,* sprinting up the steps and dragging the door shut tight behind. My hands flutter at the end of my arms until my entire body is shaking like one of those tourist junkies wandered down from the heroin hills. Is it possible to have a heart attack from swallowing screams?

I pray for no more "opportunities," as Maechi Roongdüan would put it, to overcome my own fears while developing compassion for all living creatures. No more glittering monitor lizards, their razored claws prying loose the wooden planks of my hut, no more glossy, fist-sized spiders clinging to the wall above my sleeping mat, no more packs of cave rats swarming over statues of the Buddha as I try to meditate. Tonight I have no interest in meeting the challenge of Buddhist practice!

ᘒᘒ

OVER THE NEXT few days I have even more time to think than usual, since I'm certainly not urinating, not once. It occurs to me that the first precept of Buddhist ordination—to refrain from harming any living creature—was also the first law of our household. Whereas lying, the fourth Buddhist precept, seemed to be my mother's particular pet peeve (more on this later), harming another creature was the only act that earned actual physical punishment.

wall. The wood creaks and flares.

Already close to hysteria, I jump up, grab the flashlight, and head outside. Reaching the bathroom in a few short steps, I throw open the door, flick on the torch, and stop short.

There, clinging to the wall above my head, is a muscular monitor lizard, its body a full foot long and some three inches thick. Squat bowed legs center its weight; claws dig deep into the wooden planks. Chain-mail scales shimmer blue in the circle of light from the flashlight.

In a single fluid motion, its flat snake's head swivels a smooth 180 degrees toward me, the slit eyes rotating, focusing, locking on me, unblinking.

I stumble back and switch off the flashlight. The Thai call monitors *thú-gàe,* the first syllable a rising tone followed by a fall to a guttural groan, an imitation of the resonant, prehistoric rumble of their belly call.

I hear my breath in the damp bathroom—short, wet, like a dripping faucet. My hands shake as if I were sixteen again, feverish from three hundred shots of mosquito venom in my veins.

Just like here in the *wat,* where I must monitor and plan my every act, from breathing with a veil over my orifices to standing without rocking in order not to harm the world of insects, even accidentally, my mother's rules of engagement were complicated. As with Buddhism, lack of intention or awareness was no excuse. As soon as I reached what my mother referred to as "a reasoning age"—too old for corporal punishment—I was expected to live an *actively* moral life.

I walk in meditation, eyes on the path before me, not thinking of urinating despite the rain, and come to a stop before a rain-bloated worm. Immediately I remember one of my first visits to moist Oregon, where Great-aunt Ines handed me a shaker of salt and directed me toward the mossy path mottled with slow-moving slugs. I soon discovered to my delight that the spotted blobs dissolved beneath a shower of salt (foaming and shriveling into phosphorescent ooze!). When my mother discovered me on the path, I was expected to know that what I was doing was horribly cruel. Awareness!

And I had known (to be honest), or at least suspected, but had pushed this knowing to the back of my mind, letting my fascination with color, transformation, danger, take precedence, temporarily absolving myself from awareness and responsibility. I was the classic cheater who cries he never intended to hurt anyone (least of all you, baby!). My blindness was temporary, a refusal to align action and intention, cause and effect. (Where did I imagine the slugs had gone, after all?)

Sufficiently guilt-ridden once the killing was complete, the community of benign creatures reduced to smears of paint, I got myself off on a technicality, the fact that I'd been obeying an adult (what a respectful child!). The command? Kill!

Listening to the yip-yap of the monks' dogs, I step over the worm, saying a quick prayer for the neon detritus I'd caused years before. I have limited time for repentance at present. Here comes Dreaded Anger, my old enemy and friend, stomping down the path toward me. She stops on the path, just out of reach, steaming in the cool forest air and smiling, daring me to make the connection between her and the sins of lying and killing. She knows I hate to look her in the face.

When it came to the rules governing my mother's precept against lying, sins of omission ranked equally with those of commission. The rules were complex equations: Not Volunteering the Truth = Lying! And yet, Lying to Cover Up would theoretically get me in Far More Trouble than admitting to my transgressions (usually chores left undone or smart-ass comments) while I had the chance. Speak now, speak now!

In practice, however, everything carried the same punishment. The memory floods back during the in-breath, startling me with its hot intensity. First came a period of icy silence during which my mother worked herself into a lather. Next: Forceful steps reverberated down the hallway and Mom burst into my room, a Batman comic-style balloon over her head: BLAM! Red-faced, she lobbed psychologically intricate recriminations at me as I ducked and parried, throwing up my golden bracelets, Wonder Woman-style.

I come to a standstill on the rough cement path. Unwelcome anger overtakes me. "I didn't expect you to be this impossible and irrational until you reached adolescence!" was a favorite charge of my mother's in the years preceding puberty, as if sheer will could shame hormones into making a detour and bypassing our house entirely. My role was a simple equation: Listening + Tearful Apology + Promises to Reform. Oh, how I seethed.

I resume my steps—heel up, swinging, arcing—a bit more surefooted now. The arrival of the oft-maligned puberty came as an immense relief. I took full advantage of my terrific monster status, frequently getting in the first strike (POW!) with withering sarcasm, and then refusing to allow the unannounced room invasions that ruined my entire day, leaving me furious yet terrified that my remaining parent would abandon me.

I try to focus. I can only think about the lizard's weight as it moves across the wall. The thing is cold-blooded muscle and teeth, cousin to the dinosaur.

I think about nearby Komodo in the Indonesian archipelago, where ten-foot-long monitor lizards rule an island of exiles. Travelers say they can outrun any creature on the island, claw their way up skinny *lontar* palms to snatch monkeys from the branches, submerge themselves underwater for thirty minutes at a time, then spring up, surprising a deer come to drink, gulping down its entire hindquarters as it turns to run.

The islanders, outcasts expelled from other islands, kill goats and carry them rotting into the barren hills to leave as a sacrifice; otherwise hungry Komodo dragons have been said to venture down into the settlement and carry off human babies.

The Thai say that *thú-gàe* lock their jaws during attack and nothing short of burning them off will loosen their grip. Oh God, I'm in a Buddhist temple! I can just see myself—victim of the first precept not to kill—with the damn thing latched to my forehead for the rest of my life!

I take a deep breath and two quavering steps forward, hoping to get the lizard used to me. Immediately the tail shoots up, an eight-inch exclamation point. I stop breathing. The air thickens between us. Is this a warning, a prelude to attack? How to interpret the actions of a reptile? How to anticipate them? Will a monitor attack out of pure malice, or only if provoked? What constitutes provocation? Can I assume that a temple-dwelling reptile is concerned with the acquisition of merit?

I breathe heavily, taking care to hold the veil over my nose and parted lips. I don't need to add murder to my list of defilements right now. Repelled by the All-Powerful Privacy Force Field, my mother stayed out of my room but was unable to silence her Great and Terrible Wrath. Steam emitted from ears; the sound of a boiling teakettle or factory whistled offstage. From my safe vantage point in the Thai forest, I imagine the creature in her lair laboring furiously over a strange black metal contraption. And so began the practice of typed treatises being shoved under my bedroom door. Rage clots my blood.

Eventually I realized that I could save myself a great deal of agony by simply not reading these angry lists (voilà)! I would wait a respectable amount of time, twenty to fifty-five minutes (if I waited too long she would invade anyway, enraged anew that I hadn't responded to her first set of charges), then take a deep breath and head down the hall to offer a blanket apology for whatever I had done/had not done/was thinking of doing eventually.

&

ANGER WATCHES me with interest as I piece the puzzle together, the possible origin of the great and puzzling anger shimmering always beneath my surface. Hoping to avoid her, I head up to the caves, marveling once again at their mediocrity and the misnomer, Temple of Golden Caves. I settle onto the reed mats covering the hard stone floor and squint at the gilt Buddha figures. I've always been a sucker for gold. When I was four, just learning the precepts of omission and commission, I committed my most serious crime to date, smashing the gold-and-glass locket that was my mother's finest possession.

My Finnish great-uncle had returned from Alaska with two identical lockets, one for each of his sisters. Beyond its sentimental and financial value, the locket my mother inherited looked stunning. Suspended from a heavy antique chain, delicate scrolling gold flourishes encased a double-sided wafer of glass the size of a quarter. Fat chunks of gold my great-uncle had panned himself rounded the belly of glass.

It was these jagged, glittering pieces, gently magnified by the concave swell, that caught my four-year-old eye, eventually tempting me to filch my mother's property and pick up the hammer, despite recognizing both gestures as morally wrong, not to mention clearly inviting disaster.

The afternoon I flattened my mother's locket she was camped out as usual on the living room sofa with a book. Saucer-eyed, I took a fugitive's inventory of my options. There was no hiding the deed: the glass wafer shattered, the gold dust scattered into the carpet, the scrollwork bent askew. Clearly, if ever there were a time to test my mother's much advertised policy that coming clean was better than lying, this was it!

Emerging from my bedroom at top speed, I tore down the hallway to the living room. There I did a furious lap around my mother where she sat on the couch.

She looked up and blinked.

On my second turn, I headed back down the hall. At the last minute, I half turned and lobbed the locket's remains into her lap with a flick of the wrist as if skipping a stone over the surface of a lake.

Startled, she grunted, then glanced down.

Speeding up, I continued my sprint down the hallway toward the safety of my open bedroom door. She was just beginning to bellow "FAITH!" when the door slammed shut behind me.

Though my mother credited my coming forward (of sorts) as the reason for my relatively light punishment, I myself always thanked the time it took her to make it off the sofa and down the hall, as well as the unintentional hilarity of my performance. Now, watched by the row of silent golden Buddhas, I wonder about the true lesson learned: though intentionally harming a creature was

After a few minutes more, I concede defeat. I have no idea what to do, and the monitor is giving no clues. I slide by the mass of blue steel, its tail still aloft, and return to my *guti,* thoroughly disheartened.

I often find myself wondering why we have to be braver than other women. Isn't it enough that we're different?

I stopped counting the gibbons and macaques I saw chained by the neck at Buddhist temples. Monks accepted such gifts freely from the people, sometimes believing they were doing the animal a service by caring for it. Often, however, the monks knew the value of such animals. . . . Sometimes the abbot . . . requested certain species of animals because they brought in tourists and increased . . . donations. Many temples had little zoos. . . . Then there were the buckets of frogs in the marketplace. I watched as women skinned them alive, then severed the legs from their bodies to sell. With eyes bulging, the still living naked torso was thrown into a pail to be discarded. "Why don't you kill the frogs before you dismember them?" I asked repeatedly. "It is not right for Buddhists to kill," I was told.

—ALAN RABINOWITZ,

Chasing the Dragon's Tail: The Struggle to Save Thailand's Wild Cats

my mother's most stringent prohibition, the reality was that lying—in particular lying to cover up incidental bad behavior—was to be the focus of my moral upbringing. If that's true, had I been left with the nagging dread that lying is nearly tantamount to murder?

ᚘ

DURING MEALTIME the next day I make a note to myself: *Problems faced by left-handed maechi: The over-robe doesn't allow the left arm to raise above waist level, which makes eating difficult.* I have to smile; from the smallest detail, I have been raised always to swim upstream. As a child, I learned that most of us lie out of weakness, to protect ourselves from discomfort. Not our family. "Tell the truth," my mother exhorted me. "Always dare to tell the truth."

And when the truth proved unpopular, as it invariably did, she was there to back me up. She wore a pathway between our house and Chief Kamiakin Elementary and Lincoln Middle Schools. She was forever battling principals intent on punishing me for pointing out the favoritism of teachers, forever reducing Campfire Girl troop leaders to tears for trying to circumvent policies I knew were in the official Campfire Girl Handbook. Oh, how they quaked to see us coming, my ebony curls and her chestnut cowlicks waving!

How odd, then, that ordained life terrifies, that the bravery required to maintain such honesty with oneself, not to raise one's hand with the urge to destroy a wild creature, is so daunting. Or perhaps I, telling myself the specks on the path aren't ants, chanting my little prayers to ward off snakes, have been a fraud all along. After all, at some point, despite my mother's best intentions, I learned both to lie and to kill.

When I was six, we left California and moved to my grandparents' farm at the foot of the Rattlesnake Hills. There, in the semi-desert of southeastern Washington State, Mummi waged a grim daily battle against invading insects and dust. I was always pulling back my covers, ready to spring into bed, to find a spider, hairy and angular, in the middle of my white sheets. Each time I screamed, indignant and aggrieved.

My mother would point out that it was only a house spider, not that big. "Aren't you glad it eats mosquitoes and flies?"

No, I wasn't glad! I envisioned knocking aside her rocking chair while she was at school and stomping on her latest ward. Who was she kidding? They were on death row. I wouldn't even scrape the cracked body and green pulp off the bottom of my shoes.

"Kill it!" I shrieked, pointing an unwavering finger at the intruder in my bed. My grandmother's child.

ꙮ

BUT IF I am completely honest with myself—and not just with the world outside the *wat,* which is easier—then I must admit that it was lying that proved to be my natural talent. I couldn't prevaricate about small things, daily matters, chump change. I meticulously reported the correct price of unmarked grocery items and raised my hand to admit sneaking off campus for lunch. Stupid things like the school principal putting me in charge of collecting money at assemblies are still a source of pride. "Faith," he announced to my mother, clearly pleased by his own administrative savvy, "has principles! Even if her best friend asked her to cheat, she wouldn't do it!"

But oddly, it was the big stuff where I, the great moral compass of Chief Kamiakin Elementary, felt no compulsion to honesty. I lied about my family background, life experiences where I wanted the authority to speak. After all, I had stared so intently at the television screen during that nature documentary on snakes and been so mesmerized by the mutant two-headed one, its dominant head dragging the minor one around like a spaced-out Hindu deity, that after a time I began to feel I had seen the snake for real. I had been watching; I had admitted its existence; I had felt an affinity: perhaps I did indeed see it! Certainly I see and hear all sorts of things around

The Rain Retreats
..

The Rain Retreats (also known as Phansa, Vassa, or Buddhist Lent) last three months, during which monks and *maechi* are not allowed to sleep outside their "home" temple. Traditionally, the *Sangha* and laity use this time to focus on more rigorous practice. This is the time most men and boys would ordain temporarily.

In Phansa monks change to sienna-colored robes and hunker down to wait out the rains. We're still in white. No one can leave the *wat.* The *maechi* explain that travel is restricted during Phansa because so many creatures emerge during the rains, it would be virtually impossible to move and not to kill a living being.

According to my Buddhist history book, however, long before Buddhism's spread, wandering mendicants gathered together at rain retreats during July to September, primarily because the rains made it difficult to travel. After the Buddha's extinction, his followers continued to wander during the year, then rejoin each other for the rains. A few centuries later, the *Sangha* had developed into two distinct strains: those who continued to wander all year long, and those who had permanently settled into monasteries. Wat Thamtong's population swells with the stream.

During the cold and hot seasons, Thamtong held a restrained, cool beauty. Now, during the monsoon rains, it is warmer, lusher, greener. I thought it was breathtaking before, but now it is possibly even more so: glowing, tangled greenery, birds and bugs buzzing and vibrating at the edges of my consciousness.

the world while sitting in meditation within the confines of my *guti*. Are they not true experiences? Do they not exist?

My pre- and post-*wat* lies were as carefully crafted as the first line of a story, their aim to reveal a greater truth than I believed mere facts allowed. My reality, as I justified it, was More Real, that is, closer to the truth. And a better reality was what I was after, if it took colorizing books and paper dolls, as my mother had done, to create a brown world for me, or lying to get there. Sitting in my *guti* trying not to see my spider roommate, I wonder, if the world is illusion, and memory is so subjective anyway, then how do we determine truth?

৩ৎ

WHEN I move into the forest in northern Thailand, shaving my head and eyebrows, donning white robes, and ordaining as *maechi,* I agree to live by ten precepts.

When I leave the *wat*, I will become a devout laywoman, meaning that I will exchange my *maechi* vows for the five basic precepts to which Buddhist citizens are supposed to adhere: to refrain from killing; stealing; sexual offense; lying and harmful speech; and consuming intoxicants. Even as I take the five Householder Precepts, new stubble chafing my neck, I will recognize the lie. The vows are simply a gesture, a transitional measure to reduce my anxiety at leaving ordained life. I know that for me there is no Middle Path. I am either ordained or not. A Buddhist in Asia or not. Of the spirit or of the body.

Like any tourist come to deal in flesh, I will justify my decision easily, co-opting phrases from the mouths of sex tourists: "Sin does not exist in Buddhism." I will tell myself that, since the purpose of the precepts is only to enhance the practice of mindfulness, there is no reason for me not to return to who I used to be. No reason not to drink alcohol or have sex. No reason not to shade the truth toward a larger reality. There will be no easy way, however, to justify killing.

In the decade since leaving the *wat*, I have wondered about my ragged determination not to break this first precept. I certainly don't adhere to the letter of the law a quarter as closely as I do in the *wat*—I wear shoes and drive a car, committing virtual genocide against our highway's flies and gnats; I prepare meat and wear leather (both quite well, I might add); I breathe often and with impunity—but I do not raise my hand with the intention to kill. This does not make me feel virtuous; it is in fact entirely aggravating. However, it does help to stave off some feelings of dread at the thought of destroying life.

And so, ironically, the precept that proves the hardest to keep during my tenure as *maechi,* requiring an eagle eye and a light tread on the path, a series of makeshift contraptions to keep bugs away from candles, strategies for urinating and breathing, is the only one I keep. Okay, so there was little opportunity to break the others. What was I going to steal—a fourth sarong? And though all monastic traditions have their share of sexual transgressors, sex wasn't an issue for the short length of my ordination. And to whom could I lie? About what? Was I going to brag to other *maechi* around the watercooler that I'd achieved enlightenment and was levitating in my hut? As for intoxicants, we weren't exactly brewing moonshine in the *sala*. I did, however, have, as they say, both motive and opportunity to kill.

Is this, then, why the first precept is the only one I try to keep to this day? Not because it most directly impacts the welfare of another, but because it directly impacts me, presenting a constant challenge? Reminding me of what is possible, more than a decade out of the temple, out of my mother's house.

Apparently I'll never pee again. I eat; I drink; nothing leaves.

The spider and monitor lizard have finally tired of my *guti* and departed without killing me.

Ever since the Rat Incident, I've been even stricter about my routine. I don't use the bathroom when it's dark (and since it's dark nearly twelve hours of the day—from seven at night until six-thirty in the morning—that means I really have to plan). No liquids after four in the afternoon. No trips to the toilet after eight at night. And of course, I'm still trying to pee standing up. Ah, this woman's body.

A warm rain drips steadily over the *wat* all morning, all afternoon, all evening, all night. The villagers who tramp along the pathways en route to the forest wear shower caps or plastic baggies on their heads.

Every morning I steel myself to walk mindfully through the rain in bare feet, watching carefully for upward-driven earth dwellers, and every morning it stops raining just before mealtime. The rain holds during the chanting, the serving, the blessing, the eating, the cleanup, the walk back. I close my *guti* door and, drip, drip, drip, warm rain grows the streams.

The monsoons bring insects. A huge praying mantis like something out of science fiction, spiders the size of my fist, wriggling bug larvae that dive-bomb my candle and writhe on the mat in silent agony, still smoking. I erect a makeshift candle cover from an empty saline bottle to protect them from accidental suicide.

I sit in meditation with my door open to the night, my *guti* lit by a single candle. Maechi Roongdüan comes to the opening, her face aglow in the whispering light of her own candle. "Go back to meditating," she murmurs in Thai. "I brought you juice. Do you have enough candles? Any problems?"

She beams confidence in me, so I don't tell her that I've been crying. That I'm so very, very lonely. That I finally opened my eyes while meditating in the cave and discovered that the soft noises I've been hearing and the air current I've been feeling swirl through the darkness, imagining it was a ghost, are in fact rats. As soon as the sun goes down, they emerge in packs from the recesses of the cave. I opened my eyes to see them chattering and swarming over the figure of the Buddha, curved eyes downcast in a golden, smiling face.

"No problems, right?" Maechi Roongdüan prompts.

Right. I am filled with love.

I finally feel like *maechi* and not someone pretending to move slowly, just dog-paddling in the air to kill time. When a breeze blows the white gauze at the *guti* door back and I catch a glimpse of another *maechi,* a silent figure in white, I am reminded of something mysterious, not quite human or ordinary. I feel light, indistinct, something people can't quite look at or see. The *Näga*!

On the steps of Wat Phra Singh with
Thai host family after ordination.

CHAPTER SIXTEEN

⊗ Open Doors

FROM THE MOMENT OF ENTERING THE *SANGHA* TO THE TIME OF
LEAVING IT, THE INDIVIDUAL ACTS AND IS TREATED IN A MANNER
APPROPRIATE TO THAT STATUS.

    —*Thomas Kirsch,*
       "BUDDHISM, SEX ROLES AND THE THAI ECONOMY"

THE MONASTERIES ARE ALWAYS OPEN TO ANYONE WHO WANTS
TO RETIRE THERE, EITHER PERMANENTLY OR TEMPORARILY.

    —*Phra Rajavaramuni,*
       THAI BUDDHISM IN THE BUDDHIST WORLD

IN MIDMORNING Maechi Roongdüan presents herself before my *guti* and announces that she wants me to visit her family with her. "One of our visitors has offered to take us," she explains, eyes twinkling, her smile almost shy. "Will you go?"

Speechless at the honor, I nod.

The drive feels almost sinful (to ride!). I focus on the gentle rocking of the truck in the sun until before I know it we are pulling into a middle-class neighborhood, the rice fields replaced by palm-lined streets and large compounds. It's Dr. Seuss land—smooth walls painted mint, strawberry, and butterscotch surround two- and three-story stucco bungalows of whimsical geometry. Pastel balconies drip with bowers of night-blooming jasmine. Somewhere a macaw squawks.

We climb down and thank the driver, a series of bows and *wai*

The observer has a lot of sympathy and love for the people around him, but he no longer permits himself to become entangled in their feelings and destinies.

—AYYA KHEMA,
I Give You My Life: The Autobiography of a Western Buddhist Nun

*I*t is very interesting and important to note that [in the Middle Path] thoughts of selfless detachment, love and non-violence are grouped on the side of wisdom.

—WALPOLA RAHULA,
What the Buddha Taught

I feel as if I'm finally mastering seated meditation. Now I have absolutely no pain at all, and my breathing is natural. My consciousness exists *inside* the abdomen and *underneath* the buttocks and knees. Instead of visualizing these points in my mind, my consciousness actually travels. It's as if I *were* the floor at the point it meets my body.

Suddenly everything moves off to the left, as if my consciousness that was in the abdomen moved to the corner of my left eye. As if a life-support system were taking care of life for me, breathing over on my left.

until we are safely through the intricately scrolled metal gate. The compound is gorgeous—a velvety carpet of grass sculpted around carefully placed roses, lemon and orange trees, pots of spotted orchids, shrubs of yellow and pink frangipani, bushes of hibiscus with giant ruffled lavender blossoms. Carved wooden patio furniture overlooks a fishpond strewn with pink lotus.

Maechi Roongdüan's parents and grandmother and brother emerge from behind sliding glass doors, laughing and exclaiming their way across the grass. They are like any other Thai family welcoming guests to their home—gracious, smiling, thrilled the *farang* can speak Thai. The only difference is all the *wai*-ing. Facing each other, we bow our way through the courtyard, stopping within feet of the house.

"Where will *maechi* drink water?" Maechi Roongdüan's mother inquires.

Maechi Roongdüan turns to regard me. "Outside," she suggests in English, "don't you think?"

I nod. She turns back to her mother. "We'll *düüm naam* outside, Khun Mae." Her brother whips out a handkerchief and begins polishing the patio furniture.

Maechi Roongdüan's mother serves us herself, not calling a maid or younger female relative to do it, before retreating inside with the others, their round pale faces bobbing before us. We sit in the shade, the silver tray of chilled sodas (as "drinking water" refers to any beverage) and beveled glasses forgotten, gnawing on ripe mango. The meat melts on my tongue; the golden juice dribbles down my chin.

"Though I loved spending afternoons in my father's study, I loved this garden more," Maechi Roongdüan says. "I would play here for hours. I once fell out of that tree there when climbing after bananas." She gestures at a fringed banana palm. "The fruit was still in my hand when I hit the ground."

We laugh, and she reminisces about her childhood—small, sunny tales. It is a world I recognize from my own upbringing— books on the shelves, fruit in the trees, family plump with love. The rest of the world forever disappoints.

I imagine that she has re-created her childhood at Wat Thamtong, with the loving community of *maechi* she has assembled and a garden so large we live in it.

"No," she corrects me, shaking her head. "We could live happily together forever, yes, but then destroying desires would be a slower process." She tosses the hairy mango pit into the red dirt at our feet, as if it were the rejected social experiment. "That is why we live scattered throughout the *wat*."

I wipe my musky beard of juice and suck my fingers, marveling at how she never once loses sight of the long-term picture. She is not looking to retreat from the world or to grow sluggish in the comfort of this forest sisterhood. Figuring this is the ideal opportunity to put my research question to her, I say, "Maechi, what is your goal for the Life?"

Unlike other *maechi* I've interviewed over the course of the year, who, after thinking a minute, say they want to practice well, develop discipline, find a little peace, learn the truth, improve their health, serve others, she responds immediately and concisely: *"Nibbana!"* *Nirvana!*

Her eyes get that joyful gleam that makes me want to follow her anywhere, and she repeats, "Even when I wash dishes, I do it with mindfulness, for *Nibbana!*"

My mango pit drops next to hers, rolling into a red, tentacled ball. I've never met anyone who believes that Nirvana is actually attainable—at least not in a single lifetime. *Not since the time of the Buddha,* the Thai mourn. At most, the devout hope to be reborn as a higher being with a better chance of reaching enlightenment the next time around.

When I "open" my eyes within the closed lids (that is, roll them up—I usually start out squeezing them tight or rolling them down), a pinkish haze hovers there for a while, then dissolves into darkness.

There are no articles of faith in Buddhism. In fact there is no "sin" in Buddhism, as sin is understood in some religions. The root of all evil is ignorance and false views.

—WALPOLA RAHULA, *What the Buddha Taught*

While doing walking meditation, I realize that no one can make me upset. I am *my own* (inasmuch as we own anything, ourselves included). Discomfort is nothing. Pain comes and goes quickly—legs that quiver and spasm for thirty minutes. At the time, all I can think about is release from suffering, and yet a mere two minutes later it's as if the pain never occurred.

Maechi Roongdüan warns me that if I leave my body or feel light during meditation, I should note it, as well as the accompanying sensation of pleasure, so that I will strive for such states and develop an innate dislike of "the heavy life." She explains, "If you take a big mud and put it in a glass of water, it makes a bad one." This statement serves to convince me that not all Buddhist analogies sound wise and deep—at least not in translation.

*I*t is not, I believe, that the [meditation] master loves no one, but rather that he is not clinging to anyone or to anything. He is deep in a state of detachment or non-attachment to self-interest; he is in a state of pure beholding which is not only compatible with, but necessary for, the highest love. . . . [T]he contemplative has equal love for everyone.

—WILLIAM JOHNSTON, *Silent Music: The Science of Meditation*

"This is what sets Thamtong *maechi* apart from others. When they do their chores they confront a fixed destiny," Maechi Roongdüan declares, regarding the mango. "Their goals are *Nibbana*, nothing less."

☙

THE FOLLOWING week, returning from scrubbing my laundry in the stream, I find Maechi Roongdüan waiting on the path outside my *guti*. She says quite casually, "Faith, you have two visitors waiting in the *sala*."

I stare at her, the words not quite registering, and she repeats her announcement.

After a few seconds, my heart gives a little spurt, and I turn down the path to the *sala* lickety-split. Who could it be? Has Scott broken the rules and come, bursting with gossip?

Hearing Maechi Roongdüan calling me, I turn.

"Put away your bucket and shoes," she reminds me with a smile.

I glance down to see the blue of my rubber bath sandals crisscrossing my feet, laundry in the bucket dangling from my fist. Sheepish, I return to set my laundry inside the *guti* and kick my sandals onto the step.

My eagerness is understandable, I console myself as I hit the path again. After all, she said that they were waiting—and I don't like to keep anyone waiting!

My mind switches gears. Perhaps there's been an emergency back home. Scott offered to send photographs of my ordination to my mom and take over the job of writing to her. Is she sending a message through him?

"Maechi Faith," Maechi Roongdüan calls me a second time. "You must put on your over-robe to receive visitors, and you are walking too quickly. Be mindful."

Aargh! This is becoming the longest Hundred-Yard Creep in history!

I creep inside (in my mind stomping defiantly) and wrestle with the over-robe for a good five minutes. I've finally got the right breast strapped down when it occurs to me that I should take pride in appearing to be a proper *maechi*. Isn't that one of my goals (being proper, that is, not pride), after all?

Somewhat chastened, I wrap up the left breast, flip back the robe, and extend my left arm, palm up like the Buddha. I leave for the third time, trying to walk as slowly as possible.

In the red-roofed *sala* sit Ajarn Supatra and her husband and daughter, looking dwarfed and strangely modern against the lush greenery and silvery mountain face. I am both disappointed and delighted to find that they are the visitors.

When I join them, Ajarn Supatra jumps up and presses her hands together. *"Maechi,"* she addresses me over her *wai*.

I return her *wai*, feeling ridiculous at the sight of my high school counselor bowing before me. *"Ajarn."*

Her husband, on the other hand, simply nods, looking ill at ease. Also bizarre. I wonder if his refusal to honor the robe comes of my being so much their junior, or from an inability to take a foreigner seriously in a Buddhist role, or from general male disrespect for *maechi*. I can certainly understand the first two reasons.

A big man, he stands off to the side pondering the stream as his wife chats with me and pets their daughter. Looking like a birthday cake in her lacy sweater with yellow bows, the child holds a Minnie Mouse bottle to her tiny rosebud mouth. Her dark eyes skim the surface of things, displaying the disinterest of a child who knows herself to be the center of the universe.

Ajarn Supatra explains that she called my host family but only the maid was home and couldn't describe where Wat Thamtong was. (I guess that Phii Niéw didn't feel comfortable telling Ajarn Supatra outright about the no visitor policy.) Somehow they man-

"Taste, smell, touch, hearing, sight, and mind are the six senses," Maechi Roongdüan says. "And the six elements are earth, fire, water, wind, space, and consciousness. Consciousness is essential to the senses."

"Take sound, for instance." She pinches my earlobe lightly. "You have always the ear and its nerves, and you have always the sound of the stream; but only at certain times do you *hear* the stream."

"Only when consciousness is with the ear." She pauses and we regard the stream as it undulates over rock like a giant serpent bisecting the temple grounds.

"When you are reading the book, you do not know the sound of the stream, any more than you know the pain of the mosquito who bites you. You must note, to see where the consciousness is at a given moment."

She snaps her fingers. "It cannot be two places at once, but it moves quickly, like waves of electricity, so that one receives the impression of a continuous flow of light."

I nod. The idea of consciousness being the third element in sensory awareness seems to make sense.

Both Sattipatthana and Forest Tradition practices believe that ultimate liberation is obtainable within the individual's current life, whereas for almost all Theravada Buddhists, be they monks or laity, Nirvana is a very remote goal, a goal that can only be achieved after many, many existences.

—CHARLES KEYES, "Buddhism and National Integration in Thailand"

aged to find me anyway, driving ninety-five kilometers down from the muddy government outpost in northern Chiangrai Province to which they've been assigned.

My hands, arranged properly in my lap, itch. I wish I could hug her.

"*Maechi* looks more fresh, more pale, more thin," she says. Forget paler and thinner—they're standard Thai compliments I don't want to begin to deconstruct—but I wonder if I do indeed look fresher, more at peace. She hands me several plastic bags. Thanking her, I glance inside to see tight clusters of green grapes and my favorite—mangosteen—dark purple balls as thick and hard as baseballs.

"Does *Maechi* have to pay for food?" she inquires.

At this her husband perks up. "Yes," he says, "if Wat Thamtong is not a 'supporting' *wat*, we want to sponsor you, to assume the expenses."

I smile, blinking back tears, and assure them that Thamtong treats *maechi* well, almost like monks.

We chat for twenty minutes, and I give the proper answers to the standard Thai concerns: *I am fine. Yes, I can eat the food. Yes, I can sleep on a bare mat on the floor. No, I am not lonely. Not homesick.*

When it comes time to go, Ajarn Supatra lifts the pastel bottle out of her daughter's grasp and folds her own hands around the girl's tiny golden fingers, shaping a miniature steeple inside a large one.

"*Wai maechi*," she instructs, aiming their four hands at me.

I return their *wai* and stand up slowly, breaking down each movement into its isolated components, imagining the residue energy of my movements arcing, luminescent, through the air.

I turn to her husband and thank him for the visit and the generous gifts. I *wai*, long, full, the way I prostrate myself to the Buddha, and he rushes to return the gesture.

"Yes, yes," he mumbles. "Take care."

Ꝺꙇ

ONE EVENING after meditating in the cave, I emerge to find Pranee and Theew standing on the ledge. Maechi Roongdüan has given us permission to speak for an hour.

Theew, the swan-necked one who had asked "how much" I could practice the first time we met turns out to be the one who sits prissy perfect during mealtime, a bald Miss Manners.

When I ask about her decision to ordain at such a young age, she launches into a passionate speech about the status of women in Thailand. "Women's suffering is this," she says, chin tipped down, hands folded neatly in her lap, "having to marry, bear children, work and work, and then die."

Taken aback to find such raging closet feminism anywhere in Thailand, especially the temple, I stammer a bit, then ask about any discrepancy between the status of *maechi* and that of monks.

"Yes," she admits easily, "it exists. I would like to help women get the same rights and educational opportunities as monks."

Boy, have I read her body language wrong! Most *maechi*, even if they admit to the inequity, claim that spiritual transcendence is all that matters. "Why bother with conditions of the flesh?" they console themselves. At least they have escaped the restrictions of worldly female life.

Theew's neck sways gently like a bamboo stalk next to the stream, and I realize that she is still speaking, softly confessing that she actually, actively, prays to be reborn as male.

"Why?" I croak out.

"So that I can ordain as a monk, one step closer to *Nibanna*. My question," she confides, turning those wide, guileless eyes and Mona Lisa smile to me, "is how to be reborn as a man."

I feel emboldened enough to mention the Asoke group, a radical reform faction of monks and followers who have broken away from the official church. Like the Forest Tradition, its members are

While sitting I see ultraviolet lights like the technique used in films to represent psychedelic visions—alternating waves of bright blue and green. First the green is the inner ring, then it grows to surround the blue and join the outer ring. Then the green light becomes a spiraling top of some sort, narrow at the ends, spinning and glowing.

I check the time, first noting the desire and intent: forty-five minutes have elapsed. After wiping my face with a cold rag, I decide to continue for another fifteen minutes. As soon as I close my eyes, I feel droplets of sweat rolling down my head, one on the left, one above the right ear. Or are large flies walking down my face? One down the left side of my back, the right one continuing past the ear and down my neck. Out of curiosity I open my eyes to check. No sweat. No flies in the room. Nothing.

My mind flashes over history. One afternoon in sixth grade, Mom was out of town and I had a party for my friends. Mummi came over to check on me. It was one of the only times I ever saw her cross. She burst in, made everyone go home, and took me to her house.

Immediately that reminds me of the only other time I remember having seen her upset. The same year she had come over in the evening and stormed out to her car within five minutes of having arrived. I'd been on the phone and chances are had said something flippant. It was the worst year of my adolescence. I remember my complete amazement—at my soft-spoken, peacemaking, bull-shit-taking grandmother—and rushing out to the car to apologize.

vegetarian, eat a single meal per day, and do not use money or wear shoes. Lay followers are expected to adhere to the religious precepts with care, and—as in Sri Lanka—several years' apprenticeship is required prior to ordination. Like the *bhikkhuni*, female monks, of Mahayana Buddhism, ordained females wear the orange robes of monks. Monastics and their lay followers live in two centers in central Thailand, where they publish a monthly magazine. I keep a copy under my mat, fascinated by the images of Thai women draped in saffron.

It turns out that Pranee not only knows about the sect but also wants to join them—not because of their attempts to raise the status of women ("It is neither proper nor possible for women to have equality with monks") but for the rigor of their practice.

Rigor is why she chose Wat Thamtong. "Here *maechi* are different," she stresses, twisting a stalk of grass around her finger and looking unusually serious. "They are dedicated and impressive. They live separately from the monks. They are more serious and have more opportunities to practice."

"Hard practice" is what drives her. She glances at Theew, who looks like she is meditating, oblivious to us, and continues. "Thamtong *maechi* don't drink liquids in the afternoon or accept personal gifts."

I nod and she grins, that irrepressible energy returned to her shiny black eyes. "Other *maechi*, who come only temporarily to practice, plan enough coffee to last their stay."

My mind flashes immediately, guiltily, to the cache of instant coffee and saline solution in my *guti*. The junkie unmasked.

Pranee continues: "We live *thaa ja yùu níi thalôd*." *As if we will be here forever.*

∞

UPON OUR RETURN to Wat Thamtong after visiting Maechi Roongdüan's family, the two of us stroll through the front *wat* grounds. In the cool of evening we pass jade and copper fields. Behind us, the temple birds warble in their bamboo cages, the tiny doors left open.

Maechi Roongdüan smiles at the sight. She says, "Thamtong will always welcome you."

She deepens the welcome, explaining that after I leave, I may return anytime. I can take the bus straight to her parents' house in town and her brother who lives at home will drive me here.

I nod, again struck silent by her generosity, her apparent faith in me. Does wisdom breed kindness? Is there a reason to be nice? I don't mean, what's the point of respecting others or being fair to the oppressed? I mean, what makes someone kind to strangers? Why are certain distinguished spiritual practitioners and political leaders and artists so remarkably generous? Their faces glow with gentleness.

It seems that I will forever be a Thamtong *maechi*, despite my bedraggled robe, my galumphing movements, my private goals that do not include *Nibbana*. Stranger still, I am a complete outsider—not Thai, not Buddhist, not only foreign but also black. Is it my interest and efforts alone that merit such blanket acceptance?

Ironically, I came here to learn how to survive being alone. Frayed from being pulled in opposite directions, I was praying to learn how to exist on the margins without community. Of course, the journey always surprises us. We anticipate one thing and receive another. Truly, the last thing I expected was this embrace.

In the dark driveway, I begged her to stay. She sat with her hands on the wheel, tears glinting in the corner of her eyes, and said that everything was fine; she wasn't angry.

She drove home anyway, and I hadn't understood why. She'd assured me everything was fine. I didn't think about the incident again, even after her death later that same year.

Now, finally, halfway around the world in the Southeast Asian forest, I understand. She'd been exhausted, her ovaries leaking cancer into the rest of her body, and in heavy pain. The pain of keeping quiet while knowing she was dying.

With the vision of my dead grandmother starting up her sleek yellow car and pulling out of our driveway, fading from my eyes, I resume breathing. *In. Out. In—*

Suddenly my breath catches abruptly. My face and heart feel like they're melting to liquid, like I'm about to have a vision, but instead I begin to sob. A sheet of tears burns down my chapped, bug-bitten face.

The violence of my reaction surprises me. Yes, I've thought of Mummi before (though not much, considering how central she was to my life for twelve years). And yes, I was devastated by her death, though her dying—once finally revealed to me—dragged on and on for months, numbing everyone. But that was years ago, my memory of her considerably dimmed.

Because I don't know what else to do, I note *crying, being sad, missing her.*

Where are you, Mummi? I want to see you. I want to talk to you.

A reddish light appears on the left and grows into a frontal view of a long, hooked nose, possibly hers. I keep noting, *wanting to see her,* at the same time squeezing my eyes tighter and tighter to avoid trickles of light entering.

The nose appears again. It floats to the center of my vision, turns to a third-quarter view, and grows a mouth. It resembles her, but is slightly off, like the quieted features of an invalid or corpse.

A teardrop appears, a small oval of intense color, like nothing I've ever seen in a dream. It's bright blue with sparkling clarity. Inside, the clean black silhouette of a robed figure sits cross-legged before mountains and trees. The figure holds something long and spiked—an instrument or branch—in its lap.

As I gasp at the crisp lines, the figure leans to my left, as if to rise, and disappears from view.

Immediately a shadowy figure with an extremely round head appears before tall, wavering edifices. The vision reminds me of the postcard of an old monk in front of the mini-stupas at Suan Dok Temple at dusk. Quickly this fades.

Wait, where is this? Where? I want to talk to you. I'll follow, but where?

Nothing.

I note and wait.

After a moment, I ask again, *Where are you? Is Old Pappa with you? Are you happy?*

Then the tears come, more violent than before.

"Ayutthaya, 1995" by Marcia Lippman.

CHAPTER SEVENTEEN

⊙⊙ Flying Igbos

MY COMING TO FAITH DID NOT START WITH A LEAP BUT RATHER A
SERIES OF STAGGERS FROM WHAT SEEMED LIKE ONE SAFE PLACE TO
ANOTHER. LIKE LILY PADS, ROUND AND GREEN, THESE PLACES SUM=
MONED AND THEN HELD ME UP WHILE I GREW. EACH PREPARED ME
FOR THE NEXT LEAF ON WHICH I WOULD LAND.

—Anne Lamott,
TRAVELING MERCIES: SOME THOUGHTS ON FAITH

OVERRUN WITH WILD beasts—the jungle animals roaming in and out of my *guti,* as well as the monsters creeping out of the recesses of my mind to chatter and hiss during the hours of mindfulness— it finally hits me: ordained life requires bravery. It's an odd bravery, not the kind I expected when my time came, but thorough, requiring the type of whole-life commitment I'd previously associated only with social activism. And I may very well be the wrong person for the job.

I am torn between what I see as two poles of courage in my religion of equality: peaceful resistance and the avenging sword.

As a child, first of all I wanted to be good, which I associated with my childhood icons who advocated peace: Mahatma Gandhi, Martin Luther King Jr., Nelson Mandela, imprisoned before my birth and still in jail, the hunger strikers in Ireland, all the brave, ordinary people, even children like me, with their dark, freshly scrubbed faces and neatly pressed clothes, lining up at lunch counters or marching, clapping and singing, straight into the face of

By continually focusing on the object of meditation, there comes the first moment marking a total break with normal consciousness. This is full absorption, or *jhana.* The mind suddenly seems to sink into the object and remains fixed on it. . . . There is neither sensory perception nor the usual awareness of one's body; bodily pain cannot be felt. . . . [C]onsciousness is dominated by rapture, bliss, and one-pointedness.

—DANIEL GOLEMAN,
*The Varieties of the
Meditative Experience*

Today I sat for three complete hours in one sitting!

Rapture may be experienced as raising of the hairs on the body, as momentary joy that flashes and disappears like lightning, as waves showering through the body again and again, as the sensation of levitation, or as immersion in thrilling happiness.

—DANIEL GOLEMAN,
The Varieties of the Meditative Experience

Maechi Roongdüan wants to take me on a mini-*thudong* into the deep forest, our own hard practice pilgrimage. We're to sleep under a round mosquito net and go on alms rounds. She says that meditating out in the open jungle can't be described in words: "It's a totally different kind of feeling."

hatred, as my young parents watched on television and imagined a better world for me, not yet born.

Secondly I wanted to be brave. My childhood was papered in a pantheon of icons I hoped to emulate. Harriet Tubman and Sojourner Truth, who tirelessly championed my rights, who, though illiterate former slaves, were such charismatic speakers they could lead you anywhere. "What's [intellect] got to do with women's rights or niggers' rights?" Truth asked. "If my cup won't hold but a pint, and yours holds a quart, wouldn't you be mean not to let me have my little half-measure full?"

I wasn't sure which method required greater bravery—fighting back in righteous anger or letting the blows rain down on one's body while one's mind roamed free. Did I want to be Thich Quang Duc, the Ultimate Buddhist, setting myself on fire? Could I be Harriet Jacobs, the Ultimate Black Woman, sequestering myself in a tiny crawl space for eight years to watch over my children and await freedom? Why not—what was personal danger when equality was at stake? Championing justice and the underdog were the engines driving our house.

As I watched my mother and grandfather sign petitions and write checks and subvert every committee they joined and draft scathing letters to local right-wing editors over dessert, I knew that our pens and tongues were supposed to be our swords, that I was supposed to be Ida B. Wells-Barnett documenting 230 lynchings a year or Frederick Douglass rousing an abolitionist crowd to tears, but periodically I yearned to administer the slap.

I wanted to be Touissant L'Ouverture leading 10,000 enslaved Haitians in armed revolt against France itself, the knife glinting in my fist, or Deborah Gannet, a black woman who, disguised as a man, served two years in the American Revolutionary War, or Osceola, the mixed-race Seminole who battled U.S. troops so effectively that they resorted to trickery to stop him. My heart throbbed with justice and injustice as he walked out of the Florida Everglades bearing a white flag of truce and into the waiting embrace of Jackson's troops. I wanted to taste blood, watch the enemy fall in its red coat of liberty.

My children's books gave simple, sanitized accounts of great black and Native Americans, reducing the Reverend Martin Luther King Jr. to a Father with a Sappy Dream and Harriet Tubman to Moses with a Ferry Oar. Their actions were divorced from context, they themselves reduced to icons without a flaw or fear or anger, impossible to emulate. *How does a woman make nineteen trips back into the belly of the beast and guide three hundred slaves to freedom?* I asked myself, feeling by comparison fearful and failed. I wanted to know that Tubman, beaten as a girl, suffered lifelong blackouts and was the only woman during the Civil War to lead black and white troops into battle. I needed to know that Martin was the marketable face of an entire movement of ordinary people and that by the end he had been tired, so very tired. That heroes inhabited real, vulnerable bodies!

I feared that when the time came, I wouldn't even be able to live up to my own family's fables. There was my mother, alone (my father having gone to Canada), defying Old Pappa's threats to take away everything (college, financial support, her family) if she didn't abort, defying the Salvation Army's threats to throw her into the street if she kept me. No, she said, she was not brave.

Then there was my father, choosing to run toward Nigeria, not away, after that Sunday in 1966 when Muslims invaded churches with machetes and hacked to death the Christians worshiping within, his sister, my auntie, one of them. He left the University of Ottawa and sailed for home just in time for civil war.

When our tribe seceded from Nigeria the following year, we became the Biafrans. In the American press, from the time I was four until I turned seven, Biafrans came in two shapes and sizes: sad-eyed children with distended bellies who died of starvation at a rate of fifty percent, and ragtag guerrillas who inexplicably held off

While we're waiting for an opportunity and the rains to pass, I've decided to do my own *thudong*: three days of fasting and hard practice. Seventy-two straight hours of mindfulness. No sleep. Eight total hours of seated meditation in each twenty-four-hour cycle, divided into two- or three-hour sittings.

I will ask to be exempted from the meal.

*S*hamatha is a con-
tinuum of states of
progressive settling of
the mind associated
with growth in
detachment, concen-
tration power and a
distinctive set of phys-
iological changes. At
the deep end of this
continuum, these
phenomena become
extreme, and states,
called in Pali jhanas
(Sanskrit dhyana), are
entered. In deep
jhana, the drives to
which everyone is
normally subject are
actually suspended,
though not necessar-
ily extinguished. This
may last for a few
hours or several days.
One does not feel
driven to move, eat,
sleep or think.
Indeed, the metabo-
lism so slows that the
breath seems nonex-
istent. The mind,
which in its unculti-
vated state is like a
torrential cataract,
becomes a rippleless,
limpid lake. The
deepest jhana is a
kind of trance, but by
no means is every
trance a jhana state.

—SHINZEN YOUNG,
   "How Meditation
   Works"

Nigerian federalist troops with homemade grenades and makeshift tanks. There was no question which one I wanted to be!

For three years we heard nothing from my father. And when later he turned up alive, picking through the ruins of the family compound to find our address on a scrap of burned cardboard, he wrote to say that he was staying. His place was in Nigeria, with the war orphans and burned-out shacks he'd inherited, rebuilding the hope of Africa. That too was brave, I conceded, on an appropriately grander, more public scale.

My own act of bravery—never once complaining at having lost my father to post-colonial Africa—seemed the least I could do. Heroes surrounded me on bookshelves, in the family album, in life. The summer following my freshman year, I met Benigno Aquino a few days before he planned to return to the Philippines from exile. "Yes, I'm told I'll be shot," he joked. "So let's say good-bye." And we had, and he had flashed the bulletproof vest beneath his dress shirt, and when he stepped off the plane onto Manila's tarmac three days later, a sharpshooter shot him in the soft hollow of his throat, just above the vest, the only place left uncovered, and he fell to his knees on the runway and died there.

I wanted to face down injustice, the phalanx of fire hoses and police dogs. My mother's mission statement—the ideal my grand-father had taught her and then reneged on upon disowning her—was that all men were created equal. No prejudice in our house was the message. No cowardice either!

౭౦

WHEN I was four years old, I once burst into our tiny apartment, covered from head to toe with mud (something my mother had repeatedly warned me against, given both my penchant for dripping on the new shag carpet and her complete and committed opposi-tion to housework), slammed the door shut, and threw myself against it. Panting, I slapped my arms out as wide as they would stretch—*bam! bam!*—barricading us against the ravening hordes clearly invading sleepy Ceres, California.

My mother glanced up from *The Autobiography of Malcolm X* to see me wild-eyed, a cascade of dirt sifting into a pile on the carpeting.

Her eyes narrowed.

"I didn't do it," I rasped out before she could ask. My head whipped from side to side, muddied curls askew. "I didn't hit her!"

My mother's lips danced around a bit and finally settled into careful sternness.

"*Faith,*" she said in her warning voice, sounding just like the black mothers in the projects where we used to live, dragging that single syllable down into a valley of trouble, then up, up, into the mountain of questions that was surely coming. "Tell the truth. Why did you hit that girl?"

She knows! My mouth and eyes popped open. *How?* Duly awed by this confirmation of my mother's superior powers, I speedily confessed to the whole dirty business, as it were.

The problem was this: That Girl had thrown dirt at me. Dirt, I knew from personal experience, was Bad. Just last week, I'd returned home for the third day in a row after rolling like a happy puppy across the empty lot out back. My mother had taken one look at my caked face and curls, tossed me over her shoulder, and marched down the hall. In the bathroom she'd dumped me in the shower and spun the knobs.

Rivulets of mud cascading down my face, I'd shrieked and sobbed. Icy water pounded my head and back, the closest thing to a spanking I'd ever received at that point—except for the time I flipped the bureau on top of myself and she ran barefoot and wailing across a sea of broken glass and stinging perfume to lift the confusion of drawers off me. Then she'd spanked me because I was alive.

Last week in the shower, my only crime was Being Dirty (who

THE THUDONG
Seventy-two hours

..

I hurt. I sit and meditate until I don't.

I want to stop. I continue until I don't.

I fear snakes on the path. I walk on the path until the fear subsides.

And because I want to be done quickly, I go slowly.

Deterrents in ordinary life are the very motivations in the Life. I cannot say, "I would love to sit for an hour and meditate, but my legs are asleep, my back throbs, I keep falling asleep, and mosquitoes are bleeding me dry." In regular life, those are each reasons enough to stop; in this life, they are the precise reasons to continue. For the notation.

*I*n some cases, the disciple may feel unbearable sensations of pain as soon as he gains certain progress in his *samadhi* (attentiveness). At times he may feel a choking or stifling sensation, the painful sensation of being poked by a knife or sharp-pointed stick, a burning sensation of being pricked by sharp needles, or an unpleasant sensation as if small insects were crawling all over the body. He may also feel strongly the sensations of itching, biting, intense cold. . . . [T]hese painful sensations are neither serious nor are they any form of disease. They are common factors and are always present in the body.

—MAHASI SAYADAW,
Practical Basic Exercises in Satipatthana Meditation

cared if the other white mothers eyed my filth with sharp glances, their heads jerking like pigeons?), but even so she had touched me rather than simply yelling. Worse yet—I fumed to myself, gasping for breath beneath the avalanche of mud—who ever heard of showering (something I hated in the best of circumstances) fully clothed?

From her perch on the toilet, my mother had said flatly, "I warned you."

Now, as I barricaded the door, equally dirty and additionally guilty of having raised my hand against another, I shook, scabby knees knocking in anticipation of Big Trouble. I choked out my confession, how I had ordered That Girl to stop throwing dirt, how she instead stuck out a red pointed tongue and proceeded to pelt me with handfuls of mud!

"So," my voice dropped to a whisper, "I hit her."

When the girl started crying (loudly!), I jumped up, dumped my plastic pail and shovel (evidence of the crime), and sped home.

My mother's lips jerked again. After getting the bottle of Joy dishwashing liquid, she joined me in the bathroom, where I was dutifully drawing a (kinder, gentler) bath.

"Okay," she said, taking my grimy paw in hers and extending the fingers out flat. "If someone is being bad, there are five things we do before punching that someone in the nose."

I gaped. I had assumed that I was *never* supposed to punch anyone. Weren't we a peaceful household that didn't believe in violence of any sort? Hadn't my home-reading curriculum highlighted heroines and heroes with skin colors like mine who practiced peaceful resistance in the face of injustice and danger? Hadn't I been passed from the shoulder of one bearded graduate student to another singing "Kumbaya" to protest (or support, I wasn't clear on the specifics) Vietnam and Biafra? Didn't we refuse to kill spiders and eat mealy soy patties and flat, pinkish rounds that (sadly) in no way resembled meat? Wasn't I supposed to turn the other cheek?

Not necessarily, it turned out. Not that I was old enough to "reason." My mother demonstrated a proper reasoning process: "One," she intoned, folding over my index finger. "Ask yourself if you did anything to provoke the person. Were you perhaps acting superior?"

I shook my head. I'd been playing in the lot first, but I was happy to share my shovel and pail; she'd been the one to start the trouble.

"Well then," my mother said, and I felt my middle finger curling down to meet the first, "try talking to the person. Tell her you don't like what she's doing, and ask her please to stop. Can you do that?"

"I did," I protested, "but That Girl wouldn't stop!"

Down went my ring finger. Step Three was asking any grown-up present—a parent, teacher, or playground monitor—to intervene. Given that the two of us had been alone, my mother proceeded immediately to Step Four, curling my pinkie into formation: coming home to get her to deal with it.

"And if *that* doesn't work," she said, pausing dramatically and pushing my thumb firmly across the four curled fingers, forming a tiny fist like a brioche, "then count to ten, take a deep breath, and bop the baddie on the nose!"

I giggled and slid into the water's warm embrace. We both believed that it would never come to bopping. No situation would ever progress beyond Step Four; she would never fail to protect me.

&c;

DESPITE NOT having been punished for that delicious moment of feeling my small palm crack against the hot cheek of bullydom, as a preteen my dilemma between peaceful and violent resistance intensified. When I was twelve, I came home from First Baptist to find my family playing Yahtzee in the living room and arguing about Joanne Little, the twenty-year-old black female prisoner who'd killed a white guard trying to rape her. Like the mainstream press, most of the family was initially outraged.

Poor posture hides pain. We hunch or twist to overcompensate for weakness in the body, but weakness remains. If we adopt proper posture, the weakness will eventually be repaired. Pain as we do this is natural. It can be endured.

There is no excuse not to follow the mind. Greed is pain. Notation is freedom.

*T*here are levels of consciousness that are entirely different from those people are accustomed to. Through them it is possible to learn to understand religion on a level of profundity that is completely unattainable without meditation.

—AYYA KHEMA,
I Give You My Life: The Autobiography of a Western Buddhist Nun

The truth of the Three Defilements occurs to me: anger (*dosa*), greed (*lobha*), delusion (*moha*). I see it clearly!

*V*isionary experiences can occur . . . when discursive thought continues, and so long as sustained focus on the object of concentration remains weak. . . . [A] danger to the meditator is becoming enraptured by beatific visions and so halting further progress by making them the goal.

—DANIEL GOLEMAN,

The Varieties of the Meditative Experience

I get quick, vivid images of people I don't know—foreign couples buying coconuts in the market, people drinking water, the tail end of nonsense conversation—as if I had plugged into a short-wave radio or were flipping through a constant procession of television stations.

EXPERIENCE VI
Thoughts become dissociated, weird juxtapositions of words and images occur with no apparent connection between them.

"Taking life is always wrong," huffed Tati Rauha. She busied herself with a plate of homemade *pepparkakor*.

Her husband, whom she was constantly quoting despite the fact that none of us had ever heard him speak, nodded before snatching up a warm cookie. He looked personally (albeit quietly) affronted.

"Not always, not in justified cases of self-defense," my mother pointed out, training her finger around the table, "or when your government tells you to."

"Don't try that old trick to get sympathy from the vet," Old Pappa said, upending the leather cup, dice scattering across the card table. "I do know," he conceded, "that all these people squawking about justice don't give a good goddamn about the life of a prison guard. If they did, prison work wouldn't be such a for-shit job."

He looked up from the table at me. "Quick"—he pointed to the dice—"add 'em up."

I calculated.

"Exactly!" Mom chimed in. "We all know this kind of abuse must go on all the time, and yet no one wants to talk about *that* part of the story. We're so concerned with Joanne Little's 'shocking immorality.' Well, if I were a young minority woman being routinely raped and beaten in prison, I wonder what kind of morality I'd be operating under!"

"Holly!" Tati Rauha gasped, her thin cheeks pinkening, "don't say such things, especially in front of, uh, you know, mixed company."

"Oh no!" I cried, snatching up two gingersnaps and placing one over each ear. "I might learn something!" I headed toward the hallway.

All joking aside, I was beginning to see that there was a certain shape to acceptable black and/or female resistance. We were supposed to turn the other cheek, and turn and turn. Our outrage was pathologized until we were dead; then perhaps we could become martyrs. My mother's Instructions to the Fist were an attempt to keep me alive.

&C:

LATER THAT year I created a comic strip starring a super-heroine named Super Afro. Super Afro wore (stylish!) wide-legged denim hip-huggers, drove a (not-so-stylish) minivan with the words "Afro Van" emblazoned on the side, and sported a large Afro of loose, Leslie-Uggams-style curls with special properties. Best of all, she could fly. Every few weeks I produced episodes much in demand around Sunnyside Junior High, which my mother allowed me to laminate on the machine in the school library after hours.

In the only remaining issue, *Super Afro in "The Return of the Loch Ness Monster,"* Super Afro hears that the monster has broken the peace treaty. I didn't detail his transgressions (the breaking of any agreement clearly being bad enough). Indeed, "Lochie" swims by, pleased as punch and obviously up to no good. Though a physical fight ensues (KA-PLOW!), Super Afro merely twists his long neck into a long braided pretzel (BOINGGG!). Immediately afterwards she calls for a submarine to take him to a zoo (apparently the most humane option I could formulate at the time). Even when kicking butt, I was nothing if not fair.

Physically violent, Super Afro was my own resistance narrative. As a child I memorized tales of African slaves who chose death over enslavement, those on hunger strikes, those who jumped into the sea, shackled together, or threw their babies overboard. I was haunted by the report of two entire boatloads of slaves who, upon arriving in Charleston in 1807, starved themselves to death.

"Look," my mother said, calling me to her desk one afternoon and showing me in one of her thick history books a slave owner's rating of tribes. "Can you believe this pseudoscience?" My tribe, the future and ex-Biafrans, made the worst slaves. My heart thrummed to read that the mere idea of enslavement was so unacceptable to the fiercely democratic Igbo that they (we!) would rather die on the spot!

This is a sign that one is dropping into deeper levels of the mind. It is similar to what happens during the hypnogogic (twilight) state as one falls into sleep. Take it as a good sign, but be on guard for possible sleepiness.

INTENSE VISIONS AND HALLUCINA-TIONS
There is a lot to be said about this phenomenon. Here are just a few of the most important points.

The causes are various, including physical, physiological and psychological factors. From the perspective of the ultimate goal of meditation, they are neither desirable nor undesirable, neither necessary nor impediment.
You are not going crazy.

—SHINZEN YOUNG,
"Experiences Associated with Meditating on the Thought Process"

There may arise many other strange happenings, such as: mental visions of brilliant or bright light; arising of rapturous feelings; feelings of calmness; strong devotional feelings relating to Buddha and Dhamma; great enthusiasm to carry out the practice of meditation; extremely clear perception of sense-objects; the capability of practising mindfulness without missing any sensation that needs to be contemplated; subtle pleasure in the contemplation.

—MAHASI SAYADAW,
  *Purpose of Practising
  Kammatthana Medita-
  tion*

I want to eat.

I have gone two days without food, I believe, and stupidly didn't clean out my *guti* before starting the *thudong*. The grapes from Ajarn Supatra wait across the room. The day she gave them to me, I consumed eight of them on the spot.

"Well, that certainly explains why a certain someone is so stubborn, wouldn't you say?" she teased, tugging my ear.

I grinned back. We were principled! Fearless to the end!

What little information the public school provided about American slavery focused on long-suffering (but long since Civil Righted and Affirmative Actioned—hoorah!) blacks who submitted to slavery with deep sighs and surprising alacrity, and the occasional unique creature who led the others peaceably to freedom. Where were the incessant uprisings and wars staged by slaves and free blacks, the more subversive strategies like poisoning that were so commonplace in the centuries of resistance?

Of course my favorite resistance narrative was the tale of the Flying Igbos (it had flying, plus my very own tribe—what's not to like?), later immortalized by novelist Toni Morrison and filmmaker Julie Dash. According to sources in the American South, when the last shipment of slaves arrived on the Carolina coast, the Africans saw the New World, shook their heads, and walked into the water. Some said they drowned rather than be enslaved, others said they simply walked across the water back to Africa; in some versions they soared over fields labored in by slaves and the sea. Whatever the case, they had certainly flown away from the disappointments and inequities of this country, as I often wished I could.

❦

MUMMI, MY dead Finnish grandmother, visits me in the temple, bringing with her the key to my rejection of peaceful resistance. One afternoon the year before Joanne Little and Super Afro, Mummi and I were sprawled together on the living room carpet waiting for our dough sculptures to bake. She'd been giving me one of her back rubs, and without warning, I felt her fingers grip my shoulder, pinching the flesh, heard her yelp softly like my puppy when his eye started to bulge out.

I whipped around to find her doubled over, clutching her stomach through the loose cowboy shirt she wore for our art projects. I cried out.

"I can feel them spreading," she gasped. Her soft face twisted.

"What's spreading?"

She shook her head, grimacing, speaking more to herself than to me. "All the things I never said, balled up inside me."

Not understanding what she was saying, I began to cry. For almost the first time in my life I had detected what sounded like complaint in her soft accent. Mummi, the quintessential stoic Finn who never complained, who was always ready to bake cookies, carve soap, paint rocks, sculpt dough, embroider pillowcases, make fudge, dye sand, crochet doilies, plant flowers, fry doughnuts, tint photographs, midwife cats, assemble jigsaw puzzles, frost cakes, tell family stories, sew costumes, play Yahtzee/cribbage/bridge/dominoes/Go Fish, roast marshmallows, gut fish, skin venison, drive to the movies, the library, the A&W for a root beer float, drive you to work, pick you up from work, pack your lunch, iron your something or other, vacuum the house, kill the spiders, have dinner on the table at five, write the family letters, beg her husband to ease up on the kids, let her husband disown their daughter, beg her husband to ease up.

As I stared, Mummi's face eventually smoothed itself into its familiar lines—the fine beauty-queen brows (Snow Princess of 1932!), gentle mouth, the nose like a soft beak. She smiled. "Don't worry; I'm fine."

Later I would learn that was the day she'd pleaded with her doctor to test for the cancer she claimed she could feel budding inside her. For months she listened to the quiet rhythms of her body as she worked in the garden, meticulously noting in her daily journal the cancer's growth alongside that of sugar snap peas and wax beans. The doctor and Old Pappa both scoffed at her hypochondria.

After a year of unsuccessful vitamin treatments, the doctor

Then, before beginning my *thudong*, I ate the sugar-tamarind Maechi Roongdüan gave me as a laxative. I didn't even stop to think that by giving them to me *after* noon she wasn't saying it was all right to eat them, but was instead trusting me to eat them at the correct time. So through carelessness I broke a precept. (Of course in my greed I overdid it and now have diarrhea!)

Today I have all sorts of excuses. Well, I already ate the tamarind; might as well eat the grapes! Well, I would never have *asked* for them, but since they've been *given* to me, I can't be expected to resist! Well, I *am* a fruit fiend, a serious hereditary condition. . . .

After sneaking the grapes that first day, I'd gone to the cave to meditate. At the end of paying respect to the Buddha, I looked down and saw my hands still together in a *wai*, a brown steeple against my white robes.

Here I was, going through the motions just minutes after blithely breaking a precept!

My hands fused together. "I've broken *sila*," I said. I wished that I were Catholic so I could just demand, *Forgive me*.

"And it lies only with me," I admitted.

This is the only precept I don't feel. I don't connect wrongful action with eating after noon. Eating one meal a day impresses me, and I see the difference in personal suffering, but I don't see why one cannot eat after noon. Yes, I *know* that the precept shows us that external conditions don't matter, that hunger makes us aware of the body's control over us; I just don't *feel* why.

And now I'm tempted, because temptation is here. But how can I ask for help in my meditation efforts if I can't even hold *sila*?

finally did a complete examination, which revealed that her body was trellised with cancer.

The lesson was clear: the saintly, the passive, died. Only anger could keep you alive!

After her long, slow death, shriveling away to a gray husk, I was torn. I was starting to hate the anger that sprouted in me, seeping its way beneath the crust of skin. My mother hated inheriting it from her father, but it had wormed its way in all the same. The time would come—that first year in Thailand with the letter that reached Cheryl first—when my mother herself would disown me in a fit of pique, just as Old Pappa had disowned her. The problem with the avenging sword, with all swords—is that eventually it swings back, cutting the hand that grips it, accidentally harvesting the innocent.

In the meantime, I readied myself for my big battle. Like the proverbial princesses in my mother's hand-painted tales, I practiced my swordplay in secret, living in obscurity and preparing for the Great Battle of Good Versus Evil through which my true aristocratic nature would be revealed. I fantasized about beating the hell out of the bad guys. I would bloody P. W. Botha and Idi Amin, Pol Pot and the Khmer Rouge, Papa Doc and the entire CIA, then fly high into the air like Super Afro, safe, safe! I protested and volunteered and formed organizations and wrote letters and drafted petitions and whenever I got to Step Four, I called in my mother, my own avenging angel, to make things right, make things fair.

Eventually, of course, I had to answer the challenge myself. The actual enemy, when it limps in, is so small as to be laughable, a David to the world's Goliath. As a *maechi*, every day I want to kill. Every day I want to give up. I'm constantly confronted with my own weaknesses, my hunger, my low tolerance for pain. Only my passion for justice keeps my commitment to Buddhist ideals, keeps the ants alive on my watch.

I learn that I'm a coward. Everything in the forest terrifies me—spiders, cobras, rats, dark caves, monitor lizards, fires, corpses—

though perhaps nothing more so than the contents of my own mind. What surprises me more, however, is my ability to sacrifice.

After I leave the temple and for years to come, people will ask, *Why did you do it?* their frowns deepening. *Wasn't it hard?* This is what we Westerners want to know—will it discomfit us? *Yes,* I will answer, surprised to remember that it actually was. Changing one's life is hard.

But don't forget, I will say, *I picked it.* I got to choose this particular cross to bear. Agency is always worth some pain.

Harder to answer is the first question—why did I choose something so hard? Because, for all my outrage and community involvement and paltry salaries, I have not been brave or peaceful or self-sacrificing. I have not met Harriet Tubman and Sojourner Truth even halfway! I have integrated public spaces reluctantly, indignantly, with great surliness. I have put my personal needs before the group's and turned my back on movements and causes. I have chosen the safety of a job and my own bed over jail. And I have always complained to the person in charge, my (please, God) avenging angel. So how is it that for three days, seventy-two full hours, I reached outside of myself and way back into my ancestral past, becoming a Flying Igbo? As Buddha is my witness, I flew!

Under the guise of transferring the mangosteen, oranges, and grapes to a box, I sneak two loose grapes out of the bag and pop the smaller one into my mouth.

I sit back down, clenching the other one—large, plump, juicy, appealing—in my hand. I hear two *maechi* outside, walking back and forth between my *guti* and the next, doing Buddha knows what.

"I believe in Dhamma," I had prayed in the cave, wondering to whom I was addressing myself, having never prayed before. Am I going crazy in solitude?

"I believe Dhamma can help me," I continued my prayer, "but often I'm not strong enough to do what's best. Please excuse me. Do not forgive me, but excuse that I trespass, taking advantage of my white robes."

By dusk I am rabid to eat something — grapes or tamarind or a bug if it wandered in here! The desire to transgress is more powerful than any belly hunger. Even as I write, I am planning when to close my shutters and do it.

My stomach churns and throbs. I can feel it shrinking, turning against itself. How odd that there would be sharpness inside something so soft.

I'm exhausted from lack of sleep, weak from lack of food, paranoid. With them out there, I don't dare sneak the grape. I hold it firmly, trying to picture myself slipping it into my mouth, refusing to see it connected to principle.

The *maechi* do not go away.

I place the grape on the mat before me and stare. It is no more than fruit juice in a membrane.

I make some orange juice, stirring the bottled concentrate round and round in my glass, mesmerized by the *clink-clink-clink* and the swirling orange like a sunset.

I drink it. *Dukkha*. I am not satisfied.

I pick up a book, not ignoring the grape on the mat by ignoring it.

*T*his imagery is more vivid than that of dreams in that it is much more realistic . . . "hypnagogic imagery that emerged full-blown . . . without being willed; vivid visions of people, scenes, objects, known and unfamiliar. . . . And they were changeful, as if a very private showing of slides were being run through the theatre of the mind." . . . From this it would seem that the mind is full of unconscious imagery of which we are ordinarily unaware.

—WILLIAM JOHNSTON,
Silent Music: The Science of Meditation

I go to the crate to get my pen. The pen is near the tamarind. Before I know it, my hand is in the bag, feeling for little loose pieces, the kind that don't count. Just pop them in! I can actually taste them, my transgression so real, so imminent. Just little smidgens of flavor, c'mon!

I hold a fragment of tamarind to my nose and sniff. Only then do I realize what I'm supposed to do! Notation! *Smelling, noting the aroma, wanting to eat, wanting to eat, wanting . . .*

I pick up the grape and feel its plumpness, turning it over and over, noting the fine beauty of its thinly veiled celadon skin. *Seeing, touching, wanting to eat . . .*

Perhaps three minutes only. I don't feel the earth move or hear a voice say: "And all craving stopped." I don't know if it has worked.

All I know is the true nature of fruit. I can touch it, smell it, see its beauty, imagine its taste. I know what a grape is—membrane and juice, like we are flesh and breath.

I know how its size, just a morsel, seduces. I know how tamarind catches the tongue off-guard, thick with sugar granules on the outside and a fibrous, devastatingly sour interior. I don't need to rationalize—*Oh, you're not hungry anyway.* I don't need to test my willpower—*If you can sit with this grape in front of you all night, then you'll have proven X, you'll be able to do Y in the future.* I don't need to belittle the fruit's appeal or hide or ignore it.

I see Dhamma: how the realization of the true nature of things liberates us from them. How, as Maechi Roongdüan says, "through notation desire cycles away."

I return the fruit to the bag and squat down, completely at rest. Three minutes of mindfulness has put an end to an entire day's preoccupation. A real end.

I regard the hanging bags. I see that feeling in the fingers, scent in the nose, and sight in the eyes were the basis of my craving, and that the object of craving was a grape (a delicate green membrane filled with juice that appeals in appearance and touch) and a tamarind (an aromatic, brown-sugar-covered sourness that appeals in smell and to the memory).

Now that I know this, craving subsides of its own accord. Of course, the intellect realizes that it's forbidden to eat after noon, but right action stems from wisdom, not guilt. Notation creates consciousness to act wisely and follow *sila*.

Meditation is training for the real world. The knowledge received is the wisdom you apply to free yourself from anything the world presents.

Beta [brain waves are] the most common in our waking hours . . . associated with focused attention and the active thinking of a mind turned towards the outside world. . . . Alpha is . . . described as one of "relaxed awareness" with a move towards interiority. . . . [T]o continue in alpha consciousness steadily with open eyes is not easy. Indeed it can rarely be done without ascetical training. . . . High-amplitude alpha indicates that the subject is in a rather deep state of concentration; this rhythm is associated with more advanced meditation and with mysticism.

—WILLIAM JOHNSTON,
Silent Music: The Science of Meditation

The last three times the sky has lightened I've gone outside at what I imagine is five o'clock or five-thirty in the morning to meditate under the tree. It's wonderful—a funny, dark, in-between time. Sky full of pre-light, blurry stars (but then again, since I'm no longer wearing my contacts, everything's blurry to me!).

There may occur: the vision of a brilliant light or luminous form; rapturous feelings that cause goose flesh, tremor in the limbs, the sensation of levitation, and the other attributes of rapture; tranquility in mind and body, making them light, plastic and wieldy; devotional feelings toward and faith in the meditation teacher, the Buddha, his teachings—including the method of insight itself—and the sangha; vigor in meditating, with a steady energy neither too lax nor too tense. . . . It is a pseudonirvana. . . . Finally, the meditator realizes these experiences to be a landmark along the way rather than his final destination.

—DANIEL GOLEMAN,
The Varieties of the Meditative Experience

Mindfulness is the basis of happiness.

—THICH NHAT HANH

I'm settling into this practice—no pains, calm endlessness, fondness for my spider ("Honey, I'm home . . . !"), desire for cleanliness, joy in the walls. It feels like ten o'clock in the morning, and I have the entire day for life.

It's like possessing the secret to happiness—my life full in its own thinly veiled celadon skin.

Thamtong maechi on the landing outside the cave.

CHAPTER EIGHTEEN

∞ Landing

MEDITATION IS NOT JUST AN OCCUPATION TAKEN ON ... FOR SEVERAL
HOURS EACH DAY. IT IS A WHOLE WAY OF LIFE OR, MORE CORRECTLY,
A WAY OF BEING. ONCE ONE GETS INTO IT, IT TENDS TO TAKE OVER,
TO CHANGE AND TO TRANSFORM. ANYBODY STARTING IT HAD BETTER
SIT DOWN AND COUNT THE COST LIKE THE SENSIBLE MAN WHO
WANTS TO BUILD A TOWER.

—*William Johnston,*
SILENT MUSIC: THE SCIENCE OF MEDITATION

SOMEONE MUST BE talking. Two *maechi* who heard that I'm leaving come to me with letters to smuggle out of the *wat*.

The first time it happens, it's like a punch in the gut. I glance up, wild-eyed, from my journal to see the intruder, who, having burst into my *guti* (itself a violation of *wat* rules), huddles in the doorway. It's someone I know. Maechi Roongdüan encouraged me to speak to her at great length about her devotion to the practice. My mouth drops.

She shuts the door and places a small crumpled envelope on the mat before my feet. Instantly I understand. I bite my lip to stop myself from crying out in disappointment.

"Our letters are censored," she rushes to explain. "Maechi Roongdüan wants us to write only of *ryang khuan*." *Worthy topics.*

I lift my hand from its pillowy pad and close the cover to my journal. Forbidden from sending or receiving letters, I have nonetheless negotiated this space where I'm allowed to roam free, my mind as unworthy and undisciplined as a baby monkey in a candy shop.

My visitor twists a corner of her over-robe round and round a golden finger. "I can't help it," she says. "I'm not like these *maechi* here." The cloth unravels; the finger trembles. "I need money from my family for special foods."

I say nothing. It is certainly not for me to contradict her, but if it were, I would shout, No, don't sell yourself short—you are like these *maechi* here! For even I, with my unraveling clothes and inept firefighting skills and callow resistance, am a bit like them—and part of the credit is yours.

She bows and then turns to leave. I let the letter remain at my feet, out of astonishment more than anything else. My mouth still hangs open, threatening the safety of gnats everywhere.

Finally I find the Thai words. "I have not agreed to mail it," I say. The tiny likeness of King Bumiphol stares up coolly from the blue stamp in the corner of the envelope. He's a stiff, thin man, with the thick black glasses of an intellectual and a passion for playing jazz saxophone.

The *maechi* pauses in the doorway. "I understand." She pulls the door shut behind her.

For a full day the letter lies on my mat. I give it wide berth, skirting the edge of the mat as I pad in and out. It's safe, I think, since the only person so far to violate the rule prohibiting entry to another's *guti* is the letter's owner. My mind whirls. I do not want to betray Maechi Roongdüan, who has earned her authority as my teacher. I do not want to help any *maechi* hurt her own practice. I do not want to be involved in deceit.

The second *maechi* passes me in line after the meal and, like a bald magician, palms a letter into my startled hand. *"Khob khun,"* she whispers, dipping her hand in and out of the folds of my over-robe. *Thank you.*

This convinces me. And that decision surprises me, because there's nothing magical in these two actions. I know the first *maechi* must have emboldened this one, given her the thumbs-up. Nonetheless, I tell myself the only rule they're breaking that matters is their covenant with themselves. Buddhism is about the practice, not sin. The rules of monastic living exist for the individual's liberation, not her punishment.

Besides, I ask myself, soaping my robes into a froth of white suds out behind the *guti,* who am I to judge these women? I am *farang,* the outsider, able to come into and go out of this life for a single Lenten period, my passport full of unexplored promise, my bags packed with enough coffee and toilet paper to last my stay. This is their life.

ॐ

"THE TEST is not being a good *maechi,* here in the *wat,*" Maechi Roongdüan says the evening before my departure. She rests her hand lightly on my shoulder, as if feeling for my sadness and sucking it up through her fingertips.

We sit in the gardens near the front of the *wat.* Now that I'm leaving, I tremble with both excitement and dread. Yes, I will see old friends and return to the incessant chatter and breezy green existence of the expatriate. But after that! The thought of life in America weighs heavily on my mind.

Maechi Roongdüan continues: "The test is being able to carry the peace you think you have found here with you when you leave, being able to deal with the outer world and the inner world interchangeably." She points to a small brown songbird warbling and hopping about the floor of an open cage. "If you can sit and be wise, and then you open your eyes and shudder upon seeing your enemy—of what use is your wisdom?"

I nod, slowly, slowly. I've been told this before, prior to my ordination. By a melancholy, silk-clad ex-*maechi* who warned me about chasing peace. With a rueful smile, I recall my favorite line from T. S. Eliot, from *The Four Quartets: We shall not cease from exploration/And the end of all our exploring/Will be to arrive where we started/And know the place for the first time.* Is this true? After taking the most radical departure from my life, is the beginning in fact the very place to which I've arrived at this end?

I wonder about the truth of what they have both said. The test is here.

My tears startle. Was I really that happy? Is this what pure, steady happiness (without the ups and downs to provide contrast) feels like? Is this what life is about? Is this it?

If everything is indeed impermanent, then I shouldn't cling to one place at one point in time in one small country. In a few days, the community of *maechi* themselves will change, those I associate with Thamtong leaving, new ones arriving. *Dukkha* arrives from trying to derive happiness from that which is by nature impermanent. Right?

And then I realize: it's not the place. If happiness exists only while living in a particular hut, then there is no loss beyond the isolated moment. If my happiness and peace are genuine, worth seeking through life, then indeed I carry them.

You didn't come here for happiness, Maechi Roongdüan corrects me, though surely I haven't spoken my feverish thoughts aloud. When I whip my head to stare at her, she is sitting silently in meditation next to me, lips and hands in obvious repose. The Maechi Roongdüan in my mind continues: *You came for wisdom!*

After Maechi Roondian "checks my mood" for the final time, I return to the interior of the *wat,* walking against the flow of the stream, against the sound of the water wearing stones smooth. Restless with sadness, I pick up my journal, penning in carefully that I want to be free, completely different when I go back. A psychic wish list: *I want to have that difference reveal itself on my face—so that no one has any hold over me.*

৩৫

THE NEXT MORNING, the day I leave Wat Thamtong and stop being a *maechi,* I walk barefoot in the mist. Through the drizzle I see two children playing in the *wat* fields, hear their faint, happy cries, watch their blurred outlines, like the teary flicker of a would-be thought. I've never seen children here. I blink and they are gone.

I scrub my *guti* and bathroom on my hands and knees, and load up everything except my journal, my books, and the set of lay-women's clothes I came with. I find Maechi Vilawam, who opens her arms with that shiny grin, silently, joyfully accepting my dona-tions. *"Choke dii, Maechi,"* she whispers as she bobs. *Good luck.*

Back in my *guti,* I change into my old clothes, which are big on me, and take out a pocket mirror. Tentatively, crouched low on the floor so that no passerby can accidentally see, I try an awkward smile. The reflection glows such that I nearly drop the mirror. What's this? I'm not particularly happy, nor am I unhappy. I merely exist. So how is it that I have never looked happier? As a *maechi* I haven't smiled much—not while doing chores, eating, sitting in meditation or walking—and in fact have worried that my face would begin to adopt a scared, humble frown. I look at other *maechi* and wonder why they look so good, so sweet, so friendly.

Squatting in my loose laywomen's clothes, studying that inscrutable smile, I realize that this is the best thing Buddhism has done for me—made me not afraid to look hard at myself. Until now, I've always worried—that I was fooling people, not fooling people, that I was appearing too angry, being too angry—but I didn't sim-ply look and accept. Now I admit to what's there, and yet I feel pow-erful. I have the power to save myself.

Let me admit, I am afraid. But I can pick up my life in the middle. I don't need ideal conditions, perfect comfort, a full night's sleep, an auspicious horoscope to change myself. We fool ourselves. We say, *Well, today's blown, I'll get up early tomorrow and . . .* Bullshit. Get up now!

☙☙

I WALK TO the *bod,* where Ajarn Suchin waits, Maechi Roongdüan and Mae Oey in attendance. The abbot's face lights up. Very ten-derly he asks how I am.

I reply in my best *pasat phra*.

He looks to the two *maechi*. "She practices well," he announces.

They smile and nod. "Yes, she is very dedicated," Maechi Roongdüan asserts.

"So you won't be *maechi* anymore?" he asks, lips curving upward.

I shake my head. "No, honorable sir. I'll be *upasika*." *A devout laywoman.*

"*Dii maak.*" He nods, and it's as if he'd reached across the room and touched my cheek. *Very good.*

After the brief ceremony returning me to lay life, leaving me with only the Five Householder Precepts, I receive advice and blessings from the three until Maechi Roongdüan sends me up to the caves one last time to pay obeisance to the Buddha. There's far less fanfare, but my departure is pretty much as blurry as my arrival. I move mechanically, glad to have concrete things to do.

There's some standard Thai concern about how I will get back to Chiang Mai City, am I too delicate to travel, why won't I let a car come for me, whether I will accept money for the fare from the temple coffers, why won't I eat more before I leave. I smile and shake my head. *No thank you. No thank you. No.* In the end, I hoist a canvas schoolbag with my books and journal over my shoulder, give a final, grateful *wai* to Maechi Roongdüan, and hike out to the road to flag down a bus headed north.

ॐ

THE BUS ARRIVES like a moving mirage. It is the most magnificent bus I have ever seen, more like the fancy ones you hear about in Africa or the Caribbean. I'm tempted to congratulate the driver but I am too shy to look a man in the eye, so I climb on, mouth open, glad that this bus has come especially for me. The young driver puffs out his chest and grins. He knows I'm impressed. The interior of the bus gleams proudly, and its occupants seem to beam rosily at me as I choose a seat from among the many available.

Each window on the magnificent bus is outlined in red braid, with a jingly curtain of grape-and-lime-colored beads separating the driver from his lucky passengers. Hanging from the ceiling are wreaths of plastic flowers in hot pink, yellow, and fluorescent blue. Blue bells with gold tassels adorn the ceiling above the rear window. Two mobiles dance above the driver's seat; I blink but these remain: thick-lipped black women in red bandannas.

A vase of plastic yellow, white, pink, lavender, and red flowers is glued to the dashboard, encircled by a faded pink-and-blue doily. A matching knitted contraption covers the driver's seat. The intrepid knitter, no doubt the driver's wife or girlfriend, has created a multi-colored tassel for the horn and a royal blue sock for the gearshift. A pink plastic doll with blonde hair on the dashboard wears a lime-green knit dress that actually hides a roll of toilet paper. I know this because Tati Rauha learned to crochet the exact same doll in a craft class at the Sunnyside Senior Citizen Center.

As the ticket taker bounces down the aisle in his snappy uniform and jaunty hat, clicking his puncher rapidly and making change, the driver of the magnificent bus plays DJ, smoothly manipulating the radio dials to provide us with an endless supply of cheery pop tunes instead of the usual manic Thai talk radio.

The passengers are uncharacteristically quiet, as if they sense that this is a ride to be savored. Young voices I don't recognize, crooning American songs I've never heard, catch at me, unlocking a cache of rusty emotions. *Click.* I feel as if someone has plugged my head into a shortwave radio, and I have to fight not to burst into tears and loud laughter both at once.

I prepare to tell the ticket taker that I don't carry money, but he passes me by. At my look of surprise, he offers in Thai that some-one on the bus has paid for me. I glance around. No one is looking at me; no one acknowledges this moment, my unfocused look of gratitude. Did someone pay because I was *farang,* an oddity, or because I used to be *maechi*? Which part of my identity sparked an anonymous stranger's generosity?

We jostle through a countryside as brilliant in its own way as the synthetic interior of the bus. Out the window I watch an interlocking puzzle of green and gold rice paddies broken by jagged purple mountains and lumbering water buffalo. Straw-hatted farmers in dark blue work shirts up to their knees in mud. Roadside juice and noodle stands shaded by heavy bows of fuchsia and peach bougainvillea. I feel light, light, *light.*

The beauty of the Thai countryside never fails to amaze and soothe. I remember my first sight of the north: The year of my high school exchange, I took the night train up from Bangkok, leaving a crowded, fetid metropolis at night, black oily sweat pouring down my face. I woke up in green mountains, surrounded by mist and banana fronds and guava trees and leafy ferns, to see wild dogs tearing down from the hills at the sound of the train and running alongside as the lanky, sad-eyed dining room attendant let loose a bucket of scraps. I laugh to remember my initial reluctance at being sent to "save Thailand." I had railed at Rotary's unfair system and declared my desire to move to a place where merit was rewarded! And indeed I have found that place, an entire universe constructed on merit, Thailand in turn saving me.

If the other passengers are surprised to see a lone bald black woman riding this magnificent bus with its two Mammy mobiles through the northern Thai countryside, alternately sobbing and laughing, they don't let on. *Mai pen rai.* Thai politeness conquers curiosity.

The young driver maneuvers the bus in fits and starts, speeding up, almost immediately screeching to a halt. He squeezes the psychedelic tassel cradling the horn and honks steadily at the dogs napping in the road. They are the Thai dogs seen everywhere—mangy orange creatures with strips of raw skin down the middle of their backs from constant chewing at fleas. They lie as if dead in the middle of the asphalt: legs stretched out in two directions, bellies exposed, blissful.

The driver leans on the horn, and eventually the dogs groggily lift their heads. They move as slowly as *maechi,* rolling over on their sides and lifting their front legs and climbing to all fours and ambling grudgingly to the side of the road, where they sit staring into space, waiting for the magnificent bus to pass.

As soon as we roll by, the dogs step right back in the road. Traffic weaves and speeds in both directions, the drivers paying little attention to which side of the road is which, keeping up a constant tooting on their horns. Shiny new privately owned Nissan trucks, *tuk-tuk* bulging with passengers, lumbering buses from Bangkok with sleepy passengers just waking up, motor scooters and bikes with entire families strapped on.

The dogs ignore them all, reentering the fray, throwing themselves down into instant slumber only to be awakened again and again and forced to move. Each time they invariably head to where the centerline would be, if such a thing existed. It all seems terribly futile, but then again, this must be the part of the road that's warmest to a dog—the middle.

"Bangkok, 1995" by Marcia Lippman.

🙐 Get Married, Buy a Car: Epilogue

THE EVENING OF my twenty-third birthday I'm back on the terrace of the Riverside Tea House, where *farang* and natives mingle amicably in the open air, despite the creeping tourist trade that will soon threaten the Garden of Thailand. In a trance, I gaze out at the wide Mekong. Thai folk music tinkles on the speakers, barely audible over the clink of bottles—brown liters of Singha beer, glasses of cheap Mekong whiskey. Yellow rice paper lanterns bob in the warm night breeze, their reflection shimmering across the surface of the darkening river.

In addition to Angel, Eric, Jim, Scott, and me, the table is crowded with young Thais—university students, workers, members of our host families. Daeng, Scott's perpetually drunk host brother, is telling a tale in a mixture of Thai and broken English. Chong teases him, spattering the conversation with French and *pasat nua*, the northern Thai dialect. The Thais, who love a good joke, roar with laughter.

As the birthday girl, I'm wearing garlands of sweet, waxy jasmine and a new pair of handmade leather sandals. All day I've moved as if drugged, through an afternoon spent watching pals bet at the track, through a lavish dinner banquet that will ruin me for all Thai restaurants in the United States, through the return here to the Riverside, the bar of the moment.

Jan, the Dutch owner, stops by our table to welcome me back to town. He tells the bartender the next round is on the house. Everyone immediately switches to the imported stuff.

"Jack Daniel's," Eric orders with a red face, toasting me across the table.

"Oh, oh, wine!" the Thai girls burble between giggles. "Mateus rosé!"

Scott settles on an Absolut gimlet. "Too bad you're not drinking, Faith," he notes with a grin.

I shrug and smile and stare out at the muddy swirl of the Mekong creeping north, past groves of palm trees and patchworked fields of rice, toward Burma and Laos. I'm still out of sync.

At midnight someone has a brainstorm and we pile onto motorcycles and scooters in twos and threes and head across the Mekong to Chiang Mai's nightclub strip.

The club is throbbing with synthesizers and I blink, blinded by the brilliance of the neon lights and glittery disco ball, by the Thai transvestites with their spiky gelled hairdos and heavily made-up eyes, by the prostitutes in their red sequined dresses and pink face powder. Every time the DJ spins a song I recognize from last year, I feel heat at the base of my neck and stumble, as if I've been drinking. The club kids in their bright, flowing clothes flock to Scott and Chong and me like birds, swaying in circles around us. *Where did you get your hair done?* they ask. Suay dii! *Pretty!*

This is even more overwhelming. Over the past few weeks I've grown used to small knots of university students, even faculty members, laughing as I pass by. In stage whispers they wonder if I have lice or am undergoing chemotherapy. Or am I simply mad? Apparently higher education allows them to transcend traditional Thai politeness. The kindlier ones advise me to wear a wig.

Encircled in the embrace of New York Nightclub, I close my eyes and settle into the infectious Europop. It's great to dance again, great to be back with Scott and Chong. We're young, dammit! It's always summer in Thailand.

We finally stagger back to the table to find that a strange drunk has joined the party. He has the standard teak-colored skin stretched taut over cheekbones, a glossy spray of black hair, eyes and cheeks red from drink. Leaning close to the women, he peppers them with slurred questions, Thai inquisitiveness gone sour: "How do you all know how to speak Thai so well? How do Thais and *farang* get to be such close friends?" His drink sloshes against the side of the glass. "Huh?" he presses.

Chong and a secretary from the department avert their heads, forming tiny, pained smiles.

Seeing this, Scott leans forward. *"Bai la na!"* he commands, staring the man directly in the eyes. *Get out of here!*

The drunk grins and focuses on another section of the table. "Hey, rich white lady," he greets Angel, his breath reeking of fermented rice over the table. "Buy me a drink?"

Scott and I flee back to the dance floor.

After twenty minutes, the music descends into Thai disco—bubblegum pop sung in off-key Thai—and the club kids stomp off the dance floor, doing a collective pout. The prostitutes swarm the floor, pulling their reluctant European/Japanese/Saudi/American men behind. We drag our way back to the table to find it empty. Completely. No friends, no birthday gifts, no purses. No drunk. Just a ring of empty glasses, as if someone had circled the table, draining each glass dry.

Scott does a wide turn around the nightclub, the silver lamé walls and mirrored columns fracturing him into a hundred images.

I scout in smaller circles, hoping to find our party relocated to a new table. Clusters of Thais glance up from their plush banquets to watch. *Her hair,* I see them mouth to each other. *Look at the black farang!*

From across the room, Scott shakes his head and shrugs, palms up.

As the rest of our party straggles back to our bare table, the truth emerges. *But I thought you stayed behind with the purses . . . we* say to each other. *No, I wanted to get away from that guy. I thought* you *were going to . . .*

"This can't be happening," Scott protests. This is our town, our New York Nightclub! Everybody knows us. Furthermore, this is my birthday, as well as my welcome-home party. My first time out in the two weeks since leaving Wat Thamtong.

After a few moments of silence, someone remembers the motorbikes. Scott's host brother Daeng, whose motorcycle is new, hits the door first, the rest of us a frantic knot behind.

Outside the club, the usual crew is lounging near the front steps: the club bouncer and pals, *tuk-tuk* and rickshaw drivers, most of whom double as dealers or pimps, young kids toting baskets of roses and cigarettes. They watch as we sprint to the parking lot, muttering prayers and curses, Buddhist amulets in hand. We come to a collective halt. The bikes are safe. All we need now are the keys to drive them, the women's purses, my presents.

The crowd on the steps twitches with palpable curiosity. Daeng joins them, explaining that the *farang* have been ripped off. Everyone has something to say. We soon learn that the drunk staggered out of the club with an armload of Hmong handicrafts (my gifts) and women's purses and climbed into a *tuk-tuk.*

"Why didn't they stop him?" Angel demands irritably in English. "Didn't it occur to them that *all* of those purses couldn't have been his?"

She certainly has a point, but the perpetually drunk Daeng shrugs. *"Mai pen rai,"* he says. *Never mind.*

The bouncer regards us sympathetically. "What's up with her?" he asks, jerking his head at me.

Daeng explains about my ordination.

"Oh!" The man nods. He calls to the crowd. "Anyone overhear where the drunk said he was going?"

Several people name an area of town unfamiliar to us, and someone claims to know the *tuk-tuk* driver. "He'll be back here looking for more fares," he assures us. *"Mai pen rai."*

Scott and whichever men hadn't given their wallets to a woman to carry in her purse pool the money in their wallets to pay our tab, while the rest of us settle in to wait. Exhausted from the pace of this life, I plop down on the club steps. Grinning shyly as they ask about my hair, several child vendors who remember me from before clamber into my lap or lean against me, their narrow shoulders poking through my blouse.

Soon enough the *tuk-tuk* returns, and after a lively discussion between the driver, the bouncer, and Daeng, there's a flurry of activity. Suddenly the bouncer revs up his motorcycle, Daeng somehow perched on the back. When did this happen?

"Call the police!" Daeng shouts out as they speed away in a squeal of tires and cheers from the kids. "We'll meet you there!"

The *tuk-tuk* driver grins and waves us over to him with great scoops of air. We get in back. As the *tuk-tuk* careens through the empty streets of Chiang Mai, he turns periodically to shout over his shoulder: *"Mai pen rai!"*

I cling to the intricate grillwork of the truck's canopy and battle to keep my butt on the narrow padded bench. I hadn't planned to spend my birthday crammed into the back of a Nissan truck with a dozen tipsy friends, chasing a drunken thief across town at two in the morning to get my presents back. I am, after all, just getting used to the idea of talking.

We arrive at a neighborhood of narrow streets and open canals. The wooden houses are boarded up tight, dark except for a rod of light under a door or two, quiet except for the occasional bark of a dog. The *tuk-tuk* driver decides to wait and cranks up the radio. Culture Club's "Do You Really Want to Hurt Me?" blares from the speakers.

"So," the driver says, leaning out of the cab and cocking his head at me. "What's up with her?"

Just then Daeng and the bouncer burst out of a house, dragging the thief between them. He's changed out of Western dress into rubber flip-flops and a traditional print sarong, and though his body hangs limp, his eyes look more focused than before. Daeng and the bouncer are already reliving the night's adventure, laughing and joking like old friends. The thief's wife brings up the tail, alternately praising her husband to his captors and cursing at him bitterly in northern Thai dialect.

When the thief spies the full complement of us standing in the darkened street, he begins to squirm. "Hey," he protests, "the *farang*! What's this about?"

Neighbors start unbolting their wooden shutters, yellow light and questions spilling into the street. *What's happening, hey!*

"Hey, Fate, you made it!" Daeng grins. He explains that they'd arrived at the house and were invited in by the thief's wife. How Thai! I wonder if it was Thai politeness that motivated her—or inquisitiveness. Anyway, despite the late hour, they found the thief at the kitchen table eating dinner, my birthday gifts spread before him. He seemed to be particularly attached to one of the handbags.

"You're not very smart, are you?" Daeng observed, sweeping the evidence into the apron of his shirt. As he recounts the story and dumps the loot into my arms, the knot of neighbors crows with laughter. Daeng plumps. We check our purses and wallets and discover empty interiors. There is one thing the thief managed to do correctly after all.

The neighbors are unimpressed. *Return the money, you good-for-nothing,* they jeer.

By the time the police arrive in their tight tan uniforms with braided gold trim, the thief has refunded all the money, except what he spent on the *tuk-tuk* ride home. The driver offers to return that to us as well.

"Oh no," we assure him. *"Mai pen rai!"*

It is now three o'clock in the morning and a full crowd has assembled in the streets to study the prisoner, bare-chested in faded sarong, hands cuffed behind his back and eyes red from too much Mekong, and us, the *farang*. The atmosphere is festive, everyone reliving the tale of the stupid thief trailed by a *tuk-tuk* of Thai-speaking avenging Americans. Thais love a good joke!

Since nearly everyone except me is either drunk or new to the situation, I get the job of trying to explain the entire chain of events to the two impatient policemen.

I know that the first step in a Thai story is to establish character origin. I explain that the five of us from the United States are all studying at Chiang Mai University. Next I point out Daeng, host brother and unlikely hero. From the looks on their faces, the policemen aren't buying anything I have to sell. I press on.

In the middle of my explanation, one policeman, a large, irritable man in his mid-forties, holds up his hand. "Hold it!" he says, giving his head a single violent shake as if he can't believe what he's seeing. "What *are* you?" He looks me up and down. *"Phu chay phu ying?"* Man or woman?

The street falls silent. All eyes are trained on me—policemen, university students in club clothes, the bouncer from New York Nightclub, the *tuk-tuk* driver in his decorated Nissan truck, sleepy, wisecracking neighbors, the red-eyed thief and his fuming wife. Suddenly we're not here to catch a thief, or even to stare at Thai-speaking *farang;* we're here to figure out what I am. Thai curiosity squares off against Thai politeness.

I stop in mid-sentence. My mouth, stretched wide by the strange, full Thai vowels, hangs open. Scott gives a wild snort of laughter.

What am I? I can't believe he asked. I can't believe he doesn't know! Sure, my shaven head is just now beginning to sprout curls. At this stage I'm Velcro woman—everything sticks to me; I wake up every morning with my head covered in lint. And sure, I'm wearing trousers, which Thai women are just starting to do. But I'm also wearing makeup and jewelry, using feminine pronouns and suffixes, and his eyes have not, I note, failed to notice my larger-than-standard-Thai-issue breasts.

I shoot him a look designed to burn the gold braid off his uniform. I demand to know what the hell that has to do with being ripped off, but somehow the words don't leave my open mouth.

He glares back. *"Well?"*

The others rush to speak for me. "She's just out of the temple," Chong says. Daeng offers, "She was *maechi*."

"Maechi!" the policeman snorts, his eyes widening. I know what he is thinking. Nobody becomes *maechi*!

"Maechi?" he says again, and the others nod. Scott and Chong pick up the tale of the thief, and the problem of my origin thus resolved, the policeman listens quietly, almost reverentially, to the rest of the account.

The neighbors crowd closer. This gets better and better! A black *farang* who shaved her head and became a Buddhist nun. Who then celebrated her birthday at a nightclub known for its transvestite clientele. The very idea must stun them, setting the stage for a lifetime of stunned responses.

But it is the first part of the policeman's question—*What are you?*—that haunts me, at first shaking and annoying me, and then pleasing me that for once identity can't be recognized, assumed, categorized, explained from the outside. That I have indeed accomplished my goal before returning to the West, establishing that there's no easy, static answer to the question. It's a good question and I honestly consider it, *What am I?* long after I've dropped the charges against our red-eyed thief and waved good-bye to his wife and neighbors, long after I've thanked everyone for my gifts and dropped Chong at home, long after I've driven my red motor scooter back over the silent Mekong, past the sleeping train station and now empty Riverside Tea House, through dark groves of banana and coconut palms, to my strangely soft bed.

*The yogi (disciple) is so much encouraged and elated
that he cannot remain mute and cannot help recounting his
experiences. This is just an intial or immature state.*

—MAHASI SAYADAW,
Purpose of Practising Kammatthana Meditation

Bibliography

Buddhadasa Bhikku. *The ABCs of Buddhism*. Trans. Stephen R. Schmidt. Bangkok: Sublime Life Mission, 1982.

Dhammadharo, Ajaan Lee. *Basic Themes: 3 Essays on Buddhist Practice*. Trans. Geoffrey DeGraff. Free pamphlet. Bangkok, 1982.

Friedman, Lenore, and Susan Moon, eds. *Being Bodies: Buddhist Women on the Paradox of Embodiment*. Boston: Shambhala, 1997.

Goleman, Daniel. *The Meditative Mind: The Varieties of the Meditative Experience*. New York: Jeremy P. Tarcher/Putnam, 1988.

Haas, Mary R. *Thai-English Student's Dictionary*. Stanford, Calif.: Stanford University Press, 1964.

Hamilton-Merritt, Jane. *A Meditator's Diary*. New York: Harper-Collins, 1976.

Harris, Marvin. *The Sacred Cow and the Abominable Pig: Riddles of Food and Culture*. Carmichael, Calif.: Touchstone Books, 1987.

Hinshiranan, Narumon (Pook). "The Case of Buddhist Nuns in Thailand." *Sakyadhita Newsletter* 4:1 (Summer 1993).

Horner, I. B. *Women under Primitive Buddhism*. London: Motilal Banarsidass, 1930.

Iyer, Pico. *Video Night in Kathmandu: And Other Reports from the Not-So-Far East*. New York: Vintage, 1989.

Johnston, William. *Silent Music: The Science of Meditation*. San Francisco: Harper & Row, 1976.

Kabilsingh, Chatsumarn, Dr. "Nuns of Thailand." In *Sakyadhītā: Daughters of the Buddha*, ed. Karme Lekshe Tsomo. Ithaca, N.Y.: Snow Lion Publications, 1988.

———. "The Role of Women in Buddhism." In *Sakyadhītā: Daughters of the Buddha*, ed. Karme Lekshe Tsomo. Ithaca, N.Y.: Snow Lion Publications, 1988.

Keyes, Charles. "Buddhism and National Integration in Thailand." *Journal of Asian Studies* 30:3 (1971).

Khema, Ayya. *I Give You My Life: The Autobiography of a Western Buddhist Nun*. Boston: Shambhala, 1998.

———. "The Significance of Ordination as a Buddhist Nun." In *Sakyadhītā: Daughters of the Buddha,* ed. Karme Lekshe Tsomo. Ithaca, N.Y.: Snow Lion Publications, 1988.

Kirsch, Thomas. "Buddhism, Sex Roles and the Thai Economy." In *Women of Southeast Asia*, ed. Penny Van Esterik. Center for Southeast Asian Studies, monograph series on Southeast Asia, occasional paper no. 9, 1982.

Lamott, Anne. *Traveling Mercies: Some Thoughts on Faith*. New York: Pantheon Books, 1999.

Lester, Robert C. *Theravada Buddhism in Southeast Asia*. Ann Arbor: University of Michigan Press, 1973.

Moore, Dinty W. *The Accidental Buddhist*. New York: Doubleday, 1997.

Nicholl, Charles. *Borderlines: A Journey in Thailand and Burma*. New York: Viking, 1989

Pannyavaro, Ven. "Insight Meditation Workshop." www.buddhanet.net. Buddha Dharma Education Association, 1992–2003.

Paul, Diana Y. *Women in Buddhism: Images of the Feminine in the Mahayana Tradition*. Berkeley: University of California Press, 1985.

Phra Rajavaramuni. *Thai Buddhism in a Buddhist World*. Bangkok: Mahachulalongkorn Buddhist University, 1984.

Rabinowitz, Alan. *Chasing the Dragon's Tail: The Struggle to Save Thailand's Wild Cats*. Washington, D.C.: Island Press/Shearwater Books, 2002.

Rahula, Walpola. *What the Buddha Taught*. New York: Grove Press, 1959.

Sayadaw, Chanmyay. "A Vipassana Meditation Course." www.buddhanet.net. Buddha Dharma Education Association, 1992–2003.

Sayadaw, Mahasi. *Practical Basic Exercises in Satipatthana Meditation*. Rangoon: Union of Burma, Buddha Sasana Council, 1956.

———. *Purpose of Practising Kammatthana Meditation: A Basic Buddhist Mindfulness Exercise*. Rangoon: Buddha Sasana Nuggaha Organization, 1980.

———. *The Satipatthana Vipassana Meditation*. Rangoon: Department of Religious Affairs, 1979.

Snelling, John. *The Buddhist Handbook*. Rochester, Vt.: Inner Traditions, 1991.

Swearer, Donald. *Buddhism in Transition*. Philadelphia: Westminster Press, 1970.

Tambiah, S. J. *World Conqueror, World Renouncer*. Cambridge: Cambridge University Press, 1976.

Thera, Nyanaponika. *The Heart of Buddhist Meditation*. London: Rider, 1962.

Van Esterik, Penny. "Laywomen in Theravada Buddhism." In *Women of Southeast Asia*, ed. Penny Van Esterik. Center for Southeast Asian Studies, monograph series on Southeast Asia, occasional paper no. 9, 1982.

Ward, Tim. *What the Buddha Never Taught*. Berkeley: Celestial Arts, 1993.

Wetzel, Sylvia. "The Function and Meaning of Vows." In *Sakyadhītā: Daughters of the Buddha*, ed. Karme Lekshe Tsomo. Ithaca, N.Y.: Snow Lion Publications, 1988.

Wheeler, Kate. "Ringworm." In *Not Where I Started From: Stories*. Boston: Houghton Mifflin, 1993.

Williams, Angel Kyodo. *Being Black: Zen and the Art of Living with Fearlessness and Grace*. New York: Viking Compass, 2002.

Willis, Jan. *Dreaming Me: An African American Woman's Spiritual Journey*. New York: Riverhead Books, 2001.

Wurlitzer, Rudolph. *Hard Travel to Sacred Places*. Boston: Shambhala, 1994.

Young, Shinzen. "Experiences Associated with Meditating on the Thought Process" (circa 1998–2003). www.shinzen.org.

———. "How Meditation Works" (circa 1998–2003).

Photograph Credits and Permissions